# teachers
# for the
# disadvantaged

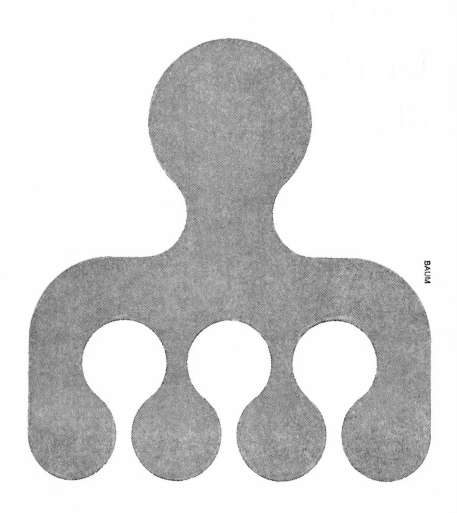

BAUM

# teachers for the disadvantaged

## JAMES C. STONE

Jossey-Bass Inc., Publishers
615 Montgomery Street • San Francisco • 1969

TEACHERS FOR THE DISADVANTAGED
*by James C. Stone*

*Jossey-Bass, Inc., Publishers*
*615 Montgomery Street*
*San Francisco, California 94111*

Library of Congress Card Number 79-92893

Standard Book Number SBN 87589-043-1

Manufactured in the United States of America
*Composed and printed by York Composition Company, Inc.*
*Bound by Chas. H. Bohn & Co., Inc.*

JACKET DESIGN BY WILLI BAUM

FIRST EDITION

*6913*

# THE JOSSEY-BASS SERIES IN HIGHER EDUCATION

*General Editors*

JOSEPH AXELROD *and* MERVIN B. FREEDMAN
*San Francisco State College*

*To*
*the components of a capable*
*and compatible research team*

*Berkeley Johnson, Jr.*
*Larry L. Leslie*
*Raymond J. Roberts, Jr.*
*William J. Schwarz*

*Preface*

On April 3, 1967, I received a call from Hobert Burns, Academic Vice President at San Jose State College, inviting me to attend a dinner meeting at the San Francisco Airport for the purpose of discussing "a possible California teacher education project which might be funded by the National Defense Education Act (NDEA) National Institute in Advanced Study of Disadvantaged Youth." The invitation was tendered me as President of the California Council on the Education of Teachers, Inc. Others attending that first meeting included William G. Sweeney, Council Vice President; John Nelson of the Council's Board of Directors; Richard Foster, Superintendent of the Berkeley Unified School District (and, like Burns, a member of the NDEA's National Steering Committee and Task Force); and Wilson Riles, Raymond Pitts, and Tom Shellhammer, then all associated with the Compensatory Education Division in the State Department of Education.

At the meeting I learned that the National Institute was making available to each of four states $50,000 for projects dealing, on a state-wide basis, with either the pre-service or in-service education of teachers of the disadvantaged. The after-dinner discussion ranged over a number of alternatives as possible projects. One idea which emerged with the unanimous support of the group was that an independent evaluation of presently funded federal grant programs in public schools and colleges ought to be the first step in any serious attempt to identify model programs, and I was asked to prepare a proposal that embodied this idea. Stimulated by the discussion, I spent the remainder of the evening writing a proposal which, with minor revisions, was approved by the National Institute the following month. Thus there came into being the California Project of the NDEA National Institute in Advanced Study of Disadvantaged Youth, and suddenly I became aware of the fact that I not only was "founder" of the project, but also its "director."

Who and what is the National Institute and how does it relate to the California Project? What about the California Project itself— its purposes, assumptions, hypotheses, and procedures? And who are the "other players" in this endeavor—The California Council on the Education of Teachers and the California Advisory Committee? Chapter I attempts to answer these questions.

*Berkeley*                                          JAMES C. STONE
*September 1969*

# Contents

PART TWO: THE FINDINGS

PART THREE: APPENDICES

# teachers
# for the
# disadvantaged

# CHAPTER I

# The California Project

In-service teacher training is the slum of American education—disadvantaged, poverty-stricken, neglected, psychologically isolated, riddled with exploitation, broken promises, and conflict.

Don Davies

1

One of the federal government's major attempts to upgrade the in-service education of teachers for the disadvantaged is Title XI of the National Defense Education Act. Since 1965, this act has provided summer institutes to train teachers of disadvantaged youth. One hundred and seventy-three such summer programs have been funded under this act. Twenty-seven of these institutes have been offered in California.

Because of the increasing involvement of the federal government in funding programs designed to improve the education of teachers for disadvantaged youth, the NDEA (National Defense Education Act) National Institute for Advanced Study in Teaching Disadvantaged Youth was established in June, 1966, under a contract between the United States Office of Education and Ball State University of Muncie, Indiana. The Institute was managed and operated by the American Association of Colleges for Teacher Education through a national steering committee. The programs of the Institute were supported by the United States Office of Education under Title XI of the National Defense Education Act.

The NDEA National Institute was established to assist colleges, universities, and school systems to expand and improve their teacher education resources and to initiate programs to meet more adequately the growing demands for teachers who are prepared to work successfully with disadvantaged children and youth.

The Institute for Advanced Study in Teaching Disadvantaged Youth was intended on a national basis to learn what fundamental issues can be resolved, what techniques and materials are more relevant, and what can be done to disseminate available information as quickly as possible. Its purpose was to help consolidate activities where possible, and to accelerate communications concerning the improvement of teaching the disadvantaged among school districts, federal and state educational agencies, and colleges and universities.

In order to accomplish its goals, the Institute sought representative leadership from throughout the country for its National Steering Committee and Task Force. This committee,[1] two members of

[1] Members of the National Steering Committee and Task Force are:

2

which were from California, planned and initiated activities that were expected to have an impact on programs for teachers of the disadvantaged and that would provide the basis for long-range efforts to make teacher education more viable, especially with respect to the preparation of teachers of the disadvantaged.

One example of the Institute's efforts was the Four-State Project, an attempt to develop recommendations for the improvement of the education of teachers, especially for the teachers of disadvantaged

Matthew J. Trippe, Chairman
Professor of Education
University of Michigan
Ann Arbor, Michigan

Hobert W. Burns
Vice President for Academic
   Affairs
San Jose State College
San Jose, California

Richard L. Foster
Superintendent of Schools
Berkeley Unified School
   District
Berkeley, California

Vernon Haubrich
Professor of Education
University of Wisconsin
Madison, Wisconsin

William C. Kvaraceus
Professor of Education
Tufts University
Medford, Massachusetts

Arthur Pearl
Professor of Education
University of Oregon
Eugene, Oregon

Saul B. Cohen
Director, Graduate School
   of Geography
Clark University
Worcester, Massachusetts

William E. Engbretson
Professor of Higher Education
Temple University
Philadelphia, Pennsylvania

F. George Shipman
Chairman, Department of
   Education
North Carolina College at
   Durham
Durham, North Carolina

B. Othanel Smith
Professor of Education
University of Illinois
Urbana, Illinois

James R. Tanner
Assistant Superintendent of
   Schools
Cleveland Public Schools
Cleveland, Ohio

Consultants to the National Steering Committee and Task Force are:

Mario D. Fantini
Program Associate for Education
The Ford Foundation
New York, New York

Harry N. Rivlin
Dean, School of Education
Fordham University
New York, New York

youth. This project, funded for $200,000, operated components in Oregon, Colorado, Wisconsin, and California. The rationale and overall purposes of the Four-State Project follow:

*Rationale*

1. ESEA Title I support to local communities through the states will probably increase during the next few years.
2. Increased support available under Title I for training purposes could be used in ways that would lead to the improvement of pre-service as well as in-service training programs for teachers of the disadvantaged.
3. Improvements in these programs will have important implications for general teacher-education programs.
4. Training funds could be used more productively if the appropriate personnel and related resources in institutions of higher education were coordinated and brought into more effective relationship with schools and their needs.
5. What is learned in each of the four state projects may be useful to other states if it is carefully recorded and reported.

*Overall Purposes*

1. To identify ways that Title I ESEA (Elementary and Secondary Education Act) training funds and others can be used more effectively in the improvement of teacher education, both pre-service and in-service.
2. To create a state structure or pattern of relationships that will facilitate the coordination and effective use of higher education resources for Title I training programs and others.
3. To develop models for achieving the above ends in the four states that may be used by other states.
4. To use these state efforts to provide the National Committee with information relevant to its fundamental purposes of clarifying issues and problems and of recommending future directions, for example, by throwing light on the question: How can the special problems of preparing teachers of the disadvantaged be dealt with in ways that also will lead to the improvement of teacher education in general?

## THE CALIFORNIA COMPONENT

The California Component of the Four-State Project was under the sponsorship of the California Council on the Education of

Teachers, Inc. Because the Council's advice was initially sought by the California representatives on the National Steering Committee, and because the Council was expected to play a prominent part in the implementation of the fundings of the study, a further word about who and what it is seems appropriate.

THE CALIFORNIA COUNCIL

At the height of the World War II teacher shortage in 1945, the State Superintendent of Public Instruction called a meeting of teacher educators from the public and private colleges and representatives from those who employ teachers—school administrators and school boards. The purpose of the meeting was to advise the State Department of Education on what might be done to recruit and train the thousands of new teachers needed for California's classrooms already bulging with pupils to be taught. From this initial meeting came the organization and purposes of the Council. Incorporated by the state in 1949 as a nonprofit educational agency, it has served as an advisory body to the State Department of Education on matters of teacher education, certification, and accreditation. It is the only statewide organization that includes representatives from all colleges and universities in the state—public and private, the State Department of Education, the public schools, the California Teachers Association and other professional organizations, learned societies, school boards, and the lay public.

The Council meets twice each year at the call of the State Superintendent. Since the beginning of the Four-State Project, the Council has received reports on its progress and was committed to give a major portion of its meetings in 1968–69 to implementing the findings of the California Component. Under an agreement between the Council's Board of Directors and the National Steering Committee, an advisory committee for the California Project was appointed by the president of the Council to be responsible for determining policies for the project and for its general administration.[2]

[2] Members of the advisory committee were:

| | |
|---|---|
| William Sweeney, Chairman | John Hemphill |
| Dean of the School of Education | Director |
| San Jose State College | Far West Regional Laboratory |

The advisory committee appointed James C. Stone, Professor of Education, University of California, Berkeley, Director, and he in turn employed Berkeley Johnson as Assistant Director and three research associates—Larry Leslie, Raymond Roberts, Jr., and William Schwarz. Jean Block, of the Institute of Human Development, University of California, Berkeley, served as research consultant.

THE PLAN

The plan for the California Project originated in the belief that an effective and coordinated state-wide effort to train teachers of the disadvantaged has a far better chance of being realized if an evaluation of existing efforts is conducted first. Without substantive evidence on the effectiveness of different kinds of teacher-education programs, it seemed unlikely that the fifty public and private universities and colleges in California would alter their own individual pre-service and in-service teacher-education programs, or that the diverse array of public school districts would do much to modify their own in-service efforts to retrain teachers.

The objectives set for the California Project were: (1) the identification of ESEA Title I, Title III, and NDEA Title XI projects conducted in California during the years 1965 to 1967 which have as a major portion of their focus, the in-service training of teachers of disadvantaged students; (2) a detailed study of those projects previously identified to the end that successful and nonsuccessful elements of the various types of programs could be reliably differentiated; (3) development of models for training teachers of the disadvantaged based upon the evidence from the previous phase of the project, that is, the identification of those elements within training programs that have demonstrated success; and (4) the dissemination of the published

---

Hobert W. Burns, Treasurer
Vice President for Academic
   Affairs
San Jose State College

Richard Foster
Superintendent of Schools
Berkeley Unified School District

Raymond Pitts
Assistant Superintendent
San Francisco Unified School
   District

Wilson Riles
Director, Office of Compensatory
   Education
California State Department of
   Education

findings through the California Council on the Education of Teachers and other professional groups, the State Department of Education, higher education institutions, and school districts.

Initial steps taken to achieve these objectives included contact with ESEA Titles I and III personnel in the State Department of Education to obtain basic information about the California programs funded under these titles. There being more than a thousand districts operating Title I projects alone in any one year, it was necessary to restrict the evaluation to those having major in-service components and, further, to those on which some evaluative data had already been gathered. With regard to Title III, the files of these programs were reviewed, and the relatively few projects that had teacher-education components relating specifically to disadvantaged students were identified. Requests were made of directors of the selected Titles I and III projects, and all NDEA Title XI 1967 institutes for project descriptions and evaluation reports. Following this initial review of the projects, considerable time was spent in deciding how best to select and study them, in view of such major limitations as: (1) the great number of programs that could be considered for investigation contrasting with the relatively modest budget for this evaluation project; (2) the differing purposes of the three titles, and of individual programs within each given title; (3) the inability, due to the timing of the grant, to do any pretesting or to use a control group, with the consequent problems of interpreting subsequent measurements and of developing relevant variables for inclusions in the research (This problem was partly overcome by an extensive pilot study which identified relevant variables. These were included in the Q-sort and questionnaire.); (4) the difficulty for outsiders to gain access to classrooms around the state and the restricted worth of post-training observations in the absence of pre-training evaluations; (5) the confounding of the effects of multiple programs in a district, some of them not even within the bounds of the study; and (6) the lack of availability, for interviewing, of out-of-state teachers and staff members who participated in NDEA Title XI programs held in California.

Accordingly, from the proposals, evaluation reports, and the experience of State Department of Education personnel, the Project staff identified the programs that appeared to possess the most substantial in-service training components focusing on the problems of the disadvantaged. Initially thirty-two Title I, five Title III, and eleven Title XI projects were selected.

Taking into account the methodological limitations previously described, a design was developed that involved a twenty-two-item questionnaire concerning demographic data about project participants and attitudinal measures concerning the direction they feel education should take (Appendix A), and a seventy-item Q-sort concerning the evaluation of the specific program in which the respondent participated (Appendix B).

About half of the Q-sort items required the respondent to estimate the changes in the participants, in their disadvantaged students, and in their schools wrought by a particular project. Changes in the areas of knowledge, attitude, and behavior were assessed by these items. The remaining Q-sort items were written to evaluate the effectiveness of particular means and methods used by the project to achieve its outcomes. These included project activities, curriculum, teaching procedures, visits to other projects and community agencies and the like. The four major groups of questions asked by means of the Q-sort were: (1) How have the participants changed as a result of the project? (2) How have the participant's disadvantaged students changed as a result of the participant's experience in the project? (3) How has the participant's school changed as a result of his experience in the project? (4) What aspects of the project proved most (least) valuable to the participants when viewed from its impact on teaching the disadvantaged?

The data from the Q-sort were factor-analyzed to provide information about the parameters of effectiveness for particular programs. The interrelationship between methods and effectiveness was assessed. On the basis of mean scores, factor scores, and other statistical procedures, particular projects were identified for in-depth study of data gathered from interviews of selected participants and program directors.

To test the evaluative procedures developed, trial runs were undertaken with one NDEA Title XI, two ESEA Title I programs, and one in-service college class for teachers of disadvantaged youth.

ASSUMPTIONS

The following assumptions undergirded the investigation:

1. The learning behavior of disadvantaged youth is predictably affected by identifiable features of the instruction they receive, particularly by the behavior of their teachers—that is, by teaching methods, procedures, styles, and techniques—as well as by curricula and materials.
2. The particularly effective methods of teaching disadvantaged youth, and also the perceptions, attitudes, and skills on which these methods depend, can be directly taught to teachers by an orderly arrangement of instruction and related experiences designed and conducted specifically for this purpose.
3. The retrospective evaluation of the participants in these programs can be accurately assessed by the combined use of the Q-sort, questionnaire, and interview.
4. The evaluation of such programs by the experienced teacher-participants will be sufficiently perceptive and accurate to warrant their use in the development of recommendations for the planning of in-service and pre-service programs for teachers of disadvantaged youth.

HYPOTHESES

With a research problem with such board dimensions as this one, with the unfeasibility of obtaining anything beyond the opinions of participants, and with no evaluation by the districts or institutions themselves, factor analytic techniques were deemed to be the most realistic and promising for determining the complicated relationships among project ends and means. While factor analysis does not offer conventional tests of significance in the manner of strictly experimental designs, there are some general hypotheses for this investigation that were at least partially testable. Among such hypotheses are:
1. Participants would express positive opinions about changes in themselves and estimate considerably less change in their students and the operations of their schools.
2. Participants would see themselves changing most in the acquisition of new knowledge about the disadvantaged and curricula suited to their special needs, less about their attitudes, and still less in their teaching behavior.
3. Projects reported as having caused the most change would be those in which there was a maximum amount of interaction be-

tween and among participants and in which there was maximum and deliberate exposure to the culture of the disadvantaged.

4. Participants who would express the most positive reaction to the project with which they were associated would be younger teachers from urban districts who taught classes with a high proportion of disadvantaged students, who came from lower social class backgrounds, and who were more desirous of changing the present school structure.

The study has identified such interrelationships as those between methods and effectiveness, between particular program components and specific school-community problems, and between methods and positive changes to the demographic and attitudinal characteristics of the teachers.

Through interviews with project directors and a sample of project participants, additional information was secured. The objectives of these interviews were: (1) To obtain some measure of the *feelings* of participants about the teaching of disadvantaged students and about the specific project, as well as the more intellectualized concepts expressed in the questionnaire. Put another way, the intent was to sample the *affective,* as well as the *cognitive,* domain of reactions of those involved, thus getting a fuller understanding of the projects being studied. (2) To confirm the written responses of certain portions, at least, of the questionnaire. (3) To gain information too sensitive to be sought by a questionnaire. (4) To determine what bias, if any, resulted from the failure of certain participants to respond to the questionnaire. (5) To expand seemingly significant leads in the questionnaire responses of the total group and of specific individuals. A unique feature of this investigation has been the effort to secure some hard data on the results of teacher training, in addition to probing via interviews for the deeper reasons for what seemed to be occurring.

Coordination among the Four-State Project and the National Steering Committee and Task Force was supplied by the NDEA National Institute. Monthly progress reports were shared, three conferences involving state directors were held, and consulting and evaluation service provided.

In the chapters which follow, we first describe selected projects and their settings to illustrate the wide range of programs, the variety of types, and the heterogeneity of the communities and clientele served.

Chapter II includes fourteen of the twenty-five (the balance are in Appendix C) ESEA Title I and the three Title III Projects finally included in the investigation; Chapter III the nine NDEA Institutes.

Armed with the picture gleaned from these two chapters, we move to the heart of the question—does teacher training train teachers?—presenting statistical answers in Chapter IV. Interview responses are in Chapter V. Our concluding chapter presents an analysis of the findings, and models of in-service and pre-service training programs most appropriate for the preparation of teachers of the disadvantaged together with recommendations for implementation.

# PART ONE

## The Milieu

# ESEA Title I and Title III Programs

S ystems die, instincts remain.

O. W. Holmes

15

$\mathcal{A}$merican public education reached a turning point in 1965 when the Congress passed the Elementary and Secondary Education Act, providing massive federal assistance to both public and non-public schools for the first time in our national history. The first section of this chapter focuses on the section of the ESEA that applies most directly to the education of disadvantaged youth: Title I—Education of Children of Low-Income Families. The second section deals with Title III Projects.

## TITLE I PROJECTS

Title I was designed to encourage and support the establishment, expansion, and improvement of special programs to meet the special needs of culturally and educationally deprived children of low-income families. Under its terms public school districts are eligible to receive payments of federal funds in support of the special programs they undertake in order to meet the special educational needs of children and youth in those of their school attendance areas having high concentrations of disadvantaged pupils. For these pupils the school districts offer special instructional activities and special supplementary services in which all children in need of them may participate. These special programs include remedial, corrective, and developmental instruction; preschool, after-school and summer school classes; cultural enrichment activities; auxiliary supportive services to pupils, their teachers, and their parents; and additional instructional personnel, facilities, equipment, and materials judged necessary for improving the educational opportunities available to disadvantaged youth.

Local educational agencies (LEA's) are eligible to receive payments of federal funds equal to one-half the average per-pupil expenditures of their state multiplied by (a) the number of children aged five to seventeen in families having an annual income of less than $3,000; and (b) the number of children in families receiving payments over $3,000 under the program of Aid to Families with Dependent Children. LEA's are required to prepare and submit annual ESEA Title I Project Plans, including basic data about their school district(s) and an application for federal funds required to support their proposed project activities; annual evaluation reports, including test and ques-

**16**

tionnaire data, statistical analyses; and narrative descriptions, commentaries, and recommendations regarding the effectiveness of their special programs. In California, these documents are prepared in accordance with guidelines established by the Office of Compensatory Education, State Department of Education, and are submitted to this office for review and approval of their compliance with state and federal requirements. Copies of these documents are then forwarded to the Office of Education in Washington, D.C. Federal funds are disbursed directly to those LEA's whose project proposals conform to the intentions and specifications of Title I, ESEA. It is the intention of the ESEA that state and local educational agencies will maintain present efforts and use the federal funds for which they are eligible to pay for additional special programs.

The California Project selected for investigation a sample of twenty-five ESEA Title I projects for 1966–67 from the more than 1,200 that have been funded in the State. These twenty-five projects were chosen primarily because they included substantial in-service teacher-training programs among their special supplementary services. A second important consideration in choosing these projects was the inclusion in their annual evaluation reports of some fairly objective evaluative data about the outcomes and effectiveness of their in-service components. Other criteria were also applied in order to assure that the ESEA Title I projects selected for inclusion in the sample represented, as fully as possible, the full range of diversity among all projects generated by the variables of particular interest to us. The variables with which the California Project has been most concerned are: (1) the types of communities whose special needs the compensatory education projects and their in-service components were designed to serve—metropolitan, urban, ghetto, suburban, and rural; (2) the racial and ethnic minority groups whose cultural and educational deprivation have been most severe and most in need of compensation by special programs—Negro, Mexican-American, American Indian, and Oriental; (3) the size of the target populations whose entitlement to special compensatory education programs determines the amount of federal funds for which LEA's are eligible; that is, the number of children residing in the district's school attendance areas who come from low-income families, the percentage concentration of these children in the district as a whole, and the average numerical concentration of these children in the district's school attendance areas; (4) the types of LEA's sponsoring compensatory education projects and their in-service components—elementary, secondary, joint, and unified school districts, and county cooperatives formed by several local school districts; and (5) the magnitude and scope of compensatory education projects and their in-service components; that is, the amount of federal funds requested; the proportion of total funds budgeted for in-service teacher training; the number and types of training activities comprising the in-service program; and the number and classifications of school personnel and others participating in these activities.

The information upon which the following descriptions of ESEA Title I Projects and their in-service components are based was gained from several sources and gathered by several means, including: (1) LEA's Project Plans and Annual Evaluation Reports which were requested from and furnished by local school districts or on file in the Office of Compensatory Education, State Department of Education, in Sacramento, and from which information has been excerpted by California Project staff; (2) questionnaires sent out by California Project staff to ESEA Title I project directors and in-service program coordinators and completed by them (or, in a few cases, by our staff, using data furnished by directors and coordinators); and (3) interviews conducted by California Project staff with ESEA Title I project directors and in-service program coordinators and also, in some cases, with school personnel who participated in in-service training activities.

Of the twenty-five ESEA Title I projects and their in-service components that were studied, fourteen are described in this chapter and the rest are summarized in Appendix C. The first eleven of the fourteen projects were those that the participants identified as particularly effective (see Chapter IV), and they are arranged in alphabetical order by the names of the local education agencies that sponsored them. The twelfth, thirteenth, and fourteenth programs (Healdsburg, Marysville, Santa Cruz) operated as learning centers. This feature was sufficiently unique to include them in the chapter.

## COLTON JOINT UNIFIED SCHOOL DISTRICT
(San Bernardino County)

Average per pupil expenditure in fiscal year 1966: $538.41
Number of schools: 19 (K–12)
Total enrollment in fall 1966: 11,501
Number of pupils from low-income families: 3,052 (25.8%)

ESEA TITLE I PROJECT, 1966–67

Title: Improvement of Communication Skills
Amount of federal funds: $172,573
Number of target schools: 3
  2 Elementary
  1 Intermediate
Number of target pupils: 942
  30 Prekindergarten
  120 Kindergarten
  666 Elementary
  126 Junior High
Percentage of minority-group pupils:
  49.0% Mexican-American
  0.4% Negro
  0.1% Oriental
  50.5% Others
Special instructional activities:
  English Language Arts
  Kindergarten
  Prekindergarten
  Social Studies
Special supplementary services:
  Lunch, service and instruction
  Physical examinations
  Curriculum materials
  Teacher aides
  In-service teacher training

IN-SERVICE PROGRAM

Amount of federal funds: $19,880

Number of participants: 47

Objectives:

To help teachers gain an understanding of themselves and their attitudes toward teaching disadvantaged children and greater understanding of the culturally unique child and appreciation of his special educational needs, and so retrain their attitudes toward meeting those needs.

To help teachers gain further understanding of the learning process and knowledge of recent research findings regarding it.

To assist teachers in learning about instructional programs, procedures, techniques, media, and materials that will enable them to implement their understanding of the learning process and express it in relation to the special educational needs of disadvantaged children.

Activities:

Spring semester and summer sessions of a Workshop on Compensatory Education, with emphasis on the language development and communicative skills of disadvantaged Mexican-American children.

Visits on released time to observe demonstration of techniques, materials, and equipment in other schools and districts, and to participate in conferences and workshops.

Consultations with specialists in teaching reading, language arts, and communicative skills.

Development of curriculum materials at the Educational Study Center.

IN-SERVICE TRAINING ACTIVITY

Colton Joint Unified School District's ESEA Title I project included among its principal activities an in-service training Workshop on Compensatory Education which was conducted in two sessions, one in the spring semester and one in the summer of 1967. The California Project asked the forty-seven teachers who participated in one or the other of these sessions of the workshop to evaluate their experience.

The district contracted with a member of the School of Education of the University of Southern California to plan, arrange, and conduct the in-service training component of its ESEA Title I project.

This consultant directed both sessions of the Workshop in Compensatory Education and also conducted an evaluation of its effectiveness.

The first session of the workshop was held during the spring semester, 1967, and consisted of eighteen weekly three-hour meetings on Saturday mornings from mid-January through mid-June. The second session held eighteen daily three-hour meetings in the afternoons of weekdays from mid-June through mid-July. Twenty-eight teachers took part in the first session, twenty in the second. The participants included some teachers from project target schools and some from schools not involved with the project. The district's reason for including teachers from both groups was given as a belief that the understandings and techniques that are effective in teaching disadvantaged children with special educational needs must be disseminated through the district, since there were a large number of disadvantaged children not attending target schools.

The program for the in-service workshop was divided into three major topics corresponding to the three broad objectives enumerated above. The first series of meetings was designed to orient the participants to the goals of the ESEA Title I project and prepare them for further instruction and training. In these meetings the participants focused on the culturally and educationally disadvantaged child himself in an effort to increase their knowledge of such matters as the self-concepts of such pupils, the barriers to their attaining a positive self-image, the meaning of education to them, their feelings about their own values and goals, failure- and success-oriented personalities, their cultural background, and the outer community's expectations of them and their effect upon them. They also worked at self-analysis and group dynamics to increase their sensitivity, awareness, and willingness and desire to change their attitudes and behaviors. The second series of meetings was designed to improve the participants' understanding of the processes by which children learn, grow, and develop. In these meetings the participants considered the findings of recent research studies in the field of child development and learning theory and the implications and impact of these findings on teaching and education in general and on the teaching of disadvantaged pupils and compensatory education in particular. The third and final series of meetings focused on specific instructional procedures, techniques, media, and materials and their appropriateness and effectiveness in meeting the special educational needs and solving the special learning problems of disadvantaged pupils. In these meetings the participants became familiar with, observed demonstrations of, and practiced with procedures, techniques, equipment, and materials that would enable them to implement their understanding of the learning process and the learning difficulties of culturally and educationally deprived children.

The various media employed in the conduct of the workshop included lectures by the director and guest speakers, demonstrations, large- and small-group discussions, informal interaction among participants, and research and writing of instructional materials.

The participants were paid a uniform hourly rate for their attendance at in-service training meetings. At the end of each session of the Workshop on Compensatory Education, the participants were asked by the workshop director to indicate and comment on the new knowledge, insights, and understandings they had gained from it, to evaluate the effectiveness of the various media employed in bringing about these gains, to speculate about the possibilities for implementing new ideas gained from the workshop in school instructional programs, and to suggest different emphases and new topics for a workshop of the same or a similar type. Principals of target schools were also asked to evaluate the effectiveness and judge the outcomes of the in-service workshop.

The district's use of a broadly experienced and widely known expert as a consultant, to whom it delegated full responsibility for planning, arranging, conducting, and evaluating its in-service program, proved a very effective means for achieving that program's objectives. It enabled the district to offer its teachers a comprehensive, coherent, and coordinated program of training activities within the relatively simple and economical format of a workshop conducted in only eighteen meetings but making efficient use of a large variety of instructional procedures and media. This means, then, seems to have achieved the comprehensiveness of an institute within the rather more limited framework of a workshop.

## FRESNO CITY UNIFIED SCHOOL DISTRICT
### (San Joaquin County)

Average per pupil expenditure in fiscal year 1966: $432.21
Number of schools: 75 (K–12)

2392

Total enrollment in fall 1966: 56,350
Number of pupils from low-income families: 12,000 (20%)

ESEA TITLE I PROJECT, 1966–67

Title: A Comprehensive Compensatory Education Program
Amount of federal funds: $1,471,805
Number of target schools: 23
   17 Elementary
    4 Junior High
    2 Senior High
Number of target pupils: 16,958
Percentage of minority-group pupils:
   35% Mexican-American
   25% Negro
    2% Oriental
   38% Other
Special instructional activities:
   Remedial Reading
   Cultural Enrichment (study trips)
   Extended week (Saturday) classes
   Extended library services
   Preschool Education
   Reduction in Class Size
Special supplementary services:
   Counseling and guidance
   School-home liaison
   Health examinations and education
   Free lunches
   In-service teacher training

IN-SERVICE PROGRAM

Amount of federal funds: $20,000
Number of participants: 131
Objectives:
   To provide in-service education for teachers and administrators.
   To modify and improve current classroom instructional programs.
   To introduce new instructional methods and techniques.

Activities:
Weekly meetings for remedial reading teachers.
Visits to observe innovative methods and materials in other class-rooms and schools on released time.
Attendance at curriculum conferences and follow-up meetings.

IN-SERVICE TRAINING ACTIVITY

The in-service program of Fresno's ESEA Title I project em-phasized the training of seven reading teachers employed especially to offer remedial reading instruction in seven target elementary schools. The California Project therefore studied the training activities of these seven reading teachers.

The remedial reading teachers attended weekly in-service meet-ings to share information and insights gained from their teaching ex-perience, to standardize their procedures, and to exchange their views regarding the merits of various diagnostic and remedial techniques and instructional materials. They also attended the California Reading Association State Conference, held in Fresno, to learn about the par-ticular kinds of reading difficulties that impede the learning of disad-vantaged pupils and about new instructional programs, procedures, techniques, and materials found to be especially effective in teaching reading to these pupils. After the CRA State Conference, these teachers attended a series of meetings conducted by reading specialist consult-ants to discuss ways and means of implementing these new instructional programs and procedures in their respective target schools. From time to time, these teachers visited other classrooms and other schools to ob-serve demonstrations of new programs, procedures, techniques, equip-ment, and materials.

The participants in this in-service program received no addi-tional remuneration or salary credit for their attendance at the regu-larly scheduled weekly meetings. They did, however, receive reimburse-ment from the project for their expenses incurred in attending the CRA State Conference—registration, lodging, meals, and transporta-tion. The project also provided substitute teachers and released time for them to visit other classrooms and schools.

At the conclusion of their participation in this training activity, which was carried out from September 12, 1966 to June 9, 1967, the seven reading teachers were asked to evaluate their experience by completing a questionnaire and to include therein suggestions for ways to improve future in-service activities—topics, speakers, procedures, and so on.

The favorable responses to the evaluative questionnaire seem to indicate that the loose and flexible structure of that program was almost entirely adequate to their needs and effective in achieving the rather limited and practical objectives it was designed to meet. The program's specific focus on the needs of teachers of remedial reading apparently made unnecessary the degree of planning, organization, and coordination that would have been required to render a more complex and comprehensive program fully effective.

## KERN COUNTY JOINT UNION HIGH SCHOOL DISTRICT (Kern County)

Average per pupil expenditure in fiscal year 1966: $608.00
Number of schools: 12 (9–12)
Total enrollment in fall 1966: 18,077
Number of pupils from low-income families: 2,400 (7.7%)

ESEA TITLE I PROJECT, 1966–67

Title: Comprehensive Instructional Program
Amount of federal funds: $459,821
Number of target schools: 5
    5 Senior High
Number of target pupils: 1,505
    1,505 Senior High
Percentage of minority-group pupils:
    18% Mexican-American
    9% Negro
Special instructional activities:
    Reading and Language Arts
    Mathematics
    Social Studies
    Home Economics
    Cultural Enrichment (field trips)

Special supplementary services:
Tutoring (volunteers)
Counseling and guidance
Neighborhood meetings
Home visits
Teacher aides
In-service teacher training
Curriculum materials development

IN-SERVICE PROGRAM

Amount of federal funds: $12,000
Number of participants: 52
Objectives:
To help teachers and counselors to a better understanding of the
characteristics, cultural background, educational needs, and spe-
cial learning problems of disadvantaged children.

To improve the attitudes of teachers and counselors toward teaching and working with disadvantaged pupils.

To assist teachers in developing innovative curricula and instructional procedures, techniques, media, and materials for teaching
disadvantaged pupils.

To help teachers carry out better assessments and evaluations of
instructional programs in relation to stated instructional objectives.

To develop techniques for achieving better relations between
school personnel and parents of disadvantaged children, on the
one hand, and staff members of community agencies working
with the disadvantaged, on the other hand.
Activities:
District-wide Saturday morning and summer workshops.

Target-school-sponsored Saturday morning and summer workshops.

Intervisitation among target school teachers to observe demonstrations of instructional procedures, techniques, materials, and
equipment in other classrooms, schools, and districts.

Consultations with curriculum specialists.

Clerical assistance to curriculum materials development projects by teacher aides.

Professional library and audiovisual services center.

IN-SERVICE TRAINING ACTIVITY

The in-service teacher training component of Kern County Joint Union High School District's ESEA Title I project consisted largely of curriculum and materials development workshops conducted during the summer and on Saturdays during the school year. Some of these workshops were district-wide, enrolling teachers from all five of the target high schools; some were local, sponsored by individual target high schools for their own teachers. The California Project asked fifteen teachers who participated in a district-wide workshop and thirty-seven teachers who participated in school-sponsored workshops to evaluate their experience.

During the fall of 1966, the project sponsored a district-wide workshop on the implications of modern approaches to language study for the teaching of English to disadvantaged students. The workshop was conducted by a professor in the English Department of the University of California at Berkeley who is a specialist in the history and structure of the English language. It was attended by fifteen English teachers from four of the project's five target high schools. The workshops met for five two-and-one-half-hour sessions on Saturday mornings. The instructor lectured and led discussions among the participants on the topic of the workshop: the contributions of modern structural linguistics, particularly transformational grammar, to innovative curricula and instructional materials appropriate for teaching English language arts to disadvantaged students.

In August of 1966 and throughout the following school year, four of the five target high schools in the project sponsored their own workshops for teachers on their staffs. (Two teachers from the fifth target high school participated in workshops conducted by the other four.) The summer workshops met for one or two weeks in late August, just before the opening of school in the fall. The school-year workshops usually met on Saturday mornings. The workshops were conducted by curriculum specialists on the faculties of nearby state colleges and universities who were engaged as consultants by the district, and were attended by from eight to twelve teachers each. The number and length of sessions varied widely from workshop to workshop, depending on the individual target school's objectives; each participant, however, spent an average of approximately one hundred hours throughout the summer and school year in this type of in-service activity. The subject matter content and the instructional procedures followed by each workshop also varied somewhat, but in all the emphasis was on such practical concerns as the writing of academic performance objectives in behavioral terms, the preparation of instructional materials, the use of team teaching and teacher aides, the use of audiovisual equipment and materials, and the evaluation and assessment of new curricula, materials, and methods. The workshops developed instructional programs and materials for teaching disadvantaged students in English, mathematics, social studies, home economics, industrial arts, business education, horticulture, and health.

Teachers who participated in the project's in-service training workshops were paid a uniform hourly rate—the rate the district customarily pays its teachers for their special contributions to the development of curricula and materials. They did not receive any units of college or professional credit toward increments on the district's salary schedule. Teachers who, as part of their participation in these workshops, visited other classrooms and schools in the district to observe innovative instructional programs, procedures, techniques, or equipment did so on released time, the project providing substitute teachers for their classrooms. Those who visited classrooms and schools outside the district were reimbursed by the project for their travel expenses.

The district's principal means of evaluating the effectiveness of the project's in-service component was by pre- and posttesting students and comparing results with baseline and comparative group information, and also by collecting data on behavioral changes such as school attendance, participation in school-related activities, and school retainment. However, since one of the project's primary objectives for its in-service training component was to improve teachers' attitudes toward teaching disadvantaged students, an objective measure of attitude, The Meaning of Words Inventory, developed by "Project Potential" at the University of Southern California, was administered to a sample of teachers before and after their participation in project-sponsored in-service activities. The results of this testing suggest that a number of significant changes in attitude toward teaching disadvantaged students might be associated with the in-service training and cumulative work experience these teachers received from their involvement in the District's ESEA Title I project.

## LOS ANGELES CITY SCHOOLS (Los Angeles County)

Average per pupil expenditure in fiscal year 1966: $571.67
Number of schools: 565 (K–12)
Total enrollment in fall 1966: 630,585
Number of pupils from low-income families: 92,347 (12.6%)

ESEA TITLE I PROJECT, 1966–67

Title: Special Education and Supportive Services
Amount of federal funds: $13,203,706
Number of target schools: 248
  181 Elementary
   41 Junior High
   26 Senior High
Number of target pupils: 178,512
    331 Handicapped
  3000 Prekindergarten
15249 Kindergarten
81057 Elementary
41872 Junior High
37003 Senior High
Percentage of minority-group pupils: not available

*Special Instructional Services*

Elementary Project 1
  English as second language
  Reading
Elementary Project 2
  Prekindergarten
  Kindergarten
Elementary Project 3
  Cultural enrichment, general
Elementary Project 4
  Reading

Prekindergarten
Kindergarten
Cultural enrichment, general
Teacher aides
Student Achievement Center
Psychological services
Guidance and counseling
Curriculum materials center services
Transportation service
Services and instruction for parents
In-service training
Health Services Team
School-Age Expectant Mothers
General elementary and secondary education
Child Welfare and Attendance Returnees
School Community Relations Specialists
Special Education—Remedial and Prevention Program
Special education for the handicapped
Work study

*Special Supplementary Services*

Elementary Project 1
Library services
Guidance and counseling
Health services
School social work services
Project administration
Elementary Project 2
Mid-morning nutrition
Psychological services
Teacher aides
Elementary Project 3
Transportation services
Elementary Project 4
Transportation services
School social work service
Guidance and counseling
Food services—other

Project administration
Student Achievement Center
Administration—secondary
Evaluation of all district projects
Administration—all projects
Health Services Team
Individual health evaluation, vision screening, audiometric test-
ing, screening for tuberculosis, dental examination, parent con-
ferences, home visits, assistance in obtaining medical follow-
up for correction of defects, providing health education to
pupils, parents, and school staff
School-Age Expectant Mothers
Health services, medical care, instruction in parental, postnatal,
and infant care
School social work services

*Services*

Child Welfare and Attendance—Returnees
School social work
Attendance services
School Community Relations Specialists
Home-school community relations
Special Education—Remedial and Prevention Program
Health services (doctors and nurses)
Psychological services
Guidance and counseling
Transportation services
Services and instruction for parents

IN-SERVICE PROGRAM

Amount of federal funds: $738,764 (+ $86,930 summer)
Number of participants: 2,059 (+ 759 summer)
Objectives:
To increase the sensitivity and awareness of school personnel and
enhance their understanding of the many dimensions and effects
of poverty, cultural deprivation, and educational disadvantage-
ment on children.
To train teachers in the use of testing and diagnostic techniques

in the assessment of specific reading and learning disabilities and also in the use of prescriptive techniques and special materials in meeting the oral language and reading skills development needs of disadvantaged children.

To help teachers gain familiarity with and skill in the use of instructional procedures, techniques, media, materials, and equipment that are especially effective in meeting the educational needs of disadvantaged pupils.

To help school personnel to become increasingly sensitive to and understanding of the characteristics, cultural backgrounds, educational needs, and special learning problems of disadvantaged children and youth.

Activities:

District-sponsored college and university seminars in multicultural relationships.

District-sponsored summer and school-year workshops, seminars, conferences, grade-level and department meetings.

Local school-sponsored in-service training sessions—workshops, faculty meetings, grade-level and department meetings.

Instructional materials development and demonstration centers.

Individual and small-group conferences and consultations with specialists in curriculum and instruction and in pupil personnel services.

Preparation and dissemination of instructional materials, curriculum guides, and planning suggestions.

Attendance at local, regional, state, and national conferences and meetings of professional organizations with particular concerns for problems of teaching disadvantaged pupils.

IN-SERVICE TRAINING ACTIVITY

Los Angeles City School Districts' ESEA Title I project for 1966–67 included an extensive and comprehensive in-service program comprised of a wide variety of teacher-training activities conducted in support of special instructional programs. From among many in-service teacher-training activities, the California Project chose six to investigate for its study. Some 445 school personnel who participated in these activities were asked to evaluate their experience.

Two of the six in-service teacher-training activities studied were workshops conducted for elementary school teachers; one was a workshop for reading specialists, the other was a workshop for teachers of English for non-English speaking pupils. A one-week session of the workshop for reading specialists was held prior to the opening of the fall semester for nine reading consultants and 155 reading teachers. In lectures, demonstrations, and small-group discussions, diagnostic and prescriptive techniques for understanding the reading needs of disadvantaged children and special materials for oral language and reading development were presented. Four bimonthly in-service meetings for the reading consultants and eight monthly meetings for the reading teachers were held throughout the school year. The agenda for these meetings included visits to special reading classes, observation of various diagnostic techniques, demonstrations of selected materials, and discussions of mutual problems. The reading consultants attended the California State International Reading Association Conference at Fresno in October and the Claremont Reading Conference in February. They met regularly with the reading teachers to help them organize and implement the special reading program and to demonstrate diagnostic procedures and remedial, corrective, and developmental approaches to the teaching of reading to disadvantaged pupils.

The workshop on English for non-English speaking pupils was planned and conducted by a teacher-consultant who was a specialist in teaching English as a second language. It was attended by twenty teachers who were responsible for organizing and implementing a special program of instruction in English for target pupils who did not speak English with sufficient ease and fluency to benefit from the regular instructional program. This workshop, too, began with a one-week session just prior to the opening of the fall semester. At this session the participants discussed the general educational needs and learning problems of disadvantaged pupils who do not speak English and surveyed the instructional programs, procedures, techniques, and materials that have been developed to teach English to such pupils. The beginning session was followed by eight monthly in-service meetings throughout the school year. At these meetings, special attention was given to audiolingual methodology, procedures for the administration of tests and screening devices, procedures and techniques for second language teaching, construction of audiovisual aids such as charts, puppets, flannel board cutouts, and tape recordings, the organization of the special instructional program, the articulation of this program with regular classroom programs, and cooperation between specialist teachers and classroom teachers of English language arts.

Three of the in-service teacher-training activities studied by the California Project were conducted for secondary school teachers: a reading-centered instruction course, a seminar on multicultural relationships, and a workshop on counseling and teaching disadvantaged students.

The reading-centered instruction course was planned and conducted by consultant-specialists in reading to provide in-service training for twenty-two teachers who were on special assignment as instructional coordinators of the reading-centered instruction program offered by the target secondary schools. The instructional coordinators attended nine monthly in-service training sessions, nine in-service meetings in their respective target schools, and two general orientation and informational sessions. They also held periodic staff meetings for teachers in student achievement centers. In all of these meetings the instructional coordinators gave special attention to the problems of teaching disadvantaged secondary school students the functional reading skills necessary for content mastery in academic subjects—not only English but also social studies, mathematics, and science. They discussed the organization and operation of the special program of reading-centered instruction, procedures for diagnosing reading difficulties, techniques for conducting remedial and corrective reading instruction, and especially the use of instructional materials, supplies, and equipment for such instruction. As in the reading-centered instruction program, the emphasis was on methods and materials for individualized instruction.

Eleven seminars in multicultural relationships were conducted by experts from local colleges and universities. These in-service training sessions were designed to help school personnel involved in ESEA Title I project activities become increasingly more sensitive to and understand better the characteristics, cultural backgrounds, educational needs, and special learning problems of disadvantaged youth. The maximum enrollment in each seminar was forty persons. Three of the eleven seminars were conducted for administrators and staff of project target secondary schools and met for one week—five consecutive days, three hours per day—just prior to the beginning of the fall semester. Six of these seminars were conducted for teachers involved with the various activities of the ESEA Title I project for target secondary schools; these seminars met for three hours on six consecutive Saturday mornings during the fall semester. Two of the seminars were conducted especially for certificated and classified employees of the Office of Specially Funded Programs, Division of Secondary Education. These people met for six hours per day on three consecutive days in the fall at California Polytechnic College at San Dimas. The seminars in multicultural relationships focused on six topics: (1) Negro history and culture, (2) the changing Mexican-American culture, (3) expectations of the dominant culture, (4) developmental tasks of adolescence, (5) self-concept, and (6) revolution versus evolution. Participants were introduced to these topics by means of a variety of media, chiefly through stimulus lectures, large-group question-and-answer discussion, small-group discussion and interaction, and informal discussion during breaks and after meetings.

The workshop in counseling and teaching educationally disadvantaged students was designed to increase participants' understandings of the many dimensions and effects of poverty on children. The workshop was planned and coordinated by counseling consultants to offer sixty-three selected school personnel—teachers, counselors, and administrators from twenty-three target secondary schools—the opportunity to explore their own attitudes and to improve human relationships in their schools. Presenters and participants shared concerns, programs, and ideas for effective school involvement in ESEA Title I project activities. This in-service training activity was conducted in two sessions, each of ten daily six-hour meetings. The first session was held from July 5 through July 18, 1967; the second from July 21 through August 5, 1967. Community resource people were used extensively in this component. Spokesmen from the disadvantaged communities presented viewpoints on more effective school involvement and the need for improving communication with parents, pupils, and school faculties. A student panel gave student viewpoints, and university professors provided insights on positive self-image. Topics considered included (1) the disadvantaged child, (2) national research efforts, (3) the Mexican-American child's self-image, (4) the student's view of school efforts for the disadvantaged child, (5) effective involvement of the teacher and counselor in programs for the disadvantaged pupil, (6) current events in the disadvantaged areas of the city, (7) participation of the clergy in the disadvantaged community, (8) the Negro as a Negro artist sees him, (9) community politics and the disadvantaged. The presentation of each of these topics by lecture, film, or panel discussions was followed by small-group discussion and interaction. In addition, field trips were made to two skills centers, one in Watts and the other in East Los Angeles, and to the International Institute, a community agency serving new foreign arrivals.

The sixth in-service training activity studied by the California Project was a workshop for teachers involved with the project's Summer Assessment Program which ran from July 5 through August 11, 1967, and served physically handicapped and trainable mentally retarded pupils from Special Education Branch schools. Seven consultants planned and conducted the workshop, which stressed communications, self-help, and pre-vocational skills. Twenty-two teachers participated in the workshop. These consultants and teachers met for a three-day session in the spring semester, prior to the beginning of the summer program. Then each of the teachers was released from classroom duties for one week for assignment to a fifteen-hour schedule of classroom observations, demonstrations, and outside visitations to prepare them for more effective teaching of trainable mentally retarded pupils. During the course of the summer program, each teacher participated in forty hours of in-service meetings, two hours each afternoon, Mondays through Thursdays. These meetings stressed occupational training, development of physical and motor skills, and the use of video tape in teaching language development. Opportunities were provided for the participants to listen to outside experts and discuss with them their common experiences and problems encountered in the program. Fifteen of the teachers were also enrolled in a sixteen-hour workshop designed to help them teach swimming to trainable mentally retarded pupils.

School personnel who participated in the six in-service training activities described above were compensated either by payment of a uniform hourly rate ($4.40 per hour) for their attendance at training sessions or by a number of units of credit on the district's salary schedule commensurate with the amount of time they were involved with these activities. Upon completion of these in-service activities, participants were asked to evaluate their experience by responding to a questionnaire. The district's Office of Research and Development designed a special questionnaire to evaluate each of the many in-service training activities conducted by the project. The questionnaires are similar, however, in that they all ask participants to judge, on an appropriate scale, the effectiveness of the topics treated and the instructional media employed; to indicate some of the outcomes of their participation; and to offer suggestions for future in-service activities of the same or a similar type.

## MONROVIA UNIFIED SCHOOL DISTRICT
### (Los Angeles County)

Average per pupil expenditure in fiscal year 1966: $561.81
Number of schools: 9 (K–12)
Total enrollment in Fall 1966: 6,908
Number of pupils from low-income families: 1,176 (15.1%)

ESEA TITLE I PROJECT, 1966–67

Title: Higher Opportunities in Monrovia Education
Amount of federal funds: $188,138
Number of target schools: 6
  4 Elementary
  1 Intermediate
  1 Senior High
Number of target pupils: 963
  100 Prekindergarten
   48 Kindergarten
  416 Elementary
  199 Junior High
  200 Senior High
Percentage of minority-group pupils:
   1% Mexican-American
  12% Negro
   0% Oriental
   0% Other
Special instructional activities:
  Reading

Prekindergarten
Speech Therapy
Reduction of Class Size
Special supplementary services:
Food service (preschool snack)
Health services (nurses aides)
Physical examinations (preschool)
Psychological testing
Home-school coordinator
Library services
Curriculum center
In-service teacher training

IN-SERVICE PROGRAM

Amount of federal funds: $12,000
Number of participants: 55
Objectives:

To provide comprehensive training in diagnostic and remedial techniques for teaching reading to disadvantaged pupils in the primary grades.

To develop curricula and instructional materials to meet the educational needs of disadvantaged pupils with reading problems.

To orient reading teachers toward research and evaluation of instructional procedures, techniques, media, materials, and equipment recently developed for use in teaching reading to disadvantaged pupils.

Activities:

Extension course on Diagnostic and Remedial Reading offered under the auspices of California State College at Los Angeles.

Workshops and grade-level meetings on instructional techniques and materials.

Lectures and discussions on learning theory and the learning problems of disadvantaged youth.

IN-SERVICE TRAINING ACTIVITY

The in-service component of Monrovia Unified School District's ESEA Title I project in 1966–67 was directly related to the program of remedial and developmental reading instruction carried out by teachers in the primary grades of the district's seven elementary schools. The principal activity in the in-service component was an extension course in diagnostic and remedial reading offered under the auspices of California State College at Los Angeles. The California Project asked the thirty-two teachers who participated in this activity to evaluate their experience.

The extension course, entitled Diagnostic and Remedial Reading—X 435, was conducted by a professor (a clinical psychologist) on the faculty of California State College at Los Angeles who also served the district as a consultant during the period of the course. The thirty-two participants in the course were teachers from all seven of the elementary schools in the district, not just the four target elementary schools; most of them taught in the primary grades. The teachers enrolled in the course were selected for their ability to communicate effectively with other members of the staff, their willingness to share the materials developed in the course with other teachers in their respective schools, and their willingness to serve as resource persons and to work with other teachers in their schools to develop the various skills taught in the course.

The course ran for fifteen weeks in the fall semester of 1966–67, meeting for three hours on a weekday evening at one of the target elementary schools in the district. In the afternoon of the day on which the course met, the instructor, in her role as consultant, visited one of the target elementary schools to test the reading skills of some disadvantaged pupils and to assist their teachers in learning and applying more sophisticated diagnostic techniques. Then, in the evening, the instructor spent about an hour or so discussing with all the participants in the course the specific reading disabilities of the disadvantaged children she had tested on that particular day, describing the techniques she and their teachers had used in diagnosing their difficulties and the methods and materials she had recommended for remedying these difficulties. The remaining time in each of the evening sessions was spent on lectures, demonstrations, and discussions covering a wide range of topics related to the diagnosis and remediation of reading problems, including general theories of learning reading, causes of various types of reading disabilities and failures, classroom procedures and techniques for teaching both remedial and developmental reading, programs of individualized instruction in reading, use of various pieces of equipment in diagnosing reading difficulties and teaching reading skills, and many of the new and innovative instructional materials that have been developed for their special relevance to the reading problems of disadvantaged pupils.

Upon successful completion of the extension course, the participants received three units of credit from the sponsoring state college. The participants and the principals of the elementary schools in which they taught were asked to answer seven questions about the effectiveness and value of the course and to make recommendations for the next year's in-service program. The nearly unanimous recommendation of "more of the same" for more teachers at all grade levels testified to the effectiveness of the format of the in-service program: using a clinical psychologist and reading specialist from the state college faculty as both a consultant and an instructor to work with the district's disadvantaged children and their teachers.

## NORWALK-LA MIRADA UNIFIED SCHOOL DISTRICT
### (Los Angeles County)

Average per pupil expenditure in fiscal year 1966: $514.00

Number of schools: 37 (K–12)

Total enrollment in fall 1966: 32,482

Number of pupils from low-income families: identified 1,491 (4.27%)

ESEA TITLE I PROJECT, 1966–67

Title: Increasing the Learning Potential of Culturally Deprived Students Through an Emphasis on Communication Skills, Preventive Counseling and Special Opportunity High School

Amount of federal funds: $316,141

Number of target schools: 6

3 Elementary

3 Senior High (including 1 Continuation)

Number of target pupils: 1,399

180 Kindergarten

684 Elementary

535 Senior High

Percentage of minority-group pupils:
20% Mexican-American
0% Negro
0% Oriental
0% Other
Special instructional activities:
Reading and Communication Skills
Preschool
Kindergarten
Opportunity High School (Continuation)
Remedial Reading and Communication Skills
Vocational Skills
Special supplementary services:
Preventive counseling
In-service teacher training

IN-SERVICE PROGRAM

Amount of federal funds: $3,000
Number of participants: 89
Objectives:
To increase the awareness of school personnel of the characteristics, cultural background, educational needs, and special learning problems of disadvantaged children.

To help teachers improve their professional skills in planning and implementing instructional programs, procedures, techniques, media, and materials that are effective in meeting the special educational needs of disadvantaged pupils.
Activities:
A series of workshops featuring lectures, films, panel discussions, demonstrations, and small-group interaction and discussion of cultural, educational, and other influences that directly affect the level of aspiration and success of disadvantaged children.

An extension course on The Mexican-American in Transition, offered under the auspices of the University of California at Irvine.

A number of workshops on curriculum materials development.

In-service meetings of target school teachers grouped by grade level or department.

IN-SERVICE TRAINING ACTIVITY

The in-service program of Norwalk-La Mirada Unified School District's ESEA Title I project featured a series of six workshops on the historical and cultural backgrounds of Mexican-American pupils and the problems arising from their educational deprivation. The California Project asked seventy-three elementary school teachers on the staff of the district's three target elementary schools to evaluate their participation in these workshops.

The workshops were conducted by consultants to the project brought to the district from colleges, universities, and other institutions. Four of these consultants were themselves of Mexican-American origin; all had had wide experience with compensatory education programs developed to meet the educational needs of disadvantaged pupils. The workshops were open to all teachers in the district; however, they were planned specifically to be beneficial for teachers from the project's target schools with the largest concentrations of Mexican-American students.

Most of the workshops met for about two hours after school in the late afternoon. They offered lectures, films, demonstrations, panel discussions, and group discussions about a variety of historical, cultural, and environmental influences on the academic performances and occupational aspirations of Mexican-American children. The knowledge and understanding gained by participants in these workshops were passed along to other teachers on the staffs of project target schools in school-sponsored meetings and workshops that dealt more specifically with instructional programs, procedures, techniques, and materials for teaching disadvantaged pupils.

## ORANGE UNIFIED SCHOOL DISTRICT (Orange County)

Average per pupil expenditure in fiscal year 1966: $473.00
Number of schools: 35 (K–12)
Total enrollment in fall 1966: 25,314
Number of pupils from low-income families: 472 (1.7%)

ESEA TITLE I PROJECT, 1966–67

Title: Educating the Bi-Lingual Child
Amount of federal funds: $142,392
Number of target schools: 3
  3 Elementary
Number of target pupils: 451
  63 Kindergarten
  388 Elementary
Percentage of minority-group pupils:
  34% Mexican-American
Special instructional activities:
  Remedial Reading
  English as a Second Language
  TA Instructional
Special supplementary services:
  In-service teacher training
  Curriculum development
  School/community cooperation
  Extended use of school facilities

IN-SERVICE PROGRAM

Amount of federal funds: $16,174
Number of participants: 32
Objectives:
  To help teachers develop a better understanding of the problems and values of the educationally disadvantaged.

  To help teachers develop rational strategies for approaching decision-making at curricular and instructional levels.

  To help teachers develop a broader range of appropriate teaching behaviors through self-observation of teacher-pupil interaction in the classroom.
Activities:
  Cooperative group inquiry seminar for staff, teachers, administrators, and consultants in the project.

  Video- and audio-taping of classroom interaction.

  Interaction analysis of classroom teaching performances.

IN-SERVICE TRAINING ACTIVITY

Orange Unified School District's ESEA Title I project included an in-service program that featured a cooperative group inquiry seminar for the staffs of its target elementary schools. The California Project asked the twenty-five teachers who participated in the seminar to evaluate their experience.

The instructor of the seminar was aided in the planning and conduct of its activities by two consultants, one from the University of California at Los Angeles and the other from the University of Arizona. The seminar held ten monthly meetings of three hours each. In these meetings the participants discussed general topics in the philosophy of education and the psychology of learning with particular focus on the formulation, in behavioral terms, of desirable instructional objectives for special programs, particularly in remedial reading, for disadvantaged pupils. The approach to this problem was first through a review of the research literature on the special educational needs and learning problems of disadvantaged pupils and then through the writing of instructional objectives for the project's special program in remedial reading and English language arts for Mexican-American children who speak English as a second language. At the conclusion of the seminar, these instructional objectives were stated in behavioral terms in a booklet assembled and printed by the project director.

The instructional objectives written by the participants in the seminar also became the basis for their self-analysis and self-appraisal of their own classroom teaching performances. Beginning in March, video tape recordings were made of each teacher's classroom activities; each teacher taped three thirty-minute sessions for self-analysis and self-appraisal. The teachers themselves, with the help of the expert consultants, replayed their own tapes and coded their own classroom behaviors, using Flanders' Interaction Analysis Codes and Roberson's System for Self-Appraisal, which had been taught them in earlier meetings of the seminar.

Participants in the seminar were paid a uniform rate of $6 per hour for their attendance at its meetings. At the conclusion of the seminar, they were asked, by questionnaire and interview, to evaluate the outcomes of their participation, particularly in the self-analysis and self-appraisal activities.

The assumption underlying the project's stated objectives for its in-service component was that traditionally trained teachers, imbued with middle-class values, probably lack the understandings and skills necessary to work effectively with culturally different and educationally deprived children. These objectives imply that rational strategies for decision making on the curricular and instructional levels require significant changes in the behavior of teachers, and that teachers will make these necessary changes only if they are helped to revise their perceptions of themselves, their roles in relation to their pupils, and their teaching performances in actual classroom teaching-learning situations. That is, by seeing for himself what he is actually doing in the classroom and how his actions affect his students, the individual teacher will have some rational basis for modifying his attitudes and changing his behavior. The use of video tape-recorded classroom teaching performances and techniques for systematic interaction analysis and self-appraisal proved a highly effective means for achieving the seminar's objectives, giving the participants a new perspective within which to see themselves, their pupils, and their teaching. It would appear, then, that self-evaluation by these means is a worthwhile addition to authoritative presentations of principles and techniques of instruction through lectures and micro- or miniteaching demonstrations, live or on film or video tape. The additional expenditures of time and money necessary to train teachers in the writing of instructional objectives in behavioral terms, in the operation of video tape recording and playback equipment, and in the use of interaction analysis codes and systems of self-appraisal may be fairly judged prudent investments in the improved effectiveness of teachers of the disadvantaged.

## PARAMOUNT UNIFIED SCHOOL DISTRICT
### (Los Angeles County)

Average per pupil expenditure in fiscal year 1966: $495.73
Number of schools: 14 (K–12)
Total enrollment in fall 1966: 9,560
Number of pupils from low-income families: 1,691 (15.62%)

ESEA TITLE I PROJECT, 1966–67

Title: Lincoln Demonstration School

Amount of federal funds: $143,373
Number of target schools: 1
  1 Elementary
Number of target pupils: 394
Percentage of minority-group pupils:
  20% Mexican-American
Special instructional activities:
  General Elementary (Enriched)
  English Language Arts
  Reading
  Cultural Enrichment (General)
Special supplementary services:
  Diagnostic testing
  In-service teacher training
  Instructional media center

IN-SERVICE PROGRAM

Amount of federal funds: $3,500
Number of participants: 30
Objectives:
  To establish constant cross-communication between teachers and paraprofessional staff members.
  To provide for attitudinal, perceptual, and behavioral changes in teachers, administrators, and staff.
  To encourage goal planning that would result in changes in the instructional program consistent with the needs of disadvantaged children.
Activities:
  In-service meetings to expose teachers to new curriculum approaches and communications media from which they could select new approaches to learning problems.
  A series of encounter group sessions to give teachers an opportunity to cross-ventilate and explore their concerns in a supportive climate.
  A teacher-student sociometric study to determine if teachers' perceptions of peer social acceptance of students was congruent with the students' social status placement by their peers.

A series of sensitivity training sessions to facilitate changes in teachers' awarenesses, insights, and attitudes and their behavior.

A summer in-service program in conjunction with the summer school session, consisting of meetings and workshops emphasizing understanding of individual uniquenesses and differences as they relate to success in learning, and creative methods in art, music, language arts, and research techniques.

A series of in-service meetings focused on research techniques, characteristics of gifted children with culturally disadvantaged backgrounds, and inquiry techniques of instruction.

A series of in-service meetings on Self-Concept and Individualization of Instruction.

Maintenance of an instructional media center.

IN-SERVICE TRAINING ACTIVITY

Paramount Unified School District's ESEA Title I project was the operation of Lincoln Demonstration School (elementary), and its in-service component consisted of a number of training activities for the teachers, teacher aides, administrators, and other school personnel on the staff of this target school. Featured among these in-service teacher-training activities was a series of encounter group sensitivity training sessions. The California Project asked the twenty-four teachers who participated in these sessions to evaluate their experience.

The encounter group sensitivity training sessions were planned and conducted by a professor of educational psychology on the faculty of California State College at Long Beach, acting as a consultant to the project. The twenty-four participants who volunteered to take part in this activity were divided into four groups of five each and one group of four. The members of each group were teachers who taught at approximately the same grade level. The original plan for this activity anticipated twelve weekly meetings of one hour each, running throughout the spring semester. Actually, however, the sessions ran from April 11 through May 23, 1967, and most of the groups held only four or five one-hour weekly meetings during that period. One group was able to meet only twice. The sessions were held after school in the late afternoon at the project demonstration school.

Stressing the achievement of openness to honest feelings and

reactions about themselves as they reacted toward children and probing current ways of responding, each group member was encouraged
to compare notes on who was his best student. What did this choice
of "best" indicate about his attitudes and values toward this and other
students? Conversely, which pupil seemed to be the greatest source of
each member's frustration and negative feelings? What ways, verbally
and nonverbally, were members employing in order to establish and
sustain teacher-pupil relationships? Which students allowed each member to feel most relaxed and unpressured in this demonstration school
setting, and which least? Specific elements of teacher-pupil relationships were emphasized in each session. Among these were relationships
that created opportunities for pupils to feed back to teachers, those that
exemplified the meaning of active listening, those in which teachers
expressed honest feelings so that pupils could use them, and those in
which the differing perceptions of teachers, pupils, and parents regarding rewards and controls in the classroom were manifested. Some
attempts at formal synthesis of these elements were made with the
idea of giving some structure to the task of becoming humanely objective about frustrating conditions in the participants themselves, in their
relationships with pupils who have various types of learning problems,
in the operation of the project demonstration school, and in relationships between school personnel and parents, other social agencies, and
the community.

In these encounter group sensitivity training sessions, the focus
was at all times on relationships between teachers and pupils and not
on peer relationships among teacher colleagues; stress was consistently
and constantly placed on helping relationships among colleagues, in
which group members could recognize and complement each other's
strengths as teachers.

The Eysenck Personality Inventory was used to take pre- and
postmeasures of participants' attitudes on three scales: Extroversion,
Neuroticism, and Lie Scales. Form A of this instrument was administered prior to the opening session; Form B, following the concluding
session. Analysis of the pre- and posttest score means, using the $t$-test
of differences between the compared mean scores, indicated a significant change in the participants' attitudes (at the .01 level) only on the
Lie Scale. However, results also indicated the likelihood that significant change would probably have occurred had the sessions been car-

ried out over a longer period of time; that is, test scores indicated changes which, though not statistically significant, were nevertheless in the desired direction.

Participants in this activity received no additional compensation of salary or college credit for their participation; nevertheless, twenty-four out of the twenty-six teachers invited to participate did so.

The demonstration-laboratory school setting would appear to be in many respects ideal for conducting encounter group sensitivity-training sessions of the type featured in the in-service component of Paramount's project. The close collegial relationship among group members—teachers on the staff of a single target school and sharing common instructional objectives—seems to have been enhanced by their participation in this activity. If carried on over a longer period of time, these sessions would probably have been more effective in bringing about changes in the teachers themselves, in their relationships with each other and with their pupils, and ultimately in the pupils' gain in learning skills from the project's special instructional program.

## REDONDO BEACH CITY ELEMENTARY SCHOOL DISTRICT (Los Angeles County)

Average per pupil expenditure in fiscal year 1966: $452.85
Number of schools: 17 (K–6)
Total enrollment in fall 1966: 9,891
Number of pupils from low-income families: 344 (33%)

ESEA TITLE I PROJECT, 1966–67

Title: Remedial Reading for Educationally Deprived Children
Amount of federal funds: $114,043
Number of target schools: 3
  3 Elementary
Number of target pupils: 456
Percentage of minority-group pupils:
  11% Mexican-American
  1% Oriental
Special instructional activities:
  Remedial Reading

English as a Second Language
Cultural Enrichment
Special supplementary services:
  Expanded library facilities and extended library services
  In-service teacher training

IN-SERVICE PROGRAM

Amount of federal funds: $5,000
Number of participants: 14
Objective:
  To provide in-service education for teachers relating to the objectives of the project.
Activities:
  District-sponsored workshops on reading methods, production of materials, use of equipment.
  Attendance at county, regional, and state conferences on reading, audiovisual instruction, and school library facilities and services.
  Consultations with specialists in the fields of reading, audiovisual instruction, and school libraries.

IN-SERVICE TRAINING ACTIVITY

The in-service teacher training component of Redondo Beach City Elementary School District's ESEA Title I project included workshops, attendance at conferences, and consultations with specialists. The California Project asked ten persons who participated in all, or nearly all, of these activities to evaluate their experience. Among these were the Deputy Superintendent of the district, the ESEA Title I project director, the principals of the three target elementary schools, three teachers from project target schools, and two librarians working in these schools.

The district-sponsored workshops on methods of teaching reading dealt with such topics as the use of Frostig materials and programmed instructional materials and the Language Experience Approach. Workshops on the production of instructional materials were concerned with photographic techniques for producing educative materials, copystand composition and subject matter, production and use of 35mm slides, filmstrips, and Super 8 single-concept films. Workshops on the use of equipment dealt particularly with the uses of the Controlled Reader, the Language Master, the overhead projector, SRA Games Kit, Lymburn records, the Tachist-O-Flasher, and listening posts.

Participants in the in-service program attended the following local, regional, and state conferences and attended sessions concerned with the following topics:

IRA California Reading Association Conference in Fresno, October 27–28, 1966:
Language Arts and the Reading Program
Miller-Unruch Law SB 205
What Makes a Good Project Proposal
Evaluation
Private and Parochial Schools Involvement
In-Service Needs
Programmed Teaching
Linguistic Teaching of Reading
English as a Second Language
Teaching Educationally Disadvantaged Children
Developmental Reading
Changes Made Through In-Service Education
Audiovisual Education Association Conference in Long Beach, November 4–5:
The Role of the Media Specialist
Lib-Visualist
Instructional Materials Centers
The Many Messages of Multi-Media
A New Look at Old Techniques
Audiovisual Education Association Conference in Los Angeles, February 2–4, 1967: Enrichment Experiences
Claremont Reading Conference in Claremont, February 10–11:
Communication Skills Project
Linguistic Diversity
Perceptual Symbols
Motor Perceptual Development
California Association of School Librarians Conference in Los Angeles, March 2–4, 1967:
Evaluation of Library Facilities, Programs, and Collections

The School Library and Language Arts
The School Library and Science
The School Library and Social Studies
The School Library—An Instructional Center
Orange County Reading Conference at Fullerton State College:
"The Language Experience Approach to Reading"
Los Angeles County Conference on Reading in Los Angeles, May
16, 1967:
Teaching Reading to Children Who Have Educational Handicaps
Selective Reading
Some Applications of Linguistics in Teaching English as a Second
Language

At district-sponsored workshops and at conferences, the participants consulted with several specialists from the State Department of Education on problems relating to the teaching of reading and English as a second language to Mexican-American children in the elementary grades. A professor at California State College at Long Beach served as a consultant for the evaluation of the entire ESEA Title I project, helping to draw up its proposal and design its evaluative instruments.

The participants in the project's in-service activities were asked to evaluate each activity and to make recommendations for improving the in-service program for the next year by responding to a questionnaire. They also met as a group to discuss and evaluate the year's in-service activities and plan for the future in late May, 1967.

From the responses participants made to the evaluative questionnaire it would appear that they regarded their attendance at local, regional, and state conferences as the most beneficial feature of the project's in-service component. They judged that the conferences had provided them particularly valuable opportunities to learn about and observe innovative classroom procedures and techniques of instruction and had been a strong source of professional inspiration. The participants, particularly the teachers and librarians, also judged the district-sponsored workshops to have been beneficial, especially the demonstrations of teaching techniques, instructional materials, and equipment. However, they felt that there had been too few workshops and that those that were offered had allowed too little time for informal meetings, small-group discussion, and interaction among participants—exchange of ideas and suggestions. They also felt that the workshops did not provide adequate opportunities for the production, field testing, and evaluation of instructional materials. The district's problem in providing for the professional growth of its project teachers and other school personnel seems to have been one of achieving a balance between theory, research, and practice in the attainment and developmnt of skill in using various instructional procedures, techniques, materials, and equipment.

## SANTA MARIA JOINT UNION HIGH SCHOOL DISTRICT
### (Santa Barbara County)

Average per pupil expenditure in fiscal year 1966: $631.02
Number of schools: 3 (9–12)
Total enrollment in fall 1966: 4,000
Number of pupils from low-income families: 120 (7%)

ESEA TITLE I PROJECT, 1966–67

Title: SMJUHSD Educational Opportunity Program
Amount of federal funds: $44,550
Number of target schools: 1
  1 Senior High
Number of target pupils: 210
Percentage of minority-group pupils:
  Not available for 1966–67
Special instructional activities:
  English Language Arts
  Reading, Remedial and Corrective
  Saturday Continuation Program (for high school dropouts)
  Summer School Remedial Reading
Special supplementary services:
  Counseling and guidance
  Vocational guidance and work experience program
  Curriculum development (individualized instruction)
  In-service teacher training

Amount of federal funds: $12,684
Number of participants: 16
Objectives:
To help teachers and counselors recognize and express their feelings and ideas and to be receptive to those of culturally deprived children.
To help them understand and accept culturally disadvantaged children.
To help them develop a positive self-image within each child.
To help them change the child's attitude toward school and education.
To help them improve the child's emotional and social stability.
Activities:
Two-week (ten-day) summer workshop for teachers and counselors, with consultants conducting sensitivity training focused on individualized instruction for disadvantaged children and using video tape-recorded materials to analyze behavior and create innovative approaches to teaching and counseling these children.

IN-SERVICE TRAINING ACTIVITY

The in-service program of Santa Maria Joint Union High School District's ESEA Title I project featured a two-week summer workshop for teachers and counselors. The California Project asked the sixteen participants in the workshop to evaluate their experience.

The summer workshop, which was held for two weeks in late August, 1966, emphasized sensitivity training for teachers and counselors on the staff of the project's target high school. It was conducted by consultants from the faculty of UCLA who were trained and experienced small-group discussion leaders. Discussion focused on matters relating to the problem of providing individualized instruction for culturally and educationally disadvantaged children. Participants were encouraged to recognize and express their own feelings and ideas concerning these matters and to pursue their interests in developing procedures, techniques, and materials for use in individualizing the instruction of their own disadvantaged students. Video tape-recording equipment and supplies purchased for use in the ESEA Title I project for the previous year (1965–66) were used in this workshop to facilitate the analysis of teachers' and pupils' behavior and the evaluation of innovative approaches to teaching and counseling.

The participants in the summer workshop were paid a salary, based on their position on the district's salary scale, for their attendance at the ten daily sessions of six hours each.

The distinguishing feature of Santa Maria's in-service program was its extensive use of video tape recording in the classroom and replay of recorded teaching performances at in-service training meetings. The dramatic immediacy and direct relevance of these video tape-recorded instructional materials not only facilitated analysis and evaluation of teacher-pupil interactions but greatly intensified teachers' interest in experimental and innovative approaches to individualized instruction for disadvantaged pupils. The use of this medium and these materials in the format of a sensitivity training workshop proved an especially effective means for achieving the objectives of this in-service training activity.

## WILLOWBROOK ELEMENTARY SCHOOL DISTRICT
### (Los Angeles County)

Average per pupil expenditure in fiscal year 1966: $401.43
Number of schools: 5 (K–8)
Total enrollment in fall 1966: 4,118
Number of pupils from low-income families: 885 (20.2%)

ESEA TITLE I PROJECT, 1966–67

Title: Willowbrook Expanded Learning Program
Amount of federal funds: $269,800
Number of target schools: 5
  5 Elementary
Number of target pupils: 762
  77 Kindergarten
  685 Elementary
Percentage of minority-group pupils:
  5.4% Mexican-American
  94.4% Negro

Special instructional activities:
Reading, Remedial and Corrective
Cultural Enrichment (study trips)
Special supplementary services:
Health and psychological services
In-service teacher training

IN-SERVICE PROGRAM

Amount of federal funds: $18,100
Number of participants: 25
Objectives:

To help meet the educational needs of teachers in order that they might feel more comfortable in working with disadvantaged children.

To help teachers understand how to use instructional media within the framework of learning situations and how to use new media to overcome the learning barriers characteristic of disadvantaged pupils.

To help teachers gain deeper insights, skill, and sensitivity in working with children from disadvantaged socioeconomic backgrounds.

Activities:

Numerous workshops and discussion meetings conducted by consultants for target school teachers, emphasizing (1) characteristics, cultural backgrounds, educational needs, and special learning problems of disadvantaged pupils, and (2) instructional programs, procedures, techniques, materials, media, and equipment for teaching specific subjects to disadvantaged pupils.

Demonstrations of instructional equipment and materials by representatives of manufacturers and distributors.

IN-SERVICE TRAINING ACTIVITY

Willowbrook Elementary School District's ESEA Title I project included a comprehensive program of in-service training activities for the teachers in its five target schools. The California Project asked the twenty-eight teachers who had participated in any or all of the various activities in this program to evaluate their experience.

The district contracted with a member of the Education faculty of Pepperdine College to plan and provide a "package" of in-service training activities to meet the broad, general objectives for target school teachers enumerated above. This consultant arranged a program consisting of a series of workshops conducted by administrative staff of the district and the project, by supervisors, by special consultants, by guest speakers, and by sales representatives of manufacturers and distributors of instructional equipment and materials. Most of the workshops in this series, which ran throughout the entire school year, were held in the late afternoon after school hours in one of the target schools. The length of the workshop meetings and the number of teachers who participated in them varied considerably, depending upon the day and date of the workshop and the subject which it treated. Some of the workshops were concerned with general topics related to the teaching of disadvantaged children, such as recommended programs and procedures for compensatory education; significant interrelationships between administrators and teachers and between teachers and children; techniques for manipulating and controlling classroom behavior of pupils; communication; constructive conflict; the structure of intelligence; perceptual and motor coordination; concept formation; evaluation of self-concept. Other workshops were concerned with the curricula, methods, and materials of specific school subjects, such as reading and the language arts, music, health and hygiene. Still others were concerned with auxiliary supporting services provided by the project for its target pupils, such as library facilities and procedures, health and nursing care, psychological testing and counseling, and school-home-community relations work. The instructional procedures employed in the workshops included lectures, panel discussions, demonstrations, large- and small-group discussions, and case studies.

At the conclusion of the series of in-service workshops, the coordinator asked the participants to respond to two questionnaires. One questionnaire asked them to evaluate the effectiveness with which the total in-service program achieved its primary objectives, to express their opinions regarding the greatest strengths of the program, and to make recommendations for improving the program for the following year. The other questionnaire asked the participants to indicate how much the in-service program had contributed to their awareness, knowledge, and understanding of culturally and educationally disadvantaged children, particularly of their personality and social characteristics; home and family structure; family attitudes and values, conflicting value systems blocking communications; the influence of their environment upon disadvantaged children; recognition of strengths in their culture; special learning problems of disadvantaged children; factors other than lack of ability that cause reading problems among disadvantaged children; and problems of planning instructional programs, procedures, and materials to meet the special needs of disadvantaged children.

Although the project's intensive and comprehensive in-service program for 1966–67 did, in the judgment of its staff and participants, achieve broad objectives, the district moved, in 1967–68, from the buckshot approach with multiple topics related to teaching the disadvantaged to a concentrated approach to the problems of teaching language arts to such children. The resulting in-service program featured training activities focused on the use of individualized instructional procedures, video taping, listening kits, and other equipment and materials for teaching language arts and skills to disadvantaged children.

## HEALDSBURG UNION AND HIGH SCHOOL DISTRICTS
### (Sonoma County)

Average per pupil expenditure in fiscal year 1966: $465.00
Number of schools: 4 (K–12)
Total enrollment in fall 1966: 2,807
Number of pupils from low-income families: 434 (13.7%)

ESEA TITLE I PROJECT, 1966–67

Title: Opportunities Unlimited
Amount of federal funds: $103,389
Number of target schools: 4
  2 Elementary
  1 Junior High
  1 Senior High
Number of target pupils: 403
  172 Elementary
   98 Junior High
  133 Senior High

Percentage of minority-group pupils:
  24% Mexican-American
  2% Negro
  0% Oriental
  4% American Indian
Special instructional activities:
  Remedial and corrective instruction in:
    Reading
    English as a Second Language
    Mathematics
    Cultural Enrichment (field study trips, performances, exhibits)
    Vocational Training
Special supplementary services:
  Counseling and guidance
  Coordinated school-community support
  Teacher aides
  In-service training of teachers and teacher aides

IN-SERVICE PROGRAM

Amount of federal funds: $20,832
Number of participants: 22
Objectives:
To strengthen the understanding and skill of teachers and other staff members working with the educationally disadvantaged.

To provide an opportunity for teachers and staff members to work with children and their families in an educational, social, and intercultural setting.

To provide a well-planned training program for teachers and teacher aides around the personal and educational needs of a specific group of disadvantaged children.

To provide an opportunity for teachers and staff to plan curriculum experiences evolving out of the observed needs of disadvantaged children.

To assist teachers and staff members in communicating effectively with members of a disadvantaged minority group and with the staff members of other local and county agencies that work with this group.

Activities:

Weekly seminar on curricular needs of disadvantaged pupils, conducted by a professor from Sonoma State College.

Workshop and practicum in teaching educationally deprived pupils in twice-weekly evening demonstration classes.

Six-week workshop and practicum in teaching disadvantaged pupils in a summer demonstration school.

Development of a curriculum planning and instructional materials preparation center in the high school library.

IN-SERVICE TRAINING ACTIVITY

During the spring and summer of 1966, the Healdsburg Union and High School Districts sponsored a workshop in teaching the disadvantaged as the in-service training component of its ESEA Title I project. The California Project asked the twenty-two participants in this workshop to evaluate their experience.

The principal activity of the workshop was a practicum in teaching Spanish-speaking Mexican-American children. This pilot in-service training project was carried out in conjunction with the ESEA Title I project's demonstration school for educationally deprived students and their parents. Throughout the twelve weeks of the spring semester, 1966, the demonstration school held classes at Healdsburg Elementary School on Monday and Thursday evenings for two hours. Approximately sixty to sixty-five parents attended classes at each of these sessions to learn English and prepare for American citizenship; their children, numbering from 135 to 156 per session and ranging in age from three to fourteen years, attended classes averaging twelve or thirteen pupils in each to learn English as a second language and to participate in a wide variety of educational and cultural activities.

The demonstration school and the in-service training workshop were under the direction of the project coordinator, who was assisted by a staff consisting of the evening program administrator (the school principal), the cultural center coordinator, a library assistant, an account clerk, two consultants who were curriculum specialists on the faculty of Sonoma State College, a bilingual county social worker assigned to Healdsburg, and five guest lecturers and demonstration speakers. Instruction for the demonstration school classes was provided by the participants in the workshop: eleven elementary and secondary school teachers on the faculties of the project's target schools and eleven teacher aides who were bilingual Mexican-American juniors and seniors in the target high school. About one-fourth of the participants—teachers and teacher aides—served in rotation as the instructors in the English classes at each session; the others worked with the children who took part in all the other activities offered by the program, such as drama (skits and short plays); music (vocal and instrumental ensembles); art (drawing, painting, ceramics, and puppet making); science (nature study and demonstration experiments); history and government (city and county); and field trips to visit local places of interest and attend community affairs and cultural events.

The workshop met each Monday afternoon for two hours for a lecture-discussion session conducted by a professor from Sonoma State College. At these sessions the participants were instructed in such matters as the educational philosophy and instructional program and practices of the ESEA Title I Compensatory Education Project: Opportunities Unlimited; the definition of disadvantaged students in the context of this project; the relation of the disadvantaged student's home environment to the objectives and outcomes of the project; the role of the teacher and the social worker in relation to disadvantaged students and their parents; the development of curricula and methods for teaching the disadvantaged; the use of instructional procedures, techniques, materials, and equipment in meeting the educational needs of the disadvantaged; the use of teacher aides, consultants, counselors, and specialists in pupil services (psychologists, psychometrists, nurses, speech therapists, and others) in working with these students; and procedures for evaluating outcomes of teaching the disadvantaged.

At the conclusion of the lecture-discussion sessions, the participants in the workshop joined with the staff, parents, and students in the demonstration school for a family-style dinner. After dinner, the parents went to their classes and the children to theirs, and the participants took up their teaching duties.

In addition to the lecture-discussion sessions on Monday afternoons and the practicum on Monday and Thursday evenings, the participants in the workshop also took part in such activities as observing demonstrations in teaching English as a second language given by Spanish-speaking consultants, hearing guest speakers present research results and new methods and materials in teaching the disadvantaged, watching the representatives of commercial suppliers demonstrate new instructional materials and equipment, visiting other schools and districts to observe similar programs and practices in compensatory education, and developing curriculum plans and preparing instructional materials for use in the project's program for 1966–67.

During the summer of 1966, the ESEA Title I project sponsored a six-week summer demonstration school involving the same staff, teachers and teacher aides, and many of the same disadvantaged students who had participated in the evening demonstration program and in-service training workshop during the spring semester. The three demonstration-laboratory classes of ten students each were divided into elementary and secondary levels and enrolled twenty continuing students from the evening demonstration school classes for Spanish-speaking educationally deprived children and ten new students from an English-speaking educationally deprived group. The programs of the summer demonstration school and the summer workshop continued all the various lines of endeavor begun in the spring semester.

Upon completion of the workshop, all participants who were qualified for admission to Sonoma State College received three units of credit for the spring semester and six units of credit for the summer session. The teachers also received salaries based on their position on the district's salary schedule and credit toward an increment on the schedule.

The workshop and practicum were evaluated in reports by the Sonoma State College professor who instructed the workshop and by the evening program administrator (school principal) of the demonstration school.

In the fall of 1966, the District's ESEA Title I project cut the allocation for its in-service training component from the previous year's $21,000 to $7,000. The teachers who participated in the previous year's in-service workshop conducted monthly meetings of workshops held in the target junior and senior high school and quarterly meetings of instructional materials production workshops held district-wide for teachers in all target schools. These staff members, and other district personnel—administrators and pupil service specialists—also attended workshops and conferences on the learning problems and educational needs of the disadvantaged held outside the district. They also served as members of the project's Curriculum Development Committee, working on instructional programs, procedures, and materials for its remedial and corrective instruction activities. These developments seem to indicate that the district intended its intensive and comprehensive in-service program for 1965–66 to serve not only the stated objectives of its ESEA Title I project for that year but also the further aim of providing its target schools with a well-trained and experienced cadre of teachers who could, in turn, carry on as local experts in the planning and conduct of more modest and less costly in-service training activities during the second and subsequent years of the project. From the district's evaluation of its projects for those subsequent years it would appear that the combined workshop and practicum format of its in-service program for the first year effectively served both the immediate and long-range purposes for which it was designed.

## MARYSVILLE JOINT UNIFIED SCHOOL DISTRICT
### (Yuba County)

Average per pupil expenditure in fiscal year 1966: $487.40
Number of schools: 25 (K–12)
Total enrollment in fall 1966: 10,800
Number of pupils from low-income families: 1975 (21.3%)

ESEA TITLE I PROJECT, 1966–67

Title: Yuba County Reading-Learning Center
Amount of federal funds: $169,000
Number of target schools: 25
    24 Elementary and Intermediate (K–8)
    1 Senior High
Number of target pupils: 821
    50 Kindergarten
    542 Elementary
    109 Junior High
    120 Senior High
Percentage of minority-group pupils:
    3% Mexican-American
    4% Negro

½% Oriental
2% Other
Special instructional activities:
Remedial Reading
Speech Therapy
Special supplementary services:
Diagnostic testing
Counseling and guidance (parents)
Reading materials production
Professional library facility and service
In-service teacher training

IN-SERVICE PROGRAM

Amount of federal funds: $6,000
Number of participants: 124
Objectives:
To increase teachers' awareness of and insights into the reading and learning problems of educationally deprived children.

To increase their knowledge of the causes and remedies of reading disabilities so that they may be able to identify, diagnose, and prescribe corrective instruction to resolve them.

To improve their professional skills and general competence and also to provide them with training in a variety of specialized approaches to the teaching of reading, particularly through individualized instruction.

To provide a professional library of reference materials, a copying and production service of instructional materials, and dissemination of extracts and excerpts from recent research monographs and specialized articles on the teaching of reading.

Activities:
An extension course, sponsored by University of California at Davis, on Case Studies in Reading.

A workshop on Individualized Reading.

Saturday morning attendance at a course on diagnosis and remediation of reading problems offered by the Ellen K. Raskob Institute, College of the Holy Names, Oakland.

Series of in-service meetings on teaching-learning variables.

Visits, on released time, to observe demonstrations of instructional programs, units, procedures, techniques, media, materials, and equipment used in other classrooms, schools, and school districts.

IN-SERVICE TRAINING ACTIVITY

Among the several in-service teacher training activities sponsored by the Yuba County Reading-Learning Center for teachers working with disadvantaged pupils was an extension course, Case Studies in Reading, offered by the University of California at Davis and conducted by the Director of the Reading-Learning Center. The California Project asked 160 teachers who were enrolled in this course to evaluate their experience.

The catalogue description of the extension course follows:

"Case Studies in Reading" was designed to serve teachers in elementary or secondary classrooms who have pupils with reading problems. Instruction will be shown as follow:
1. Individual conferences with each teacher to consider the nature of the child's reading difficulty. During these interviews the child's school records will be reviewed and all information related to his problem will be gathered.
2. Teachers will be trained in diagnostic techniques and their findings will serve as a basis for corrective measures.
3. A program of reading instruction will be put into effect by each teacher in his or her classroom.
4. Resources and materials will be developed by each teacher at the Reading-Learning Center under the direction of the course instructor.
5. Evening seminars will be held to evaluate progress throughout the course.

The course carried two semester units (three quarter units) of credit. It was offered twice, from March through June, 1966, and from September, 1966, through February, 1967.

Case Studies in Reading was designed as an independent study activity in which each teacher enrolled would work with one pupil for approximately twenty hours in an effort to diagnose and remedy his reading difficulty. Each teacher prepared and presented to the instructor and participants a two-page case summary in which she outlined the child's reading problem and made recommendations for its solution. Each teacher also kept a log of her tutoring activities, with running commentaries on their effectiveness, which she submitted to the instructor from time to time in conference and upon completion of the course. Lectures, seminars, materials workshops, and individual conferences were held at the Reading-Learning Center after school hours in the late afternoon or in the evening. Case work—diagnostic testing and remedial instruction as well as counseling of both children and their parents—was individually scheduled and carried out by the participants and their pupils. In addition to enabling the participants to study one child and his reading problems in depth, this extension course also provided intensive special care and helpful instruction for disadvantaged pupils wtih serious reading difficulties.

The Yuba County Reading-Learning Center represents the effort of the cooperating school districts and community to provide specialized compensatory and supplementary educational opportunities for those of their pupils who have been culturally and educationally deprived. Its program is designed to provide not only intensive remedial instruction and supporting services for disadvantaged pupils but also in-service training for teachers and other school personnel whose knowledge, understandings, and specialized skills may prevent a continuing high or even increasing demand upon the Center's limited resources for providing corrective help. Thus the effect of the Center's comprehensive, cooperative, and coordinated effort has been to reduce this rural county's dependence on the expertise of high-priced consultants who work in distant urban centers of education and to provide it with a growing number of local experts who, with the assistance and support of the Center's staff and facilities, work in and through their school classrooms to alleviate the reading and learning difficulties of educationally deprived pupils.

## SANTA CRUZ CITY SCHOOLS (Santa Cruz County)

Average per pupil expenditure in fiscal year 1966: $510.41
Number of schools: 11 (K–12)
Total enrollment in fall 1966: 7,550
Number of pupils from low-income families: 238

Title: Compensatory Education Program (Laurel Elementary School)
Amount of federal funds: $51,329
Number of target schools: 1
  1 Elementary
Number of target pupils: 484
  218 Elementary
  266 High School District Project
Percentage of minority-group pupils:
  16.0% Mexican-American
  14.0% Negro
  1.6% Oriental
Special instructional activities:
  General Elementary Curriculum
  Industrial Arts and Crafts
  Developmental Reading
  Instructional Materials Center
Special supplementary services:
  School-home-community relations
  In-service teacher training
    (for teachers and other school personnel in project elementary school)

IN-SERVICE PROGRAM

Amount of federal funds: $3,500
Number of participants: 8
Objectives:
  To develop an increased awareness on the part of the school staff of the nature and needs of disadvantaged children, as well as an increased competency in developing appropriate instructional programs.
  To provide teachers with the assistance of curriculum and instruction specialists as consultants and resource persons.
  To help all members of the school staff to coordinate their efforts to provide an enriched educational program for the children.

Activities:

A two-week summer workshop on Learning and the Disadvantaged Child.

Orientation and in-service training for teacher aides.

Consultations with curriculum specialists on scheduled consulting days throughout the school year.

Support and assistance to project elementary school teachers from district office personnel, particularly the elementary curriculum coordinator, the remedial reading teacher, and the speech teacher.

Participation of project school teachers in district-wide in-service programs.

Attendance at meetings and conferences of professional organizations.

IN-SERVICE TRAINING ACTIVITY

The in-service training component of Santa Cruz City Schools' ESEA Title I project was operated as an integral part of the total program of the project elementary school. The California Project asked the eight members of the staff of the target elementary school who participated in these in-service activities to evaluate their experience.

The objectives of the project elementary school program were to redesign the school's curriculum in an effort to combat the effects on its pupils of their culturally deprived environment; to provide an enriched instructional program that would promote more effective educational achievement; to provide the supplementary personnel and services that would result in more resources available to the school's staff; to develop better communication and understanding between the children's home and school environments and so create more effective staff-parent relationships. The primary objective of the school's in-service training program was to develop an increased awareness on the part of the entire school staff of the nature and needs of disadvantaged children, as well as an increased competency in developing appropriate instructional programs and procedures.

The in-service training program began with a two-week summer workshop on Learning and the Disadvantaged Child held from August 22 to September 2, 1966. This workshop was planned by the project director, with the assistance of a professor on the faculty of the University of Califorina at Santa Cruz Extension Services and a consultant specialist in teaching language arts from the Berkeley Unified School District; it was directed by the principal of the project elementary school (Laurel Elementary School), a professor on the faculty of San Jose State College, and a consultant from the State Department of Education. The eight participants in the workshop included the principal, the fourth, fifth, and sixth grade teachers, the supplemental teacher, the librarian, the nurse, and the psychologist.

The workshop was designed to orient the staff of the project elementary school to the purposes of the ESEA Title I project and to begin the in-service activities that were to be continued on consulting days throughout the coming school year. The program of the workshop consisted of lectures, panel discussions, films, and demonstrations followed by questions and discussion periods during the morning hours, and of discussions and creative sessions during the afternoon hours. The lectures and demonstrations were presented by the workshop staff and guest speakers from agencies and institutions in the surrounding area. These presentations treated the full range of topics related to the teaching of culturally and educationally disadvantaged pupils, particularly the effects of environmental conditioning and the special needs and problems resulting from such conditioning. The creative sessions, some of which were held in individual conferences, were concerned with planning instructional programs, procedures, and materials that are especially effective in meeting the educational needs and solving the learning problems of disadvantaged pupils.

Several members of the staff and guest speakers to the workshop were invited to return throughout the following school year to serve as consultants to the project elementary school staff on its consulting days. Their return visits were to provide a form of periodic reinforcement for the staff, to provide an opportunity for the staff to question the consultants after having had a chance to test their ideas in actual classroom situations, and to provide for the continual focus of the school's program on the goals set at the workshop. The schedule of consulting days was as follows:

| *Date* | *Topic* |
|---|---|
| October 3 | Teaching language arts and communication skills |
| October 7 | Teaching arithmetic and mathematics |
| November 3 | Teaching visual arts |
| December 5 | Teaching reading and using diagnostic and remedial materials and techniques |
| January 12 and 13 | Modification of behavior patterns |
| February 10 and 17 ⎱ | Teaching arithmetic and mathematics |
| May 5 and 10 ⎰ | |

These consultations were programmed as half-day sessions on school days during which the participants were released from their regular duties. The dates and topics for these consultations were selected by the participants to meet their felt need for further instruction, reinforcement, or assistance.

All participants attended the weekly staff meetings conducted by the principal of the project elementary school. These meetings were held for an hour or so every Wednesday morning before school. (The opening of school on these mornings was delayed an hour to facilitate a minimum-day schedule of classes.) Some of the meetings were devoted to discussions of general subjects relating to teaching the disadvantaged, some to matters of planning and conducting the enriched instructional program, and some to discussion of the specific learning disabilities and disciplinary problems of individual pupils. These last were carried on as case studies and were moderated by the school psychologist who, together with the school nurse, made many home visits to confer with the families of disadvantaged pupils and contributed background information to these discussions. Thus weekly staff meetings were properly considered an in-service training activity as well as a necessary feature of the school's instructional program.

In addition to attending consultations and weekly staff meetings, the school staff also participated in all district-wide in-service training programs such as Family Life Education Curriculum Committee, Art Education Committee, and State Textbook Evaluation. Furthermore, some or all of them attended a number of state and regional conferences on matters related to teaching the disadvantaged. District office personnel, particularly the elementary curriculum coordinator (who was the director of this ESEA Title I project), spent a disproportionate amount of their time in the project elementary school, providing assistance and support to its teachers and coordinating its programs with other activities in the district and the community.

The objectives and activities of the district's ESEA Title I project and its in-service component so interrelate and overlap that they must be considered as a single, coordinated, comprehensive effort to operate the project elementary school as a demonstration-laboratory center for the study of problems in teaching disadvantaged children.

## TITLE III PROJECTS (PACE)

Another segment of the ESEA Act—Title III, more commonly known as PACE (Projects to Advance Creativity in Education), was established to encourage innovation and creativity in educational practices. This focus makes Title III unique and sets it apart from other types of federal funding. PACE projects were developed to serve as catalysts for change—"to develop change consciousness and know-how in local school systems." Other unique features of Title III include: (1) the breadth of its scope, which includes almost every aspect of education—preschool through adult education, out-of-school education, and "an array of subject areas and combinations thereof that is limited only by human imagination";[1] (2) its comprehensive funding policy—Title III is a 100 per cent grant to local agencies, and involves a direct federal-local relationship; and (3) its built-in requirement for community participation, such as joint planning for school innovations.

As stated in the *Manual for Project Applications,* the purposes of PACE are as follows:

The Title III program . . . is designed to encourage school districts to develop imaginative solutions to educational problems; to more effectively utilize research findings; and to create, design, and

[1] *Notes and Working Papers Concerning the Administration of Programs Authorized under Title III of . . . the Elementary and Secondary Education Act of 1965,* Prepared for the Committee on Labor and Public Welfare, United States Senate, Washington, D.C., 1967, p. 26.

make intelligent use of supplementary centers and services. Primary objectives are to translate the latest knowledge about teaching and learning into widespread educational practice and to create an awareness of new programs and services of high quality that can be incorporated in school programs. Therefore, PACE seeks to (1) encourage the development of innovations, (2) demonstrate worthwhile innovations in educational practice through exemplary programs, (3) supplement existing programs and facilities. The heart of the PACE program is in these provisions for bringing a creative force to the improvement of schools and for demonstrating that better practices can be applied.[2]

Using this statement as a guide, the Education Subcommittee of the Senate Committee on Labor and Public Welfare published a book devoted to verifying or modifying the stated purposes through an analysis of Title III applications.

In the present investigation, the California Project has selected three of the PACE projects in California for study. These three projects—Compton, Imperial-Riverside, and Stockton—were chosen because they had both a definite in-service education component as an important aspect of their overall efforts and a clear relation to problems of the disadvantaged. The project descriptions were based on information taken from the projects' applications and evaluation reports and interviews with project directors and participants. The reader will note that these projects illustrate a variety in the communities and clientele they served and the various means used to achieve the projects' objectives.

## COMPTON UNION HIGH SCHOOL DISTRICT
### (Los Angeles County)

ESEA TITLE III PROJECT, 1966–67

Title: SCRIBE (Summer Curriculum Revision through Industrial Business Experience)
Amount of federal funds: $96,000
Number of target schools: 3 Senior High
Number of target pupils: 3,347

[2] *Ibid.*

Special instructional activities:

Place teachers of academic subjects in a summer employment situation in business and industry, thereby providing them with a practical background of student needs.

Have these teachers, working with industrial arts instructors, develop curriculum guides in their various subject matter area—these guides to be used for teaching academic subjects to occupational students.

IN-SERVICE PROGRAM

Amount of federal funds: $5,600

Objective:

To improve the high school training of noncollege-bound students in their occupational preparation.

Activities:

Place teachers of academic subjects in a summer employment situation in business and industry, thereby providing them with a practical background of student needs.

Have these teachers, working with industrial arts instructors, develop curriculum guides in their various subject matter areas—these guides to be used for teaching academic subjects to occupational students.

IN-SERVICE TRAINING ACTIVITY

The in-service component was a small project with only a few teachers involved, but a highly unusual project and one deserving of attention. The objective of the training program was to improve the high school teaching of noncollege-bound students by emphasizing occupational preparation. This was to be accomplished by putting teachers of academic subjects in summer employment in industry and business so they would receive a practical background that would enable them to make intelligent revisions of their courses for occupationally oriented students. The instructor so placed later worked with regular industrial arts teachers in changing the academic curriculum for terminal students.

Three phases are involved in the project. In Phase I, from early July to early August, teachers are employed by selected business and industrial organizations and given assignments and are supervised as are other employees. However, of the eight-hour day, six hours were used for productive work as paid employees, and two hours were devoted to school district activities, for which the teachers were paid by the district. During that two-hour period, they interviewed company supervisors, technical specialists, personnel managers, and others who could give them meaningful information about their occupational field. They then made analyses of their own job and the jobs performed by other employees whom they observed. They submitted a brief diary to the project director each week and retained a more detailed record for use in Phase II. During this initial five-week period, teachers were expected to develop a feeling for management attitudes, criteria for employee performance, and what the first-line supervisor actually expects of the new employee in an entry position. This, of course, was in addition to performing their own work and making other job, task, and human activities analyses. At the end of Phase I, in the beginning of August, teachers terminated their employment, were given exit interviews, and were separated from their organizations. The jobs secured by teachers ranged from computer typist for the *Los Angeles Times,* to laboratory assistant at the Los Angeles County Hospital, to accounting officer of a title company, to employment officer for the Los Angeles County Road Department.

For the next three weeks they were occupied full time as salaried employees of the Compton District. Meeting at district offices, they were joined by occupational teachers and three occupational counselors and began to synthesize their experiences and to modify or design completely new courses in mathematics, English, and science. Phase II was conceived as a conversion effect effort so that academic courses would closely support occupational courses.

Beginning with the fall term in September, these teachers were expected to be ready to start teaching the newly developed courses. This was Phase III—the transfer period.

A research consultant for the Los Angeles County Superintendent of Schools Office was employed to do the evaluation of the SCRIBE project. A community survey was undertaken to determine both the background and attitudes of parents of some of the children involved and also, more importantly, employment forecasts. In the latter connection, twenty-four firms were asked to indicate those occupations that were significant in the employment picture, which positions were considered to be difficult to fill, and industrial growth patterns of the future. The severest occupational shortage involved the machine trades; there was considerable talk about a move to automated and semiautomated equipment. Regardless of the firm's function, the vastly increased use of computers and data-processing equipment generally was seen to be a wave of the future. Training programs were assessed and the possible use of facilities in industry for the training of students was asked about. The reaction to this latter possibility was negative, with employers citing high production, union problems, and security clearance as reasons for not participating. The evaluation of the project indicated that teachers were not in agreement on whether the program had been effective. It was felt that parents, pupils, regular teachers, and project teachers were mostly positive, though regular teachers were the least positive of any of the groups. Teachers who had participated in the project thought that consultants were only about average in their effectiveness, though they agreed that consultants had insufficient time to devote to the program. Teachers thought they were probably better prepared to teach their subjects as a result of the program, but did not agree that they had fulfilled their role adequately. It was deemed that reasonable articulation had been accomplished with vocational education teachers, but classroom control was not facilitated by the project. Students were also polled about their reaction to Compton's vocational education; the conclusion of the evaluator was that the district is "rather adequately meeting the needs and plans of its students." It was not felt that project SCRIBE had been of sufficient scope or operated long enough that students could evaluate what effects they had actually received from it.

To disseminate the results of this project, the publication of a four-page weekly news sheet called *Scribe* has been achieved, and a half-hour 35 mm color slide-sound presentation of the project with approximately fifty slides and a magnetic audio tape has been prepared. This set of materials will be available for use in other school districts seeking to implement similar programs.

To the new instructional guides developed in high school mathematics, science, and English was added one in the social studies. This was not a part of the original project but resulted as an important side effect of the overall project.

## IMPERIAL AND RIVERSIDE COUNTIES

ESEA TITLE III PROJECT, 1966–67

Title: Operation REACH (Continuation Education)
Amount of federal funds: $48,138
Number of target schools: 1
Number of target pupils: 1,000
Special instructional activities:
   Establishing and operating an exemplary continuation high school model in Riverside, California.
   Providing in-service training for all continuation education personnel.

IN-SERVICE PROGRAM

Amount of federal funds: $3,750
Objectives:
   To develop a philosophy for and knowledge about continuation schools and the characteristics of continuation students.
   To gather and try out new, relevant, and useful teaching materials and techniques appropriate to continuation education students.
Activities:
   Visits to established continuation programs throughout the state.
   A two-week summer workshop entitled "Orientation to Continuation Education."

IN-SERVICE TRAINING ACTIVITY

This project was concerned exclusively with continuation education, which was first organized in California to permit working students to continue their education, but now assumes as perhaps its major function the adjustment of students who for various reasons are not performing satisfactorily in the regular school. The philosophy of continuation education as expressed by this project is worth considering at some length, and might be summarized in the following way. Operation REACH takes as its objective to "take the student where he is and help him develop into a contributive citizen at the highest level possible within the limits of his ability and personality." Such a project obviously cannot be selective in its choice of students but must accept the widest range of ability in students and the widest range of problems, too, for that matter. Most continuation students in the project either have been or are apt to become dropouts.

The staff of Operation REACH believed that a continuation school should be small and also have small classes with an atmosphere of sincere friendliness. When the school is small, then it can function with minimal regulations and provide the greatest degree of individual attention. Also, the general pressures of the school are reduced, and interpersonal relationships often induce a student to make a real effort where they do not in a conventional school. It is considered essential that the personnel in a continuation school be straightforward with students, who are often suspicious of the authority of adults and require honesty in relationships with them. A comprehensive counseling system is, of course, essential in such a continuation school.

A number of issues in continuation education are considered critical by the Riverside staff. In designing the project and in implementing it, the staff dealt with the following issues: first is the issue of whether or not continuation school students should be returned to comprehensive high schools as soon as possible or whether, instead, terminal programs in the continuation school should be established, with the possibility of graduation from that school. A prevailing opinion about continuation education in California is that its main function is to return students to the regular environment as soon as possible. Operation REACH disagrees, holding that continuation students' personal problems are aggravated in the larger, impersonal school, and that they will be doomed to failure again if they are returned to that institution. The staff argues that the continuation school must have the time to provide identification to the students, special opportunities, a helping relationship by the faculty, and, as a culminating educational goal, the high school diploma.

The second issue is that of vocational training in continuation education. The Riverside contention is that while continuation students badly need vocational training, that training must be of a short-term nature and simple enough so that continuation students, most of whom lack the maturity or long-range goals of regular students, will be motivated to complete the offerings which in the conventional program might require many months or years to complete. Operation REACH's director felt that short-term vocational offerings should be provided, with the opportunity for selected students to go into more intensive and long-range vocational programs.

On the third issue, the question of transfer of students in and out of continuation education programs, the Riverside approach is to permit the student who may have come from the conventional high school with a background of repeated failure to stay in the continuation program and graduate, which he is apt to do when he is successful. While continuation students should be permitted to return to the comprehensive high school at appropriate times should they desire, they should also be assured that they are welcome to return to the continuation school if they are unsuccessful, and they should not be forced to return to the comprehensive high school if they should not want to do so.

On the fourth question, that of the involvement of continuation students in group interaction in the classroom versus individualized instruction, the Riverside opinion is that continuation students, because of past failures, tend to withdraw from efforts to induce class discussion, prefer to work individually, and will accomplish more if the teacher is genuinely helpful. With exceptions, continuation students may require many months before they are willing to enter even limited classroom discussions. They are typically noncompetitive and prefer to work at their own rate without feeling that they are being compared with their peers.

With respect to the fifth issue, the mixing of adults and minors in continuation high schools, Project REACH concluded that discipline problems are reduced, larger classes can be handled, and a more economical operation results when adults are mixed with minors. The adults in a class may tend to inspire minors, and minors may occasionally get some feeling of success by being able to help their elders. A small district can more easily justify a continuation school if it has the numbers provided by adults, and a broader curriculum is consequently possible. Teachers are more inclined to treat the entire class, including the minors, as adults, with resulting benefits for the younger students. Moreover, the adults serve a valuable public relations function, and equalization funds may result.

As to the issue of whether there should be a separate continuation school or, instead, continuation classes held on the campus of the comprehensive high school, the Riverside opinion is that with the separate school the student is able to receive greater personal attention, he has higher status with his classmates, and his chances of success are greatly improved.

Operation REACH based its program on individualized instruction through the use of a contract. This is an agreement between teacher and individual student drawn up by the student and the teacher wherein the student agrees to perform to the best of his ability an assignment written into the contract, in a specified time. The contract is formal and binding and lets the student know exactly what is expected of him and when. The contract may be daily, weekly, or for as long as a semester; it may call for an arrangement whereby the student's difficulties are periodically diagnosed and different assignments provided; it may use a series of study guides as the basic unity of the curriculum; it may be cyclical in that certain increments of time are spent in group activity; it may provide different standards of achievement for different grades; it may provide for formal conference periods; and it may involve tutorials. When the work has been completed, credits and final grades are issued.

When students come initially to the continuation high school, they are ordinarily in need of some orientation to the program. The program of Operation Reach has approached this problem with an orientation class using group interaction techniques. Fifteen students meet daily for a period of fifteen sessions, each considered to be the hour when students are to be put at their ease and encouraged to speak their minds. The orientation classes proceed through several stages: first that of socialization in which students are becoming acquainted with each other, progressing to a stage when the needs of particular individuals emerge and specific help is provided by a resource teacher, and finally an intimate feeling of closeness or empathy among the group members. When this last stage is reached for any individual, when he can communicate well with others and accept them as individuals and give and take with the group, then he may at the orientation class teacher's prerogative be changed to a regular class. In addition to its use in the orientation program, group counseling is considered an effective device for employment counseling, family life education, and health and safety education. While group counseling may be done by any staff member, group work for therapeutic reasons was left for those who are specifically trained in psychology or psychiatry. It is considered desirable that everyone in the continuation school be involved in the guidance program, including of course the teachers who may use group techniques.

As for the in-service training, two separate phases were involved. The first was the opportunity for continuation educators in the two-county area to visit established continuation programs around the state. Though all administrators and teachers of continuation education in the twenty-two districts involved were notified of the opportunity and provided a list of continuation schools, they showed a lack of interest in making visits, probably because very few of the districts had entered into continuation education with any degree of interest and because of the dearth of effective or innovative continuation programs worth visiting. The second phase of the in-service training program was a two-week summer continuation education workshop, with continuation personnel from Riverside and Imperial counties, particularly, invited to attend, and also some persons from other districts in the state.

Operation REACH was initiated to extend exemplary approaches to the education of continuation students. In order to carry out this objective a continuation school was established and operated as a model high school in Riverside, California. The initial student body had approximately fifty students, three full-time teachers, a teacher counselor, and a principal. During the school year 1966–67, the school grew to approximately 160 students, five full-time teachers, a full-time counselor, and a principal.

Several evaluations of the Riverside continuation school were made, with findings that were generally positive. In a study comparing continuation classes with special classes in a regular comprehensive school the following generalizations were made:

> Continuation schools tend to be superior to special classes in regular schools in the area of improving students' attitudes and self-image, particularly those in the area of perceived educational progress. Continuation schools tend to create an environment in which students admit to having fewer contacts with law enforcement agencies than do special students who attend regular schools. Continuation schools foster high educational and vocational levels of aspiration.

Students tended to perceive the major advantages of continuation education as being outstanding teachers, shorter hours, and less discipline. Major disadvantages from the students' point of view were: too long a time required to graduate; being labeled a continuation student; and boredom. Since the samples were relatively small, these conclusions should be regarded as only tentative. In a poll of attitudes held by parents, it was found that they favored continuation education. Parents having children in continuation schools expressed a more positive attitude toward the program than that held by parents having children in regular schools. In a poll of teachers and administrators, continuation schools were favored overwhelmingly over classes in a regular school. Students in continuation schools tend to be rated higher by the teacher than are students in continuation classes, this effect holding in both "before" and "after" ratings.

Some specific results of the visitations were the amassing of innovative materials, devices, and techniques that the staff tried out (tested) and evaluated during the school year. Most useful of the materials collected were found to be supplementary reading materials. A book, *Techniques and Methodology in Compensatory Education,* was written by the project participants and published by the Office of the Imperial and Riverside Counties Superintendent of Schools. Questionnaires were used to evaluate the summer workshop. A majority of the participants felt that it was very helpful, very interesting, and an excellent use of their time. There was unanimous agreement that continuation education could be improved by projects such as REACH, by better teacher-education preparation, orientation programs, and expanded facilities.

## STOCKTON UNIFIED SCHOOL DISTRICT
### (San Joaquin County)

ESEA TITLE III PROJECT, 1966–67

Title: Demonstration Research Center Using the Initial Teaching
   Alphabet
Amount of federal funds: $44,000
Number of target schools: 19 Elementary
Number of target pupils: 2,400

Special instructional activities:

Establishing thirty-seven ITA demonstration first and second grade classrooms. In addition, twenty-one ITA classes and thirty-three equivalent traditional orthography classes were selected for research purposes. Included from the Tracy public schools were three second grade classrooms in the ITA research program and two ITA classrooms in the demonstration program; from the Catholic Diocese, one ITA research classroom and one traditional orthography research classroom; and from the Stockton schools, twenty first grade and fourteen second grade demonstration classrooms, and seventeen ITA and thirty-two traditional orthography research classes.

Sharing ideas and experiences by teachers from the two public school systems and the Catholic schools, use of special consultants, hosting the annual Northern California ITA Reading Conference, and providing observation opportunities at the Demonstration Research Center for over 500 educators from throughout the state.

Carrying on in-service education programs in new reading techniques.

IN-SERVICE PROGRAM

Amount of federal funds: $1,750

Objectives:

To prepare a group of teachers for ITA instruction in reading.

To prepare another group of teachers in terms of new trends in the teaching of reading.

Activity:

A series of one-week courses.

IN-SERVICE TRAINING ACTIVITY

A fifteen clock-hour one-week course on the teaching of beginning reading with ITA was established for the thirty-seven ITA demonstration teachers and the twenty-one ITA research class teachers. In order to accommodate these two groups, the course was offered on four separate occasions. It yielded one unit of in-service credit on the district's salary schedule, and was taught by the project director. It was offered in the summer, on week-ends, and after school. The course focused on techniques for use of ITA in teaching beginning reading, ITA writing and spelling, transfer from ITA to traditional orthography, and creative writing.

The traditional orthography teachers were enrolled in a one-credit (fifteen-hour) course on new trends in the teaching of reading. Included were new ideas on readiness and creative writing, and new approaches to language expression. The major emphasis of the course, however, was on new ideas in the use of phonetics. It was offered only once and was taught by the director with the assistance of two district elementary education consultants.

Widespread publicity was given by the director to the fact that first and second grade ITA classes were available for observation, and educators throughout the state were invited to visit and see children at all stages of reading development. The announcement stated "Beginning reading techniques can be observed in first grade classes, while in the second grade you may watch children not ready for transfer to traditional orthography, children who have just made the transfer, and children who made the transfer during the first grade." The first grade classes represented children from all socioeconomic levels, utilizing three ITA reading series: *Early to Read,* Scott-Foresman, and Downing Readers. The total number of visitors observing the specially trained ITA teachers exceeded the staff's expectations. In some instances school districts visited the project on two or three different occasions and several districts started their own ITA program.

Data on the project's success indicate that ITA is of value to Mexican-American bilingual children,[3] that first grade reading achievement results compare favorably with the average score for the state as a whole, and that the district's reason for improvement in first grade reading achievement scores is primarily due to the ITA program. However, in spite of its success, children who have difficulty in learning to read were still found to be unable to profit from a change in orthography. The results indicate that ITA is not a panacea, but may be beneficial to many children; and that the project has made all first and second grade teachers "reading conscious," and has equipped them with new reading skills and techniques.

---

[3] ITA mean scores 34.60, Traditional Orthography mean scores 27.88.

CHAPTER III

# NDEA Title XI Programs

*All things now held to be old were once new. What today we hold up by example, will rank hereafter as precedent.*

Tacitus

$\mathbf{T}$he National Defense Education Act, passed by Congress in 1958, has affected education from elementary through graduate school. Originally focusing on the improvement of instruction in science, mathematics, and foreign languages, the provisions of NDEA were subsequently expanded. Title XI, added in 1964, provided for summer institutes for teachers in a broad spectrum of subject matters beyond the sciences and foreign language. It marked one of the federal government's major attempts to improve the in-service education of teachers.

Since 1965, a major focus of the summer institutes has been the training of teachers of the disadvantaged. One hundred and seventy-three such summer programs have been funded under this act, and thirty-seven of these have been offered in California. As noted in the *Manual for the Preparation of Proposals,* the major objective of the summer institutes has been to offer "a specialized program of instruction designed to assist teachers in coping with the unique and peculiar problems involved in teaching disadvantaged children and youth." These projects were expected to be quite different from regular summer teacher education programs and to reflect the precision and insight of careful planning. A 1966 evaluation report noted: "What these programs may have lacked in flexibility they gained in a sense of direction and in generally high standards of performance."[1]

The institutes described were selected to illustrate a variety of programmatic approaches to achieve a common set of purposes. Although two of the Title XI projects were concerned with the teaching of English to speakers of other languages and disadvantaged youth, and two institutes were held in off-campus settings, the uniqueness of the nine institutes as groups was such that it was decided to simply place them in alphabetical order in this chapter.

In presenting the nine Title XI projects,[2] the intent is to give

[1] Gordon J. Klopf and Garda W. Bowman, *Teacher Education in a Social Context,* New York: Mental Health Materials Center, Inc. (published for the Bank Street College of Education), 1966, p. 75.

[2] The participants of one project (UC, American Indian) could not be interviewed readily; another project (Sacramento State) was used as a pilot group for pretesting purposes. An analysis of them is in Raymond J. Roberts, Jr., *NDEA Title XI Summer Institutes for Teachers of Disadvantaged Youth.* Unpublished Ed.D. dissertation, University of California, Berkeley, 1969.

the reader the salient features of projects for possible model-building as well as an appreciation of the milieu of the projects—to fashion for him a frame of reference within which to consider the overall findings of the investigation.

## "PREPARING TRAINING TEACHERS FOR PRE-SERVICE TEACHERS OF DISADVANTAGED AREA SCHOOLS"

Location of institute: California State College at Los Angeles
Amount of federal funds: $50,130

BACKGROUND

California State College at Los Angeles is one of the largest teacher-education institutions in the state, preparing annually approximately 700 secondary school teachers. Over the years, in cooperation with the city schools, the college has accumulated amples evidence that secondary classroom teachers who work with college students preparing to teach the disadvantaged need special help and specific training. As a consequence, in 1963–64, a pilot program to train teachers for the inner city was conducted at Thomas Jefferson High School.

The need for well-prepared supervising teachers long has been recognized and almost since the college first opened its doors in 1948, it has conducted workshops for supervising teachers. Beginning in 1964, "crash" training programs under the in-service division of Los Angeles City Schools and the college were required before students were assigned to student teaching in a poverty area school. As part of Project TEACH (Teacher Education for Advancing the Culturally Handicapped), an in-service workshop similar to the 1963 one was set up at David Starr Jordan High School (Watts). Thirty teachers took part. In both the Jefferson and Jordan efforts to prepare supervising classroom teachers the work done was what might be called a glancing blow. The need for skilled, trained, experienced teachers to supervise the learning experiences of pre-service teachers in disadvantaged area schools was judged as acute. The in-service division of Los Angeles City Schools gave financial support to similar workshops designed to meet this special need. The college held the first of its NDEA institutes in the summer of 1965. The 1967 institute was designed for both elementary and secondary teachers of disadvantaged youth. The experience of the 1965 institute proved extremely valuable in planning the one for the summer of 1967.

OBJECTIVES

California State College at Los Angeles offered a six-week summer institute for forty-five carefully selected teachers who were teaching in the Los Angeles urban area secondary schools at that time and who were working with California State College in the preparation of teachers. All had indicated a desire for further training better to prepare themselves to assist with the pre-service education of teachers. In offering this institute for these experienced teachers, the specific purposes were:

To help bridge the separation between the experienced teachers' backgrounds and those of the children they teach.

To help bridge the gaps between the teachers' backgrounds and those of the college students preparing for teaching careers.

To extend knowledge of appropriate resources including materials for classroom use in specific subject matter areas.

To extend the insights, knowledge, and skills required for working effectively in the pre-service training of teachers for inner city schools.

To provide opportunities for participants to work under supervision in the pre-service professional laboratory experience area of teacher education.

To give leadership experiences designed to extend the participants' influence and effectiveness in staff relationships upon returning to their secondary school teaching assignments.

To sharpen participants' awareness of special educational needs of children in urban area schools.

The major focus of all seven objectives was the preparation of their teachers of disadvantaged youth.

SELECTION OF PARTICIPANTS

Applicants for the institute had to meet the following criteria: have a bachelor's degree and a valid California standard or general secondary teaching credential; be currently employed in a secondary school cooperating with the college; have three or more years' experience working with environmentally disadvantaged youths; be recommended by his principal for high professional competence and leadership potential; be recommended by the college supervisor of his major teaching subject area for teaching competence, knowledge of subject matter, and leadership potential; and present evidence from the employing district that he would be assigned to a secondary school in a disadvantaged area where he would be directly involved in the pre-service education of teachers.

Applications and recommendations of those who met the basic requirements were evaluated by a special committee composed of two representatives of the college and one from the Los Angeles City Schools. The selection committee was instructed to give special attention to answers to the items on the application forms that indicated the candidate's understanding of the work to be undertaken and evidence that he may have an opportunity to apply benefits derived from participation, his experiences as a training teacher and/or evidence of high potential for this professional service, his expression of willingness or desire to assist with the pre-service training of teachers, and his interest in urban education and/or problems of economically, socially, or environmentally disadvantaged people.

The institute staff hoped to have from two to six enrollees from a particular secondary school, but this did not work out as planned. However, practically every major subject area taught in the secondary school was represented in the teachers' school assignments.

THE INSTITUTE

Early in June the director invited the accepted candidates who had the interest, time, and energy to serve on a steering committee. Ten volunteers met at the college once in the afternoon prior to the opening of the institute and again on the opening day. This committee of ten continued to serve as a means of communication and coordination throughout the six weeks.

Key persons involved in the pre-service preparation of teachers from both public schools and the colleges met with the participants during the first week. College supervisors, student teachers, and secondary school administrators served on panels and took part in group discussions. Problems were thus identified for further study. Individual differences in training, background, and interest varied greatly among participants and demanded that the institute program be flexible.

Two mornings a week were devoted to field work in school and community agencies. Many of the field experiences were closely related to special reports or projects that participants made in partial fulfillment of the requirements for one of the two education courses that were part of the institute. These courses, each taken for three units of credit, were: Problems in Education: basic issues in practices in directing pre-service education of teachers; and Directed Graduate Study. In the latter course a written report was required of each participant; each report was a result of the studies supervised by a faculty member with knowledge of and interest in the topic or subject under consideration.

Films, video tapes, slides, recordings, and other educational media were used by staff members and lecturers for instructional purposes. Participants made use of the audiovisual materials center in preparing slides, transparencies for overhead projection, charts, and similar items to take back to their various classrooms and to use in making final reports. Tape recorders were used by participants and staff in recording interviews with student teachers, training teachers, administrators, and parents. A sizable library of tapes with tape recorders had been accumulated from NDEA institutes held at the college. Demonstrations were given in the use of educational television in training teachers. On one occasion, a kinescope film was used to assist teachers in coping with behavior problems.

Four field trips were taken by the entire institute group. The tour through the east Los Angeles area was planned by Mexican-American teachers. The trip to the Neighborhood Adult Participation Project by members of the NDEA staff permitted participants to see some of the community activities in the south central area of Los Angeles. The trip to Stevenson Junior High School where a leader of the Mexican-American community spoke was arranged by a participant of the institute. The fourth field trip was to the United Jewish Community Center where an officer of the Anti-Defamation League of B'nai B'rith was the main speaker.

Although the participants were highly recommended as experienced, highly successful teachers of disadvantaged youth, and as teachers with high potential for serving as supervising teachers, the institute staff found that they varied greatly in understanding, purpose, and interests. There was therefore too much ground to be covered adequately in a six-week period. For future institutes, the staff recommended that there be only one major focus, and that it be either teaching disadvantaged youth or the pre-service and in-service preparation of teachers.

The staff was concerned about the participant selection process. A large number of urban teachers, especially men, usually need to use the summer for obtaining additional income. The objectives of the summer institute had little appeal to many. Central office administrators desirous of upgrading their schools and also anxious to have particular teachers given leadership roles appeared to overrate teacher applicants. In large measure, the institute staff depended on the recommendations of the principal and the subject area supervisor to secure strong candidates. Although aware of the difficulties involved in personal interviews, the staff would like to attempt including them should they be responsible for another NDEA institute.

The staff found that social studies teachers were generally much better informed and more sophisticated in dealing with inner city problems than were teachers in subjects such as mathematics and physical sciences. The staff felt that it would have been much easier to work with a more homogeneous group of teachers, but given the same objectives they would continue to draw participants from a wide range of subject specialties.

The Los Angeles City Schools ended the school year on the Friday preceding the Monday on which the institute began. The original proposal had called for a week's intermission, but unfortunately a change was later made in the Los Angeles City Schools' calendar. As a result, most of the teachers came into a strenuous six-week institute exhausted, with professional and personal classroom frustrations fresh in their minds. This unfortunate turn of events had a deleterious effect on the outcomes of the Institute.

## "TEACHERS OF DISADVANTAGED YOUTH FROM MIGRATORY FARM-LABOR AND RURAL COMMUNITIES"

Location of institute: Chico State College
Amount of federal funds: $63,316

BACKGROUND

The sponsorship of this institute by Chico State College was a natural extension of the college's history of interest in helping teachers do a more effective job of teaching disadvantaged youth. The college's active involvement had begun in the summer of 1963 with a special summer program at the Gridley Farm Labor Camp, Gridley, California. This program was later expanded, in the summer of 1965, by a grant from the Rosenberg Foundation. Further expansion of such programs, under the college's sponsorship, resulted in NDEA institutes for teachers of disadvantaged youth during the summers of 1965 and 1966. Chico State is the only four-year college serving the large area of central California north of Sacramento where there exist many pockets of rural poverty and several growing semiurban areas with high concentrations of minority group families. The 1967 institute was one successful program operated by the college to provide educational leadership in this region.

OBJECTIVES

The controlling purpose of the 1967 institute was to explore with participants the understanding and the techniques necessary for encouraging the development of positive attitudes toward learning in disadvantaged children. To accomplish this purpose the following six objectives were pursued:

To develop participants' skill in adopting appropriate techniques and materials for working with disadvantaged youngsters.

To increase participants' understanding of evaluation criteria appropriate for use with the culturally handicapped.

To develop participants' sensitivity to feelings and attitudes of children and youth living in impoverished socioeconomic settings.

To provide participants with the experience of working with parents of culturally deprived children.

To develop leadership potential of participants so that they will be effective in sponsoring action programs in their local communities.

To give teachers an opportunity to develop curricula to meet specific needs of culturally deprived youngsters in the participants' school districts.

SELECTION OF PARTICIPANTS

Applicants to the institute were screened in terms of holding a bachelor's degree or the equivalent from an accredited institution; recommendations from school supervisors and college teachers in the fields of professional competence and, when possible, from parents of children they had taught; evidence of professional commitment through courses completed, record of positions held, and special achievements indicative of interest in the specialized purpose of the institute; and evaluation of an essay submitted by the applicant indicating his current involvement with culturally handicapped children, how he was attempting to meet the needs of these children, and the kinds of personal problems he felt he had in working with such youngsters. The applicants were asked to indicate why they felt that they had some success in working with these children and what they believed to have been the reasons for their failures.

Preference was given to teachers with experience in schools serving culturally handicapped children. Diversity of experience and background was maximized by selecting participants from different size school systems, from different geographical parts of the United States, and from private as well as public schools.

Some applicants were recruited rather than screened. They were deliberately selected by the institute staff from teaching positions in schools primarily serving culturally deprived youngsters. Recruitments were made on the basis of recommendations from college supervisors who felt that they were doing an ineffective job in their teaching situations. Applications from teachers judged to be highly effective were also recruited.

During the 1965 institute, a deliberate attempt was made to select no more than one teacher from any given school. In 1966 and 1967, preference was given to applicants from designated schools in a geographic area in an attempt to enable these teachers to assist each other in inaugurating new programs in their schools.

In order to make follow-up easier, the staff tried to recruit both summer school children as well as teachers from the three schools that had been designated as the off-campus centers. A deliberate effort was made to select institute participants with different specialties, such as music, art, mathematics, and science, and school nurses working in a teaching capacity.

THE INSTITUTE

The 1967 institute was a seven-week session. A total of thirty-six teachers and administrators participated in the institute and three off-campus school centers were established. The participants were divided into three groups of twelve; Group A was assigned to Gridley School Center, Group B to Chapman School Center in Chico, and Group C to the Burbank School Center in Oroville. The twelve participants in each group were divided into three teaching teams. Three quite different types of disadvantaged children were involved in each of the three centers—migrant children at Gridley, Negroes at Oroville, and Caucasians at Chico.

One major problem concerning the location of the centers came about on the last day of May. At that time the director was told that he would be unable to hold classes for the Gridley Center at the migratory camp itself. Plans had provided that the Gridley District, by a program financed through Compensatory Education funds of the California State Department of Education, would have portable classrooms at the labor camp site. At the last moment, the State Department of Education revoked permission for this plan, maintaining that this represented segregation. As a result, the migrant labor children were taught in regular classrooms at Gridley. Bus service was provided, and the institute participants and teacher aides moved around the camp for the first few days of the institute inviting and encouraging the children to take the trip into town. A study of attendance indicates that their efforts were successful in transferring operations from the labor camp to the school.

Sixty children were at each of the centers. Twenty children, then, worked with each of the three teaching teams. In addition to this contact with twenty children in the team-teaching situation, each institute enrollee was assigned five children for more concentrated study. It was his responsibility to work closely with them and visit their homes. Each participant worked with the parents of these five children, took them on field trips, and learned to play and work with them in their own neighborhoods. Each participant also consulted with the representatives of public agencies who were or should have been involved with these children in their own geographic areas.

A major part of each morning was devoted to group instruction, with all members of the team assisting and observing the assigned master teacher for the day. The afternoons and evenings were devoted to individual work by each participant with his assigned children or to lectures, discussions, planning, and evaluation. When participants were on the main college campus they were encouraged to acquaint themselves with the college's facilities, especially its curriculum center, reading laboratory, and closed circuit television.

In all of these activities, participants were encouraged not only to verbalize new concepts and insights, but also to seek ways to utilize these concepts and insights as they worked with their disadvantaged students. A regular institute staff member was assigned to each of the three centers, and special consultants were made available when needed.

Each participant was asked to prepare a case study for each of the five children assigned to him. This study, along with the recommendations for working with the child, was forwarded to the child's regular teacher and, where appropriate, to other interested professional persons such as guidance counselors and social workers.

Throughout the program, participants met for weekly group discussions. Four groups, composed of nine participants each, were organized to meet for two hours a week. These discussions focused on personal feelings, attitudes, and beliefs of the participants, especially as these affected their current interpersonal involvement with students, other participants, and staff. The principal objective of each group was to provide a "safe" atmosphere for the free expression of personal feelings. In these sessions participants were encouraged to share their effective experiences. In addition, each participant wrote a daily log of his reactions to the institute experience. This log was shared with the staff member working with each group.

## "TEACHERS OF DISADVANTAGED MEXICAN-AMERICAN YOUTH"

Location of institute: Fresno State College
Amount of federal funds: $81,291

This was the third consecutive year in which Fresno State sponsored an NDEA institute. It has been the feeling of the staff that the need for qualified personnel for leadership roles in the education of disadvantaged youth has become increasingly apparent. In-service training is necessary, and resource speakers and instructors from colleges will not be able to fulfill all the requests for assistance. Local supervisory and administrative personnel and teachers must be prepared to give the desired leadership necessary.

Another important consideration in planning the 1967 institute was the lack of qualified supervising teachers to work with student teachers. In schools where there is a concentration of disadvantaged youth, it is difficult to find supervising teachers who are qualified to give the desired training to student teachers. Even though the college supervisor may be well qualified in the area of teaching disadvantaged youth, his effectiveness in influencing the values and behavior patterns of student teachers will be very limited if the student does not see an experiment with "theory in action" in the classroom. All too often, the supervising teachers operate on the basis of stereotypes, biases, and misunderstandings. Many of them have had no training in techniques of guidance and supervision.

This institute was developed and organized to meet the specific areas of need. The seventy-two participants were selected on the basis of providing leadership in the ESEA programs throughout the Fresno Valley area. Also, in training supervising teachers the institute gave impetus to pre-service teacher education in the college. It was hoped that this will at least help to eliminate one major barrier to adequate teacher-preparation programs.

The institute staff felt that it has definite responsibility for serving the community and area. Since this valley has a large concentration of disadvantaged youth, particularly of Mexican-American background, teachers must be trained to meet the unique needs of these children. This third summer institute made it possible for the college to be of service in meeting this acute need.

OBJECTIVES

The major objectives of the Fresno State College Institute were the following:

To increase the participant's understanding of the concepts of sociology and anthropology that are relevant to the teaching-learning situation of disadvantaged children.

To increase the participant's understanding of the principles of learning as applied to the unique needs and interests of lower socio-economic ethnic groups.

To increase the participant's skill in utilizing a wide variety of materials, methods, and techniques in effective teaching-learning situations for disadvantaged youth.

To increase the participant's skill in evaluating pupil progress—including the ability to appraise and interpret results of various evaluative techniques when utilized with culturally different children.

To develop the participant's understanding of techniques for supervising student teachers who work with disadvantaged children.

To develop the participant's ability to relate to student teachers in a manner that will promote changes in values, behavior, and classroom efficiency with disadvantaged children.

SELECTION OF PARTICIPANTS

The criteria for the selection of participants included a bachelor's degree granted by an accredited institution, a contract to teach in a school whose population includes a substantial number of pupils who qualify as disadvantaged youth, and three years of teaching experience in elementary schools. A committee of three college professors assumed the responsibility for evaluating the applications and making the final selection of participants and alternates. The institute coordinator served as an *ex officio* member of the committee. The committee used the criteria listed above as a basis for making any initial selection. Preference was then given to those who were teams of two from one school, recommended as open-minded and willing to learn, and would be (according to the recommendations and transcripts) easily encouraged to become a leader in his own district.

THE INSTITUTE

The program of the institute was organized into three distinct but interrelated phases. They were a seminar in classroom methodology, a participation and observation practicum, and a "Foundations of Education" course. These three phases were designed and taught as integral parts of the total program—directed toward the development of the objectives and specifically related to the education of the culturally disadvantaged. Attention was given to planning the sequence in order to maintain optimum coordination among the different experiences and phases of the program. Total staff planning was stressed in order to help maintain continuity in the learning process.

Participants spent two hours in the classroom each morning. They observed the demonstrating teacher first; then they took over the classes and demonstrated ways of applying the principles of the foundation sciences in maintaining effective learning-teaching situations. There were ten or eleven participants assigned to each grade level—kindergarten through grade six—and to one demonstration teacher. The institute was housed in the elementary school, in a deprived area, which was used as a laboratory school.

During the morning, 8:30 until 12:00 noon, the participants remained with the same demonstration teacher. During the two hours in which they were not observing or participating they were involved in seminar discussions with the demonstration teacher as seminar leader. At this time, participants in the previous year's institute took over the instruction of pupils. As seminar leader, the demonstration teacher guided participants in diagnosing problems, developing objectives, planning classroom procedures, and evaluating performance in the light of the principles presented through lectures, readings, and seminar discussions of the foundation sciences—psychology, sociology, and anthropology. The instructors for the morning seminars in methodology also participated in the afternoon sessions, listening to lectures and participating as resource persons in the seminar discussions. This involvement made it possible for the demonstration teacher to integrate the varying phases of the program.

The coordinator participated in the morning sessions as a resource person; he lectured in the afternoon sessions. The director did some work as a resource person in the morning—as much as time permitted—and lectured in the afternoon session. The entire faculty was thus involved in all phases of the program, certainly contributing to the effectiveness of the institute and promoting continuity of learning.

Maximum fusion of content seemed to depend on the demonstration teacher's depth of insight into the theory so that he could clarify the application for others.

Field trips, except for a tour of the district, were primarily planned as learning excursions for children. Participants had the opportunity to plan with the demonstration teacher and then to guide the children in their planning for the excursion, in taking the excursion, in participating in the dialogue experiences, and in evaluating. The participants learned to use such experiences as an integral part of the learning sequence and as a springboard for the development of numerous language, reading, writing, spelling, and creative skills.

Child study was an important phase of the practicum. Each participant was asked to do a trial study as part of the practicum experience. The purpose of the case study was to aid the participant in becoming emotionally involved with the disadvantaged child and his family as a means of promoting value change, aid him in seeing the necessity for studying each child, and to illustrate the real necessity for adjusting classroom materials, techniques, and methods to meet the needs of each individual child.

The staff of the institute felt the child study did much to help participants feel at ease with both children and parents. It made apparent the teacher's real need to understand a child's problems, values, and cultural behavior patterns before planning a learning situation for him. The staff felt the close association was very effective in changing participants' attitudes toward an acceptance of children and parents who are disadvantaged.

The child study experience, however, was generally rated low in the evaluation of participants. Nonetheless, staff members were of the opinion that the case studies made participants more cognizant of the learning process, and they are confident that the participants will find that the study did produce value changes.

Home-school relations were stressed as an important part of the institute experience. The staff felt that teachers can work effectively with children only when there is real respect for and very close cooperation with the home. Several techniques were utilized to involve participants in working with parents. During the first week a visitation day was held. All parents were invited to visit the school, and a large number of them came. During the second week there was a picnic for children and their families; about 500 people attended. Many participants were surprised at how thoroughly they enjoyed the picnic and the fellowship with parents. Each participant was asked to make a home call as part of his child study. Some were hesitant, some fearful, before they went. However, they found the home visit quite rewarding. Reports of the children's progress were made through parent-teacher conferences. Most of the parents came to school for the conference. For those whose parents did not come, a participant or demonstration teacher, or both, went to the home. Parents seemed very happy about the conferences. During the last week parents were again invited to visit the school. Grandfathers, grandmothers, fathers, mothers, sisters, brothers, aunts, and uncles came.

The lectures, the seminar discussions, and the foundations course were held in the afternoon. Lectures and discussions centered on concepts from psychology, sociology, and anthropology. The lectures were followed by small-group seminar discussions in order to encourage feedback, application, and reinforcement of previous learnings. There were six groups of twelve participants and a staff member for each seminar discussion. Care was taken to see that the participants' morning group assignments (which were the same throughout the institute) were different from his afternoon group assignments. The afternoon groups also were changed at the end of the third week to promote a maximum interchange of ideas and crossculturalization.

There were several rather unique features of this institute: (1) It was centered in the same elementary school that served as the laboratory school. (2) The site of the institute was in the heart of the disadvantaged area of Fresno; children who attended the school were those who normally attend the school; most were disadvantaged. (3) Demonstration teachers were regular institute staff members participating in all phases of the program. (4) Demonstration teachers were college professors or supervisors in the public schools. (5) Participants from the previous summer's institute were hired as regular classroom teachers. They aided demonstration teachers and took complete responsibility for the classroom when the seminar groups were in session.

## "TEACHERS OF DISADVANTAGED YOUTH WITH INTERRACIAL ENCOUNTER GROUPS"

Location of institute: Pasadena College
Amount of federal funds: $83,965

### BACKGROUND

The history of the development of the 1967 institute is significant in itself. In 1964, Pasadena College and the Pasadena Unified School District decided to extend their cooperative efforts beyond the traditional teacher-education format of observation, participation, and directed teaching, by marshaling the resources of the district and of the college to improve the education offered by both. A third partner to the new effort was the Pasadena Education Association through the work of its TEPS Commission. The involvement of the college faculty, the district administration, and the TEPS committee resulted in a number of important outcomes.

A thorough look was taken at the population of the Pasadena Unified District and the metropolitan area of which it is a part. The Los Angeles Basin, in which Pasadena is located, encompasses an ever-changing population that exceeds seven million persons. Constantly shifting population results in weakened educational work in the schools of deprived areas. Recent statistics show that an average of 750 persons move into the basin daily. A large fraction of the new population is composed of low socioeconomic groups. Included are Negroes, Orientals, migrant Mexican workers, and Cuban refugees. That the Pasadena Unified School District is affected by this influx of deprived persons is illustrated by the changing population of the HOPE schools that carry on special programs for the education of the disadvantaged. For example, the Abraham Lincoln School, in which participants in the 1965 and 1966 institutes at Pasadena College worked, has more than 65 per cent change in enrollment each year. Garfield School, which has a high percentage of Mexican children from non-English-speaking homes, also has an extremely high rate of change. These are only two of the eight schools in the HOPE program.

This metropolitan area is composed of large segments of ethnic minority groups who are becoming aware that the move to California has removed neither the causes nor the results of segregation, either intentional or de facto. The recent events in the Watts and Willow-brook areas of Los Angeles had their effects on Pasadena, and the more recent hostilities between Negro residents in these areas and the Mexicans of the Boyle Heights area of East Los Angeles had definite effects on similar ethnic groups in Pasadena.

An examination of the educational opportunities available to children in the district made evident the importance of both continuing and enlarging the program. Hundreds of children in Pasadena are incapable of participating successfully in a regular school program because of a lack of environmental stimulation and cultural orientation toward education. This, of course, has resulted in large annual additions of teen-agers and young adults to the army of those who, because of a lack of education, are unemployed or unemployable.

Serious consideration was given to the Pasadena College program for the education of teachers. The college, since its founding, is committed both academically and philosophically to the task of lifting man to his highest potential and, consequently, the education of teachers has been and is the area in which Pasadena College makes a major contribution. Even though more than 50 per cent of the graduates of the college enter the teaching profession in the schools of Southern California, it was felt that the traditional program of teacher education was not adequate to equip teachers to meet the needs of children such as those in the HOPE schools of Pasadena.

A number of changes and relationships have grown out of this new tripartite cooperative arrangement. These include a tutorial system, some teacher aide assistance, interchange of consultants, opening and maintaining clear channels of communications, and the conducting of NDEA Institutes for Advanced Study of Teachers of Disadvantaged Youth—summers of 1965, 1966, and 1967.

OBJECTIVES

The 1967 institute at Pasadena College was designed on the basis of experience provided by 1965 and 1966 NDEA institutes. The general objectives of the institute were to encourage participants to recognize the limitations of their own middle-class orientation, to increase their knowledge of the applicable principles of learning and human development, and to bolster this knowledge by rigorous and specialized training and experience with disadvantaged children.

The specific objectives of the seven-week institute were as follows:

To aid participants in achieving new psychological and sociological insights into the social, economic, and cultural background of children from deprived areas.

To familiarize participants with the knowledge and resources (social, political, legal, cultural) that are available and can be used effectively to complement the educational work of the school.

To provide teachers with an understanding of the sociological and psychological backgrounds that underlie many of the educational problems of such youth.

To teach skills needed to organize experiences lacking in the background of disadvantaged children so that they can compete successfully in the mainstream of our culture.

To introduce new media and materials appropriate for meeting the educational needs of disadvantaged youth.

To provide opportunities for self-understanding and a means for self-evaluation in terms of teachers' relationships to disadvantaged youth.

To provide opportunities for participation in and evaluation of a program that is geared to effective instruction among persons, as contrasted with a program that centers on content only.

SELECTION OF PARTICIPANTS

The program enrolled forty-five participants who were teachers in kindergarten through sixth grade. Of the forty-five participants, seventeen were Negroes. The criteria for the eligibility were possession of a bachelor's degree or higher degree from an accredited college or university; possession of or the eligibility to possess a teaching credential valid in the state of residence; completion of at least one full year of successful teaching and the recommendation by the principal of the school (however, other things being equal, those with three years of successful experience were given preference); and the possession of a valid contract for the year 1966–67 or evidence of employment in a kindergarten through sixth grade school situation involving disadvantaged children.

The selection of participants was done at two levels. Initial screening was done jointly by representatives of Pasadena College and the Pasadena Unified School District. Final selection was the responsibility of a committee composed of the director and associate director of the institute and one additional college staff member. The committee considered the following factors:

1. the potential of the individual to receive maximum benefit from the institute;
2. the evident willingness and the desire of the participant to become involved actively in the education of disadvantaged youth; and
3. the possibility of the applicant's receiving an assignment by the local school district in which the learnings from the institute could be applied.

THE INSTITUTE

The intitute ran from June 21 to August 4. The activities of the institute consisted of lectures, demonstrations, small-group seminars, supervised experience with children, and other activities that were designed to vitalize the theoretical learning process. Field trips, use of new materials in media instruction, readings, research, and work with audiovisual equipment were used when appropriate.

The curriculum consisted of three major areas:

1. Education 293: Social Psychology of Deprivation (2 semester units). This course concentrated on the principles of human growth and development as related to the unique situation of "the child of deprivation": the ways in which disadvantaged children react to their environment, their school, and their teachers; the effects of deprivation on learning; the place of the school within a total community context; the unique needs of disadvantaged youth as a means of defining the roles of the school and the teacher; and consideration of social class, mobility, acculturation patterns, intergroup relations, and social delinquency.
2. Education 294: Modern Techniques in Development and Evaluation of Interpersonal Relations (2 semester units). This included group process theory and procedures including T-group process, interaction analysis, and inquiry training. It also included the analysis of classroom behavior as proposed by Taba

and Bellak; experience in analyzing group behavior with emphasis on understanding the effects of group process on learning; use of processes developed by Flanders, Suchman, and Bellak for analyzing behaviors within the classroom. That portion of the institute program devoted to intensive work in sensitivity training required on-campus residency of all participants.

3. Education 295: Curriculum and Materials in the Education of the Disadvantaged (2 semester units). This course included consideration of the curricular needs of the disadvantaged child; methods and materials for meeting these needs; consideration of the newer teaching materials and media; directed observation, participation, and teaching of disadvantaged children under the direction of superior teachers selected for their maximum contribution to the Pasadena HOPE (Higher Opportunities in Pasadena Education) program. Specific procedures and content were provided that were appropriate for all grades, kindergarten through sixth grade, with major emphasis on the cognitive areas of language enrichment and music.

Supervised experiences consisted of working with children who were eligible for enrollment in the Pasadena HOPE program. This program was designed to offer special assistance during the regular school year to disadvantaged children. The institute participants were both observers and teacher aides in the program for culturally and educationally deprived children. The principal emphasis of the demonstration school was on language enrichment and the arts, although instruction in mathematics and science was also included. The ratio of participants to children was sufficiently low to provide an ample opportunity for personal identification between participant and child. Special attention was given to the use of library resources.

During the first two weeks of the institute, a "cultural island" situation was provided by requiring all participants to live in the dormitory at the institute. This set the stage for a major emphasis in the use of the basic encounter as an agent for participant and staff change. The staff had spent six hours together on the Saturday prior to the opening of the institute, in addition to numerous other staff planning meetings.

The staff, including the ten elementary school teachers, participated in six hours of basic encounter during the first week of the institute. Many continued in subsequent hours of sensitivity training which, for participants, totaled twenty-eight hours. An almost equal balance of Negroes and Caucasians was maintained in each of the basic encounter groups. This was considered by interviewed participants to be a valuable aspect of the encounter groups. Participants felt that they were able to communicate effectively regarding their prejudices due to the presence of minority-group or majority-group members.

At the conclusion of the institute, participants expressed the belief that longer blocks of time were needed for basic encounter sessions. Two-hour sessions were felt to be too brief. Four- to five-hour sessions were suggested. Also, the participants and staff felt that in addition to the two-week "live-in" situation in the dorms, all participants should spend the night in the dorm when basic encounter is held in the afternoon.

In the institute questionnaire, to the question "What features of the institute did you feel were unique and distinctive?" basic encounter received thirty-one votes. (There were forty-five participants.) The item rated second highest was "special guests," which received ten votes. To the question "What was the most important thing that happened to you during the institute?" twenty-two answered "self-awareness and awareness and acceptance of others." When asked to list the major strengths of the institute, twenty-six listed "basic encounter." The next highest was "good staff" with fourteen, and "getting to know others," fourteen. Five people mentioned that there should be more basic encounter time allotted.

## "TEACHERS OF NEGRO AND MEXICAN-AMERICAN YOUTH"

Location of institute: San Diego State College
Amount of federal funds: $81,951

### BACKGROUND

The city of San Diego is an urban center with a population of nearly 700,000 with nearby suburban population of more than a million. It is at the southernmost tip of a megalopolis that extends from Tijuana, a Mexican city of 100,000, 14 miles south of San Diego, to

100 miles north of Los Angeles, 120 miles to the northwest of San Diego, an area of 10,000,000 population.

San Diego is growing at a phenomenal rate. From 1950 to 1960, the city grew from 334,000 to 573,000. The last five years have added another 100,000. The economy that has produced this growth depends on aircraft and space vehicle production—General Dynamics, Ryan, Rohr, and Solar; Navy and Marine installations; electronics plants; fishing; tourism; along with the great, but fluctuating, building industry.

All of these have attracted a wide range of people to this area, from highly trained research scientists to large numbers of unskilled and semiskilled laborers who sought and are seeking a better way of life in the West. The majority of these laborers are truly disadvantaged Americans coming from disadvantaged areas, bringing with them four to five thousand disadvantaged children per year. Among the new residents in this border city are a large Negro population and a large Mexican-American population. Many others are itinerant, transient, and short-time residents; all are disadvantaged.

On the other hand these people have been thrust into an area of rich community and cultural resources unknown to them and, incidentally, to half their teachers, whom the San Diego area must recruit from east of the Rockies. These community resources range from aeronautics, numerous armed services installations, art and music centers, astronomy installations, natural history museums and the Museum of Man, import and export concerns, multiple communications media (newspapers, three television stations, radio), fishing industries, foreign consulates, Scripps Institute of Oceanography, Salk Institute, all the way to the world-famous San Diego Zoo, and to four senior colleges and seven junior colleges, each of which has a separate evening adult school.

These two culturally discordant elements—a large and growing culturally starved population and a culturally rich environment—recommend San Diego as a likely laboratory for antipoverty programs. Another relevant factor is that unemployed workers tend to remain in this area because of its pleasant climate. The result—the unemployment rate has been between 7 and 8 per cent over the last few years, as compared with national averages of around 5 per cent or less.

A large majority of the San Diego disadvantaged Americans are concentrated in an old, cheap-rent, high-density section of southeast San Diego in the Logan Heights area, an area of 30 square miles in San Diego's total of 169 square miles, an area akin to the Watts area in Los Angeles, the scene of the summer riots of 1965.

In this depressed area are two of San Diego's twelve high schools and two of San Diego's seventeen junior high schools. All four have student bodies composed predominantly of a lower socioeconomic class, with minority groups, chiefly Negro and Mexican-American, in a distinct majority. Compensatory education programs were held in these four schools. These four secondary schools and seven elementary schools in the depressed area, their programs, their teachers, their students, and their communities served as laboratories for part of the field work for the twenty-seven Title XI Summer Institute secondary school participants.

OBJECTIVES

The general objective of the institute was the development of certain philosophies, values, attitudes, insights, competencies, methods, techniques, skills, and materials in institute participants (and improving the educational opportunities for achievement in disadvantaged youth) such as:

A philosophy of educational opportunity commensurate with the needs of the disadvantaged in American society;

Basic psychological, sociological, and anthropological knowledge and understanding of factors related to such learners, their cultures, their parents, their community;

Increased knowledge and understanding of and practice in accepted methods and techniques of working with the disadvantaged in and out of school situations;

The application of these knowledges, understandings, skills, and abilities in improving the educational curriculum of these disadvantaged learners and practice in the experimental use of them;

An understanding of the role and programs of public and private social service agencies which serve the disadvantaged community including ways to develop school-community-agency cooperation.

The specific objectives of the institute were:

To study methods for raising the aspiration level of disadvantaged children, their parents, their community.

To develop teachers with higher levels of competence in counseling, managing, and teaching these students, both cognitively and affectively.

To develop methods of involving the community, lay, religious, and parent leaders in these problems.

To develop methods of broadening the experiential backgrounds of disadvantaged learners.

To learn ways of effective utilization of the cultural and individual assets of these learners, including ways to make self-understanding as well as cultural backgrounds a part of the curriculum and how to use available methods and materials, especially reading methods and materials.

SELECTION OF PARTICIPANTS

The institute enrolled fifty-four participants. A study of the number of elementary and secondary schools in this area having significant numbers of disadvantaged students was made by San Diego State in cooperation with local district administrator personnel and the San Diego County Department of Education. To limit the number to fifty-four participants was a cooperative decision to emphasize leadership potential among participants.

Twenty-seven of the fifty-four participants were recommended by the administrative staff of the San Diego Unified School District. They were the teachers and supervisors already working in the schools in depressed areas or chosen for assignments in this area in the near future. Plans called for the selection of small teams in selected schools to serve as cadres for future in-service improvement programs in these same schools. Some of the field work was done in these schools, creating a depth dimension to the institute experience not usually available.

Some of the institute participants were recommended by the staff at the San Diego County Department of Education. These participants were selected from nearby small school districts. These small districts did not have a California compensatory education program in 1965, but many of them now have programs under ESEA Title I.

Participants were selected from those schools using these Act funds. They were selected so that they might serve as resource people in the future development of their schools.

To be eligible for admission the candidate was required to satisfy these criteria: (1) certification, by the appropriate authority in San Diego County and City School Districts, that the applicant was or would be teaching or supervising in a school serving disadvantaged youth during the 1967–68 school year; and (2) ratings by principals and curriculum coordinators on the applicant's potential for exerting a leadership role in the school in providing in-service training for other teachers of disadvantaged youth, and ratings on potential for innovation.

Data and rankings described above were reviewed and evaluated by the institute selection committee. The committee recommended fifty-four participants and fifty-four alternates. The institute staff attempted to make the program a unified experience rather than a series of fragmented lectures and activities. To achieve this an instructional program consisting of five integrated parts was devised—formal instruction, field work, practicum sessions, seminars, and group work.

THE INSTITUTE

Fifteen to twenty hours of formal instruction were provided during each week of the institute, consisting of lectures, lecture-discussions, and seminars. Three types of field work were provided, occupying three to four hours each day. The three types included those listed below.

*Social Agency Orientation.* The afternoons of the first week were devoted to field trips to social agencies serving disadvantaged youth. The relationship of such agencies to disadvantaged youth and their effects on them were discussed in presentations during the morning instructional sessions.

*Classroom Field Work.* Each morning during weeks two through five, the institute was held at Gompers Junior High School, which was known as the educational field work center. On Monday, Wednesday, and Friday during these four weeks, from 8 to 9 A.M., practicum sessions were held at Gompers. The same period on Tuesdays and Thursdays was scheduled for seminar meetings.

During this four-week field work program all participants were assigned on an individual basis from 9 to 12 each day to a classroom serving disadvantaged youth; this meant fifty-four different classrooms. The participants were scheduled in schools offering summer compensatory education programs for disadvantaged youth in the San Diego Unified School District—six elementary schools, two junior high schools, and two senior high schools. Many of the 1965 and 1966 institute participants were teaching in the classes used by the 1967 institute.

The emphasis during the field work was on a case study of a disadvantaged child and his family; working in a classroom with disadvantaged youth; experimenting with materials, methods, and techniques in teaching these youth, especially in reading and language arts; and relating the theoretical principles covered in the formal instruction to the learning and personal problems of disadvantaged youth.

Six staff members were assigned to plan, direct, and supervise the daily classroom field work. Participants were divided into six groups of nine each on the basis of teaching area and level. The six groups were organized the first week of the institute and met together throughout the institute in seminar sessions for discussions of formal instruction and to plan and evaluate the field work experiences. The field work leader, a staff member, worked with the same group during the seven weeks of the institute.

*Social Agency Field Work.* The afternoon sessions of weeks six and seven were set aside for work with disadvantaged youth through social agencies. During these two weeks each participant assisted as an agency staff member in such agencies as the Boys' Club, recreational centers, Neighborhood Houses, child care centers. The purposes of this type of field work were to provide participants an opportunity to work with disadvantaged youth in an out-of-school setting; to acquaint participants with the program, purposes, and problems of social community agencies serving disadvantaged neighborhoods. The six seminar field work staff members supervised this experience.

The practicum sessions were held from 8 to 9 A.M. on Monday, Wednesday, and Friday during each of the four weeks of the classroom field work. The practicums were devoted to demonstrations, panels, and discussions of materials and techniques that have proved successful in teaching disadvantaged youth, with particular emphasis on reading and language arts. The institute staff, teachers, supervisors, and consultants presented the demonstrations and provided resource leadership for special interest groups. Programs and materials for Spanish-speaking pupils were also included.

Twelve seminars were conducted during the institute. Participants were divided into six seminar groups of nine each. The seminars were led by a staff member who worked with the group throughout the institute. The seminar group, with its staff leader, formed the basic institute unit in which field planning, interpretation, application, supervision, and evaluation took place, as well as planning for the 1967–68 school year. The purpose of the seminar sessions was to relate the theoretical aspects of the formal instruction and the field work to the particular problems of grade and level subject area instruction.

Participants were also divided into special interest groups such as primary, upper elementary, junior high, and senior high, and scheduled for eight one-hour sessions. These groups studied and developed instructional techniques and materials for use in specific grade levels and various subject areas.

A unique feature of the institute was a very high degree of staff-participant interaction in seminar and class sessions. The seminars allowed for free interactions, and some developed into sessions not unlike sensitivity training groups. Other unique features were the social agency field experiences and the involvement of community resource people in the institute program.

Staff members indicated that the most significant accomplishment of seminars was the exploration of participants' values and attitudes as they sought greater self-awareness. The freedom of expression resulted in a high degree of give and take among them. The seminars were rated as the most valued aspect of the institute by the participants. For a number, the small-group seminar experience was one they had not encountered previously in their teacher education preparation.

Staff members felt that future institutes might wish to give greater consideration to having new and experienced teachers in combination, to have more minority-group teachers as participants, and to encourage experienced tenured teachers to transfer to disadvantaged schools by making an institute available to them.

On the whole, the NDEA institute, though highly successful, provided such an intensive program that the participants had little time to read, to think, and to reflect—to sort out and relate new theoretical content to actual practice as well as to assimilate it. This reaction was common to both the institute staff and a large number of the participants.

## "TEACHERS OF DISADVANTAGED AMERICAN INDIAN YOUTH"

Location of institute: San Fernando Valley State College
Amount of federal funds: $69,660

### BACKGROUND

Since San Fernando Valley State College is located in metropolitan Los Angeles, its sponsorship of an in-service project serving two counties that are the most sparsely populated in the entire state, Inyo and Mono, both of which are geographically isolated from the rest of the state by the Sierra-Nevada Mountains, demands a bit of explaining. Although the college is approximately 250 miles from Independence, the county seat of Inyo County, because of geographical vagaries and the lack of transportation through the Sierras it is the state college most accessible to the region. As a consequence, the college has for a long time provided extension courses in this remote area. These courses, covering a wide range of academic and education subjects, have usually been requested by the county superintendent of schools. Although these classes have been of help to teachers and administrators, providing them with opportunities to stimulate their thinking and to update their educational objectives, they have been limited in number. Too, it has been difficult to persuade qualified instructors to spend ten hours driving and cover 500 miles round trip for nominal recompense. The institute came about as a result of the direct request of the superintendents of Inyo and Mono counties.

The site chosen for the 1967 institute, which was to be a live-in experience, was Camp Inyo in Big Pine, California. Camp Inyo is on a 98-acre former apple ranch, and is located on a gently sloping plateau of 4,450 feet altitude on the west side of the Owens Valley. An all-weather road extends three miles to Big Pine and an additional twelve miles to Bishop. It is near the lowest and highest points of the continental United States, the oldest known trees, extinct volcanoes and lava beds, the oldest Indian excavations, Cal Tech electronic telescopes, Indian reservations, and historic monuments. The camp provided complete kitchen and dining room accommodations for eighty people, as well as eighty bunk beds.

Bishop, California, the largest town in Inyo County, is the site of an 875-acre reservation where approximately 600 Paiute Indians live. Many of these Paiute children attend Bishop public schools, and make up the majority of disadvantaged children in the area. The elementary schools of Bishop have long sought aid in developing programs for helping these disadvantaged youngsters. For example, using state compensatory education funds, the district has initiated an in-service education class on the problems of disadvantaged youth for the teachers under its jurisdiction. While there are three other smaller reservations in Inyo County, many Indians do not live on reservations, but among the general population. They are scattered throughout both Inyo and Mono counties and make up a substantial number of the poverty stricken. According to the 1960 U.S. Census of Population, Indians living in California had the highest unemployment rate—over 15 per cent—and the lowest median annual income—less than $2700—of any ethnic group. The education attainment levels of California Indians was also very low, with more than 43 per cent of the population seventeen years old or older not having gone beyond the eighth grade.

OBJECTIVES

The institute's program was planned to assist teachers in developing positive attitudes and in designing curriculum patterns that would provide an optimum learning environment for disadvantaged American Indian youth. This general objective involved formulating realistic objectives and organizing a curriculum based on an understanding of the unique problems of culturally disadvantaged youth.

The institute staff believed that to help build realistic objectives and experiences for learning, teachers of the disadvantaged should be aware of their own feelings, attitudes, and assumptions as they observe and work with children who differ from the middle-class norm; should develop an understanding of the motivational problem of disadvantaged youth as it relates to school achievement; and should expand their understanding of how disadvantaged youth perceive the world and the factors that influence their perspective.

The institute staff also felt that to organize and implement curricula for disadvantaged youth, the teacher should be able to do the following:

To study, understand, and apply current research findings of programs for the disadvantaged (for example, in the area of language development and cognition).

To diagnose individual styles of learning in order to encourage the students' development of confidence and independence.

To understand the psychological and sociological background of the student.

To use teaching techniques that engage students in active learning in concepts, skills, and attitudes.

To be familiar with new instructional materials and procedures, develop appropriate ways of evaluating them, learn how to adapt them for their own purposes.

To develop skills and resources for leadership roles in effecting curriculum change.

The purpose of the institute was to provide teachers of disadvantaged Indian youngsters with specific and specialized assistance necessary for them to meet the many problems that they encounter in their daily teaching duties. According to the philosophy of the program, the wide gap between the tarditional education of teachers and the realities of a classroom that is inhabited mainly by pupils from disadvantaged homes can be bridged only by teacher training directed toward the development of teachers with specialized attitudes and skills.

SELECTION OF PARTICIPANTS

Thirty-six participants were chosen for the six-week institute; about half were from California and the rest were from six other states. All worked in elementary schools. This number was selected in order to provide an optimum number for large-group presentations such as lectures and demonstrations, for small-group activities such as seminar discussions and study sessions, and for the flexibility of program that this size would allow.

A bachelor's degree from an accredited institution was required for consideration for admission into the program. Applicants were required to have at least two years of teaching experience at the elementary level. Applicants were also required to provide evidence that they would be teaching a substantial number of disadvantaged Indian children during the following school year. The final selection of the participants was made by a committee composed of the director, co-director, and two other members of the institute staff.

THE INSTITUTE

The live-in character of the institute as well as its organization reflected the beliefs of the director and the staff that in order for teachers to become more effective with their students, they must first understand themselves better and become more sensitive in understanding the behavior of others. Also, the location of the institute at Camp Inyo was selected, among other reasons, because it is near a substantial American Indian population, because approximately half of the participants were from that area, and because it offered live-in facilities where staff and participants could share meals, living accommodations, and recreational facilities. The location fitted in well with the structure of the institute in that it provided a relaxed, informal setting where staff and participants could live together, have many opportunities for informal talk sessions, mutual counseling, and intense sharing of ideas and experiences. The Big Pine area is scenic, beautiful, and in the words of a staff member, "gives one a heightened awareness of Indian values related to the earth's beauty and bountifulness."

In addition to the live-in characteristic, some of the other unique aspects of the institute included two field trips. One was to the Nevada Indian Agency School at Stuart, Nevada, which provided the participants an opportunity to see the Bureau of Indian Affairs School and listen to one of the academic department heads tell of the program offered. Although the school was not in session, several students were available to talk to participants and to help conduct the tour of the school facilities. On the same trip a visit was made to Carson City to see the Nevada museum which has an extensive exhibit of Indian artifacts. The second trip, to Mammoth Mountain, was largely recreational in nature. The Mammoth area is high in the Sierra Mountains and is the scene of much skiing, even in July. This trip, coming about halfway through the institute, was refreshing and relaxing and served to help buoy participants and staff.

Extensive use was made of a variety of lecturers and consultants at the institute site. However, due to the relative isolation of the institute and the lack of public transportation, some lecturers were unavailable. Two days of teaching experience was also provided for the participants at the Lone Pine Elementary School. Here, most of the participants were able to take part in team-teaching situations and were able to work with small groups of children in new and different ways. The children were heterogeneously grouped, not only according to ability but also according to age, and were in ungraded groups that covered the elementary age range.

A wide variety of audiovisual materials was employed during the course of the institute. Among these were 16 mm sound films, loop films, records, filmstrips, and video tapes. An extensive collection of professional books and journals was also provided.

Seven types of activities were conducted to achieve the institute's objectives: teaching, lectures and discussions, seminars, field trips, task groups, conferences, and individual study. All activities were conducted in and around Camp Inyo, and all participants and staff members lived, for the entire six weeks, at Camp Inyo. The live-in experience provided an opportunity for maximum communication among participants and staff and allowed persons who differed markedly in age, race, religion, geographic origin and school location, type of school, professional competence, and personal beliefs and attitudes an unusual opportunity to become better acquainted.

Notwithstanding the idyllic charm of Inyo, there were some inconveniences. The heat (usually 100 degrees Fahrenheit or above), insects (often in enormous swarms), wind, and dryness could, it might be argued, provide the participants and staff many opportunities to empathize with the residents of the area, including the many Indians who live in the Owens Valley. While these natural inconveniences might be discounted as quirks of nature, the inconveniences that resulted from man's inability to cope with his environment were not so forgivable. These included lack of screens on doors and windows, inadequate and nonoperating toilet facilities, poor ventilation in the dining hall/meeting room, lack of reading lamps for evening study, and double deck beds (a type of sleeping arrangement that participants beyond the age of Campfire Girls found uncomfortable, especially if they had to sleep on the top bunk). There were, of course, many complaints about the physical facilities; however, they were endured good-naturedly and their very existence, since they were shared by everyone, helped to engender a feeling of group solidarity in the face of hardships.

One seminar leader commented: "The uniqueness of the Institute was the live-in aspect. This proved a real asset since we were really able to know each other well much sooner. I can say this because as a participant in last year's Institute, I know it took us much longer to really know each other."

## "ENGLISH FOR SPEAKERS OF OTHER LANGUAGES AND DISADVANTAGED YOUTH"

Location of institute: University of Southern California
Amount of federal funds: $75,325

BACKGROUND

The institute at USC was planned to meet a need that was felt by the staff—a need for teachers of English to gain skills in the teaching of speakers of other languages. It was also felt that there was a need to train teachers to deal with speakers of substandard English dialects in Southern California and other urban areas on the Pacific Coast. The University of Southern California is uniquely available for service to these areas of linguistic deprivation. The campus is located in south central Los Angeles, an area that contains 97 per cent of the Negro population of Southern California, and 63 per cent of the Negro population of the West Coast. The university is within the riot zone controlled by military troops during the Watts crisis. It is also located within ten minutes by automobile transportation from the center of the Mexican-American community of east Los Angeles. This area of the city contains 89 per cent of the Spanish-speaking population in Southern California. The inner city Mexican-American population numbers approximately 718,000.

A realistic survey of the need for teachers of English as a second language must also count other major sources of heterogeneity in English-as-a-second-language classes: for example, 310,000 speakers of Oriental languages live in the greater Los Angeles area. In these cases as well, the location of the University of Southern California allows for immediate involvement in the problems of the surrounding community.

Recent disturbances emanating from racial tensions gave evidences of the need for such institutions as the University of Southern California to seek avenues of interracial and intergroup understanding, improved assistance to the linguistically deprived and their need for acceptable language usage, and increased emphasis on educational and social developmental programs.

OBJECTIVES

This institute attempted to enhance the quality of instruction by fifty-four teachers of English for speakers of other languages and disadvantaged youth. The program sought to produce teachers who would have a sound foundation in linguistics, be adept at methodology and classroom dynamics, be knowledgeable concerning the latest techniques for technological support in foreign language teaching, be sensitive to intercultural and intergroup relations, and be concerned with the importance of cognitive behavior in second language training.

There were four courses offered at the institute. The courses and their goals are listed below.

The Linguistics course objectives of the institute were:

Introduce the participants to the basic concepts of phonemics, morphemics, tactics, and contemporary English grammar.

To assist the participants in developing skill in the basic procedures in the analysis of linguistic systems and contrastive rhetoric as applied to speaking, reading, and writing a second language.

To assist the participants in the development of sound linguistic concepts of language and language learning so that they may better plan teaching procedures in the teaching of English to speakers of other languages.

The Methodology course objective was to enhance the participants' professional growth and help them encompass objectives, course content, materials, classroom dynamics and techniques, and tests and measurements related to an English-as-a-second-language program. To be included in this instruction were the following:

Methodology to use effectively the audiolingual approach for the teaching of standard English pronunciation and structure.

Investigation and development of techniques and devices for evaluating progress in English-as-a-second-language training.

Examination and evaluation of available commercial material.

Preparation of instructional materials for the teacher's own class.

The goals of Cultural Anthropology and Educational Process, an advanced sociology of education course, were:

To foster awareness of the cultures with their patterns of behavior, values, and attitudes influencing the target groups of English language instruction.

To provide knowledge of the concept of culture, role expectation, self-concept, influence of cultural patterns, transmission of culture, problems of articulation (especially of Mexican-American, Oriental, and Negro subcultures) in relation to patterns of the more dominant culture, retarding the effects of environmental deprivation, socialization processes and agents (especially the family and the school).

To develop strategies to draw on the socializing agents as sources of positive, developmental influence or at least to neutralize the unacceptable values and patterns transmitted by these agencies or the community.

To provide course study to integrate actual experience in the home and community affected by the environmental and linguistic deprivation or handicap.

To increase familiarity with the possibilities of economic and social acceptance and effectiveness resulting from language improvement programs.

The Instructional Technology course was designed to aid participants

To gain knowledge of latest research in the field of instructional media and its implications for the teaching of English as a second language.

To establish criteria for evaluation of media and gaining knowledge of sources and materials pertinent to teaching English.

To produce simple audiovisual materials such as art and paste-ups using a photomechanical copy process, and picture stories, overhead transparencies, aural tapes for presentation, and single-concept 8 mm films.

SELECTION OF PARTICIPANTS

The institute was conducted for fifty-four participants who were then under contract to be teachers of English to speakers of other languages and disadvantaged youth in elementary and secondary schools.

Candidates were selected from those applicants who seemed to have the highest possibility of profiting from the program and the greatest possibility of contributing to the teaching of English to non-English-speakers and disadvantaged youth. All public and private school teachers of English to speakers of other languages and disadvantaged youth were eligible to apply provided that they held a bachelor's degree, could offer evidence of satisfactory scholarship (as shown by transcripts), were of sound character (as supported by letters of recommendation from responsible persons), and were willing to live and eat in housing arranged by the institute.

In order to draw together a group that would be homogeneous in terms of previous training, the University of Southern California limited their acceptance to individuals with little or no training in linguistics or methodology of English-as-a-second-language teaching.

Before the completed applications were received, plans were made for an elaborate evaluation system. Four members of the institute staff were designated as an evaluating body, and they established specific criteria to be employed in determining eligibility. Unfortunately, a huge flow of applications in the relatively brief time between the closing date for applications and the time in which the participants had to be notified made the elaborate system less effective than it might have been.

It was also felt that care taken in the selection of participants was somewhat negated by the fact that a number of participants had applied to several institutes. In a significant number of instances, first choice participants had been rated by other institutes as their first choices. This became particularly confusing in relation to the Institute for Disadvantaged Youth at the University of Southern California, since both it and the English for Speakers of Other Languages and Disadvantaged Youth Institute, also, of course, at USC, were to a large extent serving the same population.

THE INSTITUTE

The program at the institute was seven weeks long and consisted of courses, workshops, laboratory experiences, demonstration classes, and directed teaching and informal cultural experiences related to English-as-a-second-language teaching.

One of the most interesting aspects of the institute itself was the experimental program involving the Teacher Education Program prepared by the English Language Services. TEP is a self-instructional program composed of a console (including a tape deck, an 8 mm film projector, and appropriate headphones and speakers), 160 8 mm film cartridges, 140 tapes, five workbooks in twenty-six volumes, and approximately 500 pages of expendable materials. The program requires approximately 200 hours to complete. Ten participants from the institute as a whole were chosen to participate in the TEP. The institute participants were asked to volunteer for the program; the first ten volunteers were selected. Approximately half of the fifty-four participants in the total institute ultimately volunteered for participation in this program. The ten selected participants were given a special orientation by representatives from English Language Services. A special program was prepared for these ten participants, allowing them articulation with the main body of the institute in all areas except the courses of modern English grammar, phonetics, and methodology. These latter areas of training were provided through the TEP. Ten other participants were also selected, again on a volunteer basis, to serve as a control group. Both groups of ten, in addition to filling out the initial and terminal questionnaires required of all participants, took initial and terminal examinations administered by the English Language Services.

The standard curriculum of the institute provided instruction in a number of areas: methodology, instructional technology, phonology, sociology of education, modern English grammar, and field methods. The methodology classes were combined with instructional technology for the most part, although additional sections in the language laboratory were scheduled. The combining of instructional technology and methodology proved to be an effective means of presenting both areas. Participant response to the methodology class and its attendant instructional technology was good. All participants were required to prepare terminal projects as part of the institute experience. Projects were designed in such a way that finished material could be taken back to the participant's school for his own classroom use in the coming school year. The great majority of the participants chose to do their projects in the methodology-instructional technology area.

The phonology classes were somewhat less successful. According to the staff, this was in part a result of the fact that phonology is simply not an exciting discipline for most people. In brief, the course consisted of an introduction to language, a study of the physiology of speech, a detailed study of the English phonological system, a study of phonological change, and a detailed study of contrastive analysis. Part of the difficulty involved in the phonology component arose from inadequate coordination between the phonology and methodology classes. The staff felt that the phonological principles discussed in the phonology class were never adequately demonstrated in the observation classes or adequately incorporated into the application of the various other components of the institute.

The sociology of education class proved to be among the best received of the courses. The curriculum was divided into three components. The first dealt with the sociological problems of the Negro speaker of non-standard English, the second dealt with the Mexican-American dialect speaker. The last served as a summary of the first two and extended the implications of sociology to all linguistic minorities. The content of these components was so distinct from the theoretical and applied linguistic segments that no extensive attempt was made to correlate it with the rest of the program.

The instructor in this course was able to involve the students personally in the classroom discussion, which was especially important as the class contained members of both minority groups. Initially, the instructor apparently evoked a negative response as he openly attacked many deeply ingrained concepts held by the participants. As the course progressed, however, the negative rapport became positive, and the results of the course were extremely satisfying to the participants. Statistical data derived from terminal reports of the participants clearly indicate that this instructor was the most popular of the faculty.

Probably the single most effective class in the institute program was the class in modern English grammar. In this class, the specific stated goals were "to change attitudes toward language which teachers of English have held sacred for years." The popularity of the instructor contributed much to the success of the class. Grammar is a subject frequently regarded by many, even by many teachers, as inherently dull. This segment of the institute program demonstrated that grammar can be exciting. The participants were introduced to the structure of modern English grammar in such a way that they themselves not only came to have a greater understanding of the ways in which languages function, but also were able to take away with them specific information and materials that would serve them when they returned to their own classrooms.

The work in field methods was both rewarding and frustrating. Part of the frustration resulted from inadequate coordination of this segment of the program with other areas of instruction. Nevertheless, the work in this area appears to have been of interest to the participants, and a great deal of valuable data were collected. In brief, this segment was specifically designed to train the participants to collect and analyze linguistic data so that they might be able to prepare their own classroom materials. Informants—teen-agers willing to serve in this capacity—were brought in from teen posts in south central Los Angeles. They were brought to the university, where the participants worked with them on a one-to-one basis, employing a previously prepared linguistic questionnaire. The questionnaire was an attempt to evoke lexical, phonological, and syntactic items from the informants. The informants were speakers of non-standard, Negro English. All of the data collected were recorded on tape. Participants then worked with tape material in an attempt to understand the lexical, syntactical differences between non-standard, Negro English and general (white middle-class) American English. Finally, some of the participants attempted to prepare classroom teaching materials based on the contrast.

The project appeared to be successful in terms of the participants, since it not only provided an opportunity to collect and analyze linguistic data, but also provided an opportunity to work closely with Negro children, in some cases for the first time.

The instructional technology and language laboratory suffered from inadequate coordination with other segments of the institute curriculum, according to the final report of the institute. Nevertheless, a number of interesting projects were undertaken as a result of the information acquired in this segment. Several participants were able to produce visual aids of potential significant value in the teaching and testing of elementary school students for whom standard English is not a native language. The instructional technology seemed to be of far greater value to elementary school teachers in general; the language laboratory appeared to have been of greater value to the teachers of upper grades.

The segment of the institute entitled "Social Internship," the most exciting component when in its planning stages, proved to be among the least successful parts of the program. The concept, according to the staff, was probably a good one, but the implementation was extremely difficult. It was originally planned to allow all the participants the experience of actually living in an economically deprived area. The original plan called for participants to live three weeks in Watts and three weeks in east Los Angeles. The proposal began to draw fire from the local community almost at once. It was quite correctly pointed out that in most cases it would be impossible to reach those members of the community who would provide the most valuable experience. It was further pointed out that families in extreme poverty could not physically accommodate boarders in their homes. It was further noted that individuals in the community would not like to expose themselves to clinical observation. Nevertheless, it was felt that the program had so much potential value that it was worthwhile to pursue it further. Unfortunately, adequate financing had not been provided to allow for the necessary support staff and program. Ultimately, twenty-one participants did spend one weekend in Watts. Twenty of the participants were housed with Negro families in the Watts-Willowbrook area. Those participants who took part in the social internship found the experience rewarding and profitable.

Should this segment of the program be repeated, the staff felt it would be necessary to provide much more complete staff assistance.

At least one full-time coordinator was thought to be necessary to undertake the arrangement for this segment. Elaborate preplanning must be scheduled well in advance of the dates of the social internship. As part of the preplanning, contact would need to be made in advance with responsible community agencies in order to provide the community support essential to the success of this operation.

The institute staff felt that a rather crucial problem was caused by their failure to anticipate the flow of applications and inquiries. More than 12,000 inquiries were received, and more than 400 completed applications were finally processed. Telephone calls began to be received shortly after the initial announcement of the award was made by the Office of Education, long before the institute staff was organized to receive them, and before a secretary had been employed to answer the correspondence. The staff felt that in the future either the announcement from the Office of Education should be delayed until initial funds were available to the universities, or initial funds should be made available simultaneously with early announcements of award. Thus adequate support staff could be arranged at once, and fewer applicants would be disappointed or misinformed.

Furthermore, the staff felt that the propensity of school administrators to recommend all their teachers as superior tends to invalidate at least one third of the available information from which the selection is to be made. The final report of the institute strongly urged that the forms to be completed by school administrators carry a personal statement urging honesty, and indicate that it is perjury to misrepresent applicant qualifications.

The institute staff felt that although it was probably impossible and perhaps undesirable to prevent participants from applying to several institutes, some sort of central clearing house might be established to prevent the unnecessary overlap and the confusion that inevitably result from multiple applications.

Initial and terminal questionnaires indicated general approval of the TEP program by the ten participants. Members of the control group, who were carefully prevented from being exposed to the TEP, felt that they preferred contact with a live teacher, that they needed the interaction between teacher and class, and were reluctant to receive instruction from a machine. In general, the TEP proved to be quite successful. The staff recommended that the Office of Education lend its support to the further development of the TEP, and that other NDEA institutes be encouraged to experiment with the program. In future experiments, however, the staff felt that it might be necessary to make a teacher available to supplement the TEP or to use the TEP as a supplement to the regular program of instruction. The staff believed that the program as a whole has great promise and importance for English-as-a-second-language training in the future.

## "TEACHERS OF DISADVANTAGED YOUTH AND SOCIAL-CULTURAL MILIEU"

Location of institute: University of Southern California
Amount of federal funds: $78,305

BACKGROUND

The University of Southern California is located within the riot zone of the Watts area and near the largest community of Mexican-Americans in the United States. (Looting and burning took place within a block of the university in the summer of 1966; National Guard troops were quartered on the campus.) Most of the prospective teachers prepared by the university do their student teaching and internship teaching in the depressed urban schools in the immediate area. The staff of the institute had served extensively as consultants to these schools, and saw a need for more intensive programs for experienced school personnel.

This institute provided a unique opportunity for participants to see an environment through new eyes and to hear it through new ears. Slides, film, and tape recordings—subjected to individual analysis and classroom discussion—were used to gain a fresh insight into the environmental and sociological factors of cultural deprivation. Eight groups of four persons each worked on a day-to-day basis, broadening their approaches to and interpretations of poverty culture by the introduction of many new points of view.

OBJECTIVES

The institute was designed to meet four specific needs, the first of which was a team approach to studying the educational problems of disadvantaged youth. The institute personnel consisted of a combination of experienced teachers, administrators, and indigenous school community members. This was seen as a most natural combination for the study of an educational process. The institute director felt that there had often been a sharp division between teachers and administrators on one hand as manipulators, and the indigenous population, on the other hand, as the manipulated. Community action programs had suggested to him that such a division is not effective; what was needed was an approach in which each group took part in achieving solutions to community problems.

The institute participants were therefore divided into eight teams, each consisting of one administrator, two teachers, and one indigenous school community member who acted as resource person. The latter served to introduce the teams to the community and to help the professional members of the teams see the community and its problems through the eyes of a resident. These indigenous team members were carefully selected high school seniors, persons who were thoroughly familiar with the community and close enough to their own educational experience to see the relevance of community study to the improvement of educational procedures. A particularly significant aspect of this team approach was the opportunity for administrators and teachers to work with indigenous youth in other than an authority-subordinate relationship. No teams working in the Negro area were all-white or all-Negro, and similarly, participants of other ethnic backgrounds were spread throughout all the teams.

The institute's second area of study was the poverty community itself. Each team therefore focused on one census tract consisting of approximately 5,000 people living in the heart of the depressed area. Four of the tracts were in the Watts area, and were predominantly Negro; the other four were in the Avalon area, and were predominantly Mexican-American. Tracts were selected for the degree in which they represented poverty culture as a whole, and for their accessibility to the university.

A third function of the institute was to familiarize participants with new media. Since anthropologists have made extensive use of cameras and tape recorders to document their observations for later detailed analysis, since the camera records more than the eye can see, and since a recorder preserves shades of meaning and emphasis beyond human memory and the printed word, the study of such media was assumed by the staff to be most appropriate as a means of teacher retraining.

The institute's fourth specific function was the development of new classroom procedures. The institute continually focused on the implications of what was occurring for both the school and the classroom. The material gathered from the community study phase and the team interpretation provided sources of insight into the improvement of educational experience.

The specific objectives of the institute were these:

To assist teachers and administrators in understanding both cognitively and affectively the social milieu of educationally disadvantaged children in a depressed urban area, particularly where social class combined with racial and ethnic factors operates to create conditions mitigating against substantial educational progress.

To place teachers, administrators, and young people indigenous to the depressed areas together in a meaningful, task-oriented situation so that from this relationship—one most conducive to attitudinal change—each will emerge with a greater understanding and appreciation of the other's role and significance as a human being.

To suggest to teachers and administrators how camera and tape recorder assist both in sharpening cognition and altering affective behavior.

To acquaint teachers and administrators with community resources such as community houses, family aid services, public health facilities, EOA projects such as Teen Post, and child aid and care centers (for participants from southern California, this familiarity proved useful for referral purposes; for those from other urban areas, it served to introduce them to new ideas valuable for their own home communities).

To analyze all the materials and experiences provided by the institute and from these to develop bold, imaginative approaches to be used in the education of disadvantaged youth.

To help the participants develop unique materials by which to disseminate the outcomes of the institute more effectively than by the conventional oral and written forms.

SELECTION OF PARTICIPANTS

The institute included twenty-four professional members who normally work with pupils in grades seven through twelve, and eight nonprofessional, indigenous community members. In selecting participants for this institute, an attempt was made to find people who had a rural or small-town orientation and who had little or no work experience outside of teaching. Also, participants were sought who had been certified prior to 1955 and who had little subsequent graduate work; persons having no courses on the sociology of education were given preference. These criteria were used because the director of the institute felt that their specific purpose was to upgrade experienced teachers who had an inadequate background to deal with the complexities of the disadvantaged community.

In screening participants for the institute, a rather unique method was used to determine the teacher's reasons for wishing to attend. Each applicant was asked to write about a critical incident that happened in his professional life that caused him to realize that he needed additional training to become more effective in working with disadvantaged children.

THE INSTITUTE

The major vehicle used for the presentation of the bulk of formal course work in the institute was a course on the Sociology of Education. A second course served to expose participants to experience in the community and was entitled Field Work: Sociology. A third major area was included in the course Special Studies in Instructional Technology. In this course, much of the formal instruction and theory of the use of audiovisual media for factual reporting was handled. Each of the eight groups prepared a media document of about ten minutes in length in order to share their experiences with other teachers and with their home communities. Each participant was provided with a personal copy of this document at the end of the institute.

In addition to these more formally organized study areas, a seminar was offered to integrate all the experiences provided by the institute as a forum for community specialists and other resource consultants. The emphasis in the seminar was on group process. It was largely unstructured to permit a free flow of ideas from every participant.

Analysis and evaluation seminars were also conducted to develop field work skills, particularly those relating to the collection and organization of field materials, observation and interviewing techniques, and the problems of translating field-work experiences into useful educational concepts. In this seminar, materials gathered by the teams were used to help institute participants interpret their value orientations and attitudes, particularly those who had before held latent and unexamined attitudes and orientations.

Undoubtedly, the single most unique element in the institute was the emphasis on the use of media. Audiovisual equipment for the teams' use was selected on the basis of reliability and simplicity of operation. Cameras that took sharp, correctly exposed pictures were needed. It was necessary for tape recorders to have high sensitivity, fidelity, and automatic volume control for recording. Procedures had to be set up for storage and for checking equipment out. Equipment for viewing, listening, and duplication; film processing and maintenance; and other services required much advance planning. Additional equipment was needed beyond that which was budgeted, although thousands of dollars worth of equipment was loaned to the institute by other departments of the university.

Groups began to explore the environs of the university with cameras and tape recorders on the first afternoon, indoors and outdoors, on busy streets, buses, supermarkets, hot dog stands, and a snooker hall. Members had had only one half hour of formal instruction, yet pictures came back consistently good. Tape recordings were more variable because of background noise, and the fear that a close microphone would be too conspicuous. These tools were mastered by all participants in the first four days, and in a week they had made a picture story contrasting the affluent and disadvantaged environments, accompanied by a soundtrack of interviews and narration augmented by natural sounds and music. These projects showed a high level of competence, both in documentation and the presentation of ideas. Production of the final media document was an important part of the experiences; it required participants to analyze the various field experiences and to make selective value judgments on the significance of their raw material. In the synthesis of the final document, insights were expressed that might otherwise have been passed over.

The use of media documentation as the "meaningful task" proved to be of inestimable value. It may have created anxieties for some, but provided an external focus and as such often became the scapegoat for group conflicts that might otherwise have become personal. It provided a motivation as well as a measure of group interest and participation. In psychological terms, the slides and films processed overnight were a strong positive reinforcement. Another very positive value was the avoidance of the verbal stereotype. Many participants, when they arrived, spoke "the language" very well, but often they had had little direct experience and relatively little understanding of the socioeconomic milieu of disadvantaged youth. The visual and sound record came very close to reality and preserved nuances of meaning not possible with written copy. Also, the final presentation forced the selection of central themes and a deeper exploration of the significant ideas surrounding it.

Participants were encouraged to use, and, in fact, did use these visual documentations as in-service vehicles for the staffs at their own schools. Many indicated a very high degree of effectiveness in their use. The director of the project also indicated that there was great interest in the use of these documentaries by people other than institute participants for such activities as the pre-service and in-service training of teachers.

# PART TWO

## *The Findings*

# CHAPTER IV

# Q-Sort and Questionnaire Findings

The highest happiness of man as a thinking being is to have probed what is knowable and quietly to revere what is unknowable.

Goethe

135

Q-sort and questionnaire returns were obtained from 1,443 project participants. Their backgrounds are shown by the demographic data in Table 1.

For this group of subjects whose school situation is outlined below, mean scores on all Q-sort and questionnaire items were determined and then corrected for response bias by standard calculations involving the results of a poll of a sample of nonrespondents.

The 1,443 respondents represent 47 per cent of the persons to whom questionnaires and Q-sorts were initially mailed. If those whose packets were returned by the post office as undeliverable were subtracted from the overall number, it could be said that almost exactly half of those who presumably received materials sent back responses that could be scored. While this return is lower than had been hoped for, the length of time required to complete, especially the Q-sort, makes the rate understandable.

By using standard equations from sampling theory, it was found that returns from thirty-one of the nonrespondents would be necessary in order to be able to apply response-bias corrections if a 5 per cent Type I error were assigned. Thirty-one persons were selected randomly from the list of nonrespondents, therefore, and those persons were solicited again, some several times, by letter and phone. Twenty-six eventually returned the materials, and those responses were used to calculate corrected means. There are only slight differences between the mean responses of the original 1,443 subjects and the corrected means. For each item, the mean response and its standard deviation are reported in Table 2, along with the corrected means.

Items are grouped according to whether they provide estimates of change in students, participants, or the schools; opinions on the value of the curriculum; teaching methods, or general procedures of a given project; evaluations of the project; or attitudes about educational issues. Furthermore, items are listed within each group in descending order of the degree of agreement with their statements.

Items number 1 through 70 were subjected to the modified ranking procedure of the Q-sort, whereas Items 71 through 90 permit

136

answers that are independent of one another. Table 2 shows the results for items except those already used to report demographic data in the preceding table. The items are listed in descending order of their corrected mean values. Uncorrected mean values also are shown.

While the mean responses speak for themselves, certain results might be singled out for special attention. First, participants are convinced that the in-service projects did affect them—by making them less critical of disadvantaged students, increasing their effectiveness with *all* students, making them more knowledgeable about the subcultures of disadvantaged groups, leading them to give children more individual attention, showing them the effects of a deprived home environment on children and providing instructional materials and curricula to overcome those negative effects, and generally changing the ways in which they teach, counsel, or administer.

Participants also thought, though with less certainty, that the projects had had some positive effects on their disadvantaged students, feeling that problems of unsureness about self, hostility toward teachers, disinterest in school, inefficient learning, and, to some extent, discipline, had been ameliorated. It was doubted, however, that disadvantaged students got along better with teachers or classmates, had higher educational aspirations, participated more in school activities, understood their own ethnic backgrounds better, or had improved their attendance records much as a result of the in-service projects.

And though project participants were thought to have exerted some positive influence on the attitudes of other teachers and administrators, and enjoyed some success in getting instructional materials and curricula introduced that were more appropriate for disadvantaged students, and while other in-service programs may have benefited to some extent, no other appreciable changes suggested by the items were felt to have been accomplished.

As for instructional procedures and curricula, all were approved of, most of them strongly.[1] In fact, stronger support was given to the idea that the instructional procedures and curricula were valuable than to the thought that positive change had been brought about in participants, disadvantaged students, or schools.

---

[1] This is not to say that every project was lauded for its instructional procedures and curricula, but that respondents gave mean approval on each relevant item.

## Table 1

### NUMBER OF RESPONDENTS IN EACH INDICATED CATEGORY OF DEMOGRAPHIC DATA

**School position**

| Teacher Aide | Teacher | Counselor | Administrator | Other |
|---|---|---|---|---|
| 0 | 1144 | 94 | 127 | 78 |

**Teaching or other school experience**

| 0–4 yr. | 4–8 yr. | 8–12 yr. | 12–16 yr. | 16–20 yr. | More Than 20 yr. | No Response |
|---|---|---|---|---|---|---|
| 247 | 320 | 296 | 227 | 123 | 224 | 6 |

**Grade level of pupils taught**

Preschool 18.  Kindergarten 40.

| 1 | 2 | 3 | 4 | 5 | 6 | 7 | 8 | 9 | 10 | 11 | 12 | No Response |
|---|---|---|---|---|---|---|---|---|---|---|---|---|
| 148 | 208 | 208 | 92 | 80 | 75 | 66 | 178 | 59 | 101 | 132 | 10 | 28 |

**Present school setting**

| Rural | Town | Suburban | Prosperous city area | City ghetto | No Response |
|---|---|---|---|---|---|
| 119 | 332 | 266 | 117 | 583 | 26 |

**Per cent of disadvantaged students taught**

| 0–10 | 10–20 | 20–30 | 30–40 | 40–50 | 50–60 | 60–70 | 70–80 | 80–90 | 90–100 | No Response |
|---|---|---|---|---|---|---|---|---|---|---|
| 85 | 116 | 140 | 113 | 107 | 104 | 125 | 113 | 206 | 298 | 36 |

**Racial and ethnic background of respondents**

| White | Oriental | American Indian | Mexican, Spanish-speaking | Negro | Other | No Response |
|---|---|---|---|---|---|---|
| 1083 | 39 | 26 | 43 | 200 | 4 | 48 |

**Socioeconomic status of respondents during childhood**

| Lower Class | | | Middle Class | | | Upper Class | No Response |
|---|---|---|---|---|---|---|---|
| 78 | 202 | 448 | 525 | 154 | 25 | 8 | 3 |

## Table 2

### MEAN RESPONSES ON INDIVIDUAL ITEMS

| Item Number | Item Statement | Mean | Corrected Mean |
|:---:|:---|:---:|:---:|
| *Estimate of changes in participants:* | | | |
| 6 | This project increased my effectiveness with *all* students, not just the disadvantaged. | 5.5 | 5.8 |
| 12 | This project has led me to give disadvantaged students more individual attention. | 5.2 | 5.2 |
| 1 | This project increased my knowledge of the subcultures of disadvantaged groups. | 5.2 | 5.1 |
| 8 | I am more self-confident in the classroom (or office) as a result of this project. | 4.9 | 5.0 |
| 14 | As a result of this project, I have become more of a leader in my school in improving the education of disadvantaged students. | 4.4 | 4.3 |
| 9 | I like disadvantaged students better as a result of this project. | 4.1 | 4.3 |
| 4 | This project convinced me that disadvantaged students have more learning ability than I had given them credit for. | 3.9 | 4.1 |
| 5 | This project showed me that disadvantaged students are actually *superior* to other students in certain ways. | 3.3 | 3.5 |
| 13 | My relations with the parents of my disadvantaged students are unchanged in spite of the project. | 3.1 | 3.5 |
| 11 | Before this project began, I collected as much background information on my disadvantaged students as I do now. | 3.6 | 3.3 |
| 15 | I teach (or counsel, etc.) about the same way I did before the project started. | 2.9 | 3.1 |

| | | | |
|---|---|---|---|
| 7 | I have had little success in using what I learned in the project to change the attitudes of my colleagues regarding disadvantaged children. | 3.2 | 3.0 |
| 2 | I learned very little from the project about instructional materials and curricula for disadvantaged students. | 2.6 | 2.6 |
| 3 | I learned very little from the project about the effects of a deprived home environment on a student's school life. | 2.4 | 2.5 |
| 10 | I have to admit that I am as critical of disadvantaged students as I was before this project began. | 2.1 | 2.0 |

*Estimate of changes in disadvantaged students:*

| | | | |
|---|---|---|---|
| 23 | My disadvantaged students read better because of this project. | 4.6 | 4.9 |
| 17 | My disadvantaged students have higher educational aspirations as a result of this project. | 4.0 | 4.3 |
| 21 | My disadvantaged students like me better as a result of this project. | 4.0 | 4.2 |
| 26 | My disadvantaged students participate more in school activities as a result of this project. | 4.0 | 4.0 |
| 22 | My disadvantaged students get along better with their classmates because of the project. | 4.0 | 3.9 |
| 24 | My disadvantaged students are absent from school as often as they were before the project began. | 3.7 | 3.9 |
| 16 | My disadvantaged students have greater knowledge of their own ethnic backgrounds as a result of this project. | 3.8 | 3.8 |
| 25 | My disadvantaged students cause as many discipline problems as they did before the project started. | 3.2 | 3.4 |

Table 2 (cont.)

MEAN RESPONSES ON INDIVIDUAL ITEMS

| Item Number | Item Statement | Mean | Mean Corrected |
|---|---|---|---|
| 19 | My disadvantaged students are as hostile toward teachers as they were when the project started. | 2.8 | 2.6 |
| 18 | My disadvantaged students are as uninterested in school as they were when the project started. | 2.8 | 2.5 |
| 27 | This project has had little influence on how well my students learn. | 2.8 | 2.5 |
| 20 | My disadvantaged students are as unsure of themselves as they were when the project began. | 2.7 | 2.5 |

*Estimate of changes in participants' schools:*

| | | | |
|---|---|---|---|
| 28 | This project has led my school to collect more comprehensive data on our disadvantaged students. | 4.2 | 4.2 |
| 29 | Project participants have gotten parents of disadvantaged students to participate more in our school's activities. | 3.9 | 3.9 |
| 34 | Project participants induced my school to establish, or enlarge, a cultural enrichment program for disadvantaged students. | 3.9 | 3.9 |
| 35 | This project has raised the morale of the whole school staff. | 3.7 | 3.8 |
| 31 | This project has had little effect on the (other) in-service programs at my school. | 3.3 | 3.3 |
| 33 | Project participants have had little success in my school in achieving a curriculum that would be more appropriate for disadvantaged students. | 3.2 | 2.9 |
| 30 | Project participants have had little effect on | | |

the attitudes of other teachers and administrators concerning disadvantaged youth. 3.1 2.9

32 Project participants have had little success in getting special instructional materials for disadvantaged students introduced in my school. 2.8 2.7

*Opinion of instructional procedures used in the project:*

45 The actual teaching or tutoring that I did as part of the project was valuable. 5.5 5.9

51 Visiting homes, neighborhoods, or communities of disadvantaged students was worth while. 5.6 5.8

50 Meeting agency workers, community leaders, or other nonschool personnel who work with the disadvantaged was worth while. 5.7 5.7

40 The reading that I did as part of the project was of value. 5.7 5.6

53 Consultants who worked with teachers individually or in small groups were helpful. 5.4 5.6

39 The films, records, tapes, etc., were valuable to me. 5.3 5.6

48 Working together in small groups was important to me. 5.6 5.5

52 Visiting other projects similar to ours was worth while. 5.4 5.5

36 The lectures in the project were valuable to me. 5.5 5.4

38 The discussion following formal presentations was valuable to me. 5.5 5.4

37 The panel discussions in the project were valuable to me. 5.2 5.3

46 Observing the teaching of disadvantaged students was worth while. 5.2 5.3

43 The encounter group (sensitivity training, T-group, etc.) was helpful to me. 4.8 4.8

*Table 2 (cont.)*

MEAN RESPONSES ON INDIVIDUAL ITEMS

| Item Number | Item Statement | Mean | Corrected Mean |
|---|---|---|---|
| 41 | The replaying of activities through video or audio tapes was of value. | 4.5 | 4.7 |
| 44 | Doing the assigned written work was worth while. | 4.2 | 4.4 |
| 47 | Being together in one large group for activities was important to me. | 4.2 | 4.4 |
| 49 | Working by myself was important to me. | 4.2 | 4.4 |
| 42 | The role-playing that we did in the project was of value. | 4.3 | 4.1 |

*Opinion of the curriculum of the project:*

| | | | |
|---|---|---|---|
| 55 | The material on the learning problems of disadvantaged children was valuable. | 5.8 | 5.8 |
| 58 | The special instructional materials for disadvantaged children were valuable. | 5.4 | 5.7 |
| 54 | The material on the history and characteristics of minority-group peoples was valuable. | 5.4 | 5.4 |
| 57 | The material on reading improvement was valuable. | 5.3 | 5.4 |
| 60 | The material on teaching methods for disadvantaged children was valuable. | 5.3 | 5.4 |
| 59 | The material on curricula for disadvantaged children was valuable. | 5.0 | 5.1 |
| 56 | The material on teaching English as a second language was valuable. | 4.8 | 5.0 |
| 61 | The material on how to teach specific subjects (mathematics, social studies, etc.) to disadvantaged students was valuable. | 4.5 | 4.5 |

*General attitudes regarding the project:*

| | | | |
|---|---|---|---|
| 80 | What overall rating would you give the in-service project in which you participated? | 5.4 | 5.4 |
| 69 | Those sessions when participants were absolutely frank, and even angry, were valuable. | 5.1 | 5.0 |
| 65 | Persons who were themselves members of minority groups offered valuable advice on teaching disadvantaged children. | 4.9 | 4.8 |
| 62 | A better project would have resulted if participants had had a bigger part in its planning. | 3.9 | 4.0 |
| 66 | I learned more from my fellow participants than I did from the leaders and other experts who spoke to us. | 3.6 | 3.8 |
| 63 | A better project would have resulted if participants had made more of the decisions about its day-to-day operations. | 3.7 | 3.7 |
| 67 | The leaders put too much emphasis on dispensing information and not enough on getting us to explore our feelings. | 3.2 | 3.4 |
| 68 | The activities that "just happened" were of more value than those that were planned. | 3.4 | 3.1 |
| 64 | Too often in the project, I was just listening or watching, rather than actively *doing* something. | 3.3 | 2.9 |
| 70 | The project was too middle-class in its philosophy and operation. | 2.9 | 2.7 |

*Attitudes on certain educational issues:*

| | | | |
|---|---|---|---|
| 84 | The best thing schools could do for disadvantaged children would be to put them in smaller-sized classes. | 5.9 | 5.9 |
| 90 | Teachers-in-training can learn more in local schools than they can in colleges or universities. | 5.4 | 5.4 |

## Table 2 (cont.)

### MEAN RESPONSES ON INDIVIDUAL ITEMS

| Item Number | Item Statement | Mean | Corrected Mean |
|---|---|---|---|
| 83 | No expense should be spared to provide special help for disadvantaged students in the schools. | 5.2 | 5.1 |
| 86 | Disadvantaged children should begin school at an earlier age than they now do. | 5.1 | 5.0 |
| 89 | Unstructured interaction groups should become more a part of teacher-education programs, even at the expense of some traditional topics. | 5.1 | 4.9 |
| 88 | A disadvantaged student learns best from a person who has a similar cultural background. | 3.5 | 3.7 |
| 85 | Children should be bused outside their own neighborhoods if that is the most practical way to attain racial integration in a given school district. | 3.5 | 3.6 |
| 87 | The age at which students are legally permitted to leave school should be lowered. | 2.5 | 2.7 |

When given various opportunities to comment adversely on the projects, participants in every case declined, on the average, to do so. Evidence of general approval is given by the mean rating of 5.4 for all projects.

In taking stands on certain contemporary educational issues, participants overwhelmingly favored smaller classes as the best thing to be done for disadvantaged children; called for an earlier school starting age while rejecting the suggestion of a lower age, for legal withdrawal; were disinclined either to bus children outside their own neighborhoods or to accept the idea that children from a disadvantaged environment learn best from a person from the same milieu; called for more unstructured interaction groups in teacher education; and seemed to feel that teacher-education programs would be more effective if based in the schools rather than in the colleges and universities.

## FACTOR ANALYSIS AND DEVELOPMENT
## OF ATTITUDE DIMENSIONS

While the mean responses on individual items yield a good deal of information in themselves, the *pattern* of responses on various groups of items can also be significant. A basic intent of this study, for example, was to ascertain if particular project curricula and teaching procedures produced certain effects—in participants, in students, and in the schools—and a way of making that determination is to see if there is consistency between estimates of change and evaluations of features of the projects. The standard statistical technique for accomplishing this end—a factoring of the correlation matrix for the full set of variables—was therefore performed.

Data from the Q-sort and questionnaire responses were subjected, first, to Tryon's "cluster analysis,"[2] and then, independently, to a principal axes factoring with varimax rotations. The factors resulting from the two methods were virtually identical, with the items in the clusters having slightly higher loading coefficients than did the factor items. In addition, the available cluster analysis computer program provided more options for subsequent treatment of the data, so that method of analysis was chosen over the principal axes solution.

Table 3 shows the nine clusters, or factors, which resulted, with the oblique factor coefficient[3] being shown for each item and a definition of high and low scores[4] on each cluster being offered.

---

[2] For a description of this system, see: Robert C. Tryon, *Cluster and Factor Analysis* (book draft), Berkeley: University of California, 1964; Robert C. Tryon, *Theory of the BC TRY System: Statistical Theory*, Berkeley: University of California, 1964; and Robert C. Tryon and Daniel E. Bailey, *User's Manual of the BC TRY System of Cluster and Factor Analysis*, Berkeley: University of California, 1965.

[3] There is some ambiguity, both here and in the literature, in the use of the terms *cluster* and *factor*. Having made the distinction between two statistical procedures which used them, the terms will hereafter be used more or less interchangeably.

[4] High scores result from agreement with items having positive factor coefficients and disagreement with items having negative coefficients. The reversal of responses produces low scores.

*Table 3*

ATTITUDE CLUSTERS RESULTING FROM FACTORING OF THE Q-SORT
AND QUESTIONNAIRE DATA

| Item Number | Item Statement | Oblique Factor Coefficient |
|---|---|---|
| | *Cluster 1 (Change in Students):* | |
| 18 | My disadvantaged students are as uninterested in school as they were when the project started. | .74 |
| 20 | My disadvantaged students are as unsure of themselves as they were when the project began. | .72 |
| 25 | My disadvantaged students cause as many discipline problems as they did before the project started. | .71 |
| 19 | My disadvantaged students are as hostile toward teachers as they were when the project started. | .70 |
| 22 | My disadvantaged students get along better with their classmates because of the project. | —.68 |
| 24 | My disadvantaged students are absent from school as often as they were before the project began. | .67 |
| 17 | My disadvantaged students have higher educational aspirations as a result of this project. | —.62 |
| 23 | My disadvantaged students read better because of this project. | —.61 |
| 27 | This project has had little influence on how well my students learn. | .59 |
| 26 | My disadvantaged students participate more in school activities as a result of this project. | —.54 |

*High scorers* on this first dimension are skeptical about their disadvantaged students having changed for the better—in self-esteem, attitudes toward school, relations with peers, behavior, or school achievement—as a result of the in-service project under consideration.

*Low scorers* believe that the project achieved substantial changes for the better in their disadvantaged students.

*Cluster 2 (Evaluation of Project)*:

63    A better project would have resulted if participants had made more of the decisions about its day-to-day operations.      .71

62    A better project would have resulted if participants had had a bigger part in its planning.      .71

67    The leaders put too much emphasis on dispensing information and not enough on getting us to explore our feelings.      .71

64    Too often in the project, I was just listening or watching, rather than actively *doing* something.      .59

80    What overall rating would you give this in-service project in which you participated?      —.55

70    The project was too middle-class in its philosophy and operation.      .48

66    I learned more from my fellow participants than I did from the leaders and other experts who spoke to us.      .41

*High scorers* on this dimension are critical of the in-service project in which they participated—of its planning, the way decisions were made, its leaders and expert speakers, its "middle-classness," and its overall operation.

*Low scorers* approve of the project, declining to criticize it in the ways cited above.

*Cluster 3 (Relationships with Disadvantaged Students)*:

79    What percentage of your students are Negro?      .79

74    In what setting is your school located? (Rural, 1, to city ghetto, 5)      .62

75    What percentage of your students do you estimate to be disadvantaged?      .57

82    What is your own ethnic background?      .48

*High scorers* tend to teach in cities, and in ghettos, have a higher percentage of students who are disadvantaged and black, and are themselves more likely to belong to minority groups.

*Low scorers* tend more to be white, to teach away from the cities, and to have fewer students who are disadvantaged or who belong to minority groups.

*Table 3 (cont.)*

ATTITUDE CLUSTERS RESULTING FROM FACTORING OF THE Q-SORT
AND QUESTIONNAIRE DATA

| Item Number | Item Statement | Oblique Factor Coefficient |
|---|---|---|

*Cluster 4 (Value of the Project's Curriculum):*

| 60 | The material on teaching methods for disadvantaged children was valuable. | .78 |
| 58 | The special instructional materials for disadvantaged children were valuable. | .76 |
| 59 | The material on curricula for disadvantaged children was valuable. | .74 |
| 61 | The material on how to teach specific subjects (mathematics, social studies, etc.) to disadvantaged students was valuable. | .59 |
| 57 | The material on reading improvement was valuable. | .58 |
| 55 | The material on the learning problems of children was valuable. | .47 |

*High scorers* found the material on disadvantaged children and methods of teaching them to be valuable.

*Low scorers* were unenthusiastic about the material presented by the project.

*Cluster 5 (Change in the Institution, i.e., School):*

| 30 | Project participants have had little effect on the attitudes of other teachers and administrators concerning disadvantaged youth. | .63 |
| 31 | This project has had little effect on the (other) in-service programs at my school. | .63 |
| 33 | Project participants have had little success in my school in achieving a curriculum that would be more appropriate for disadvantaged students. | .62 |
| 34 | Project participants induced my school to establish, or enlarge, a cultural enrichment program for disadvantaged students. | —.62 |

| 32 | Project participants have had little success in getting special instructional materials for disadvantaged students introduced in my school. | .61 |
| 35 | This project has raised the morale of our whole school staff. | —.60 |
| 28 | This project has led my school to collect more comprehensive data on our disadvantaged students. | —.57 |
| 7 | I have had little success in using what I learned in the project to change the attitudes of my colleagues regarding disadvantaged children. | .51 |
| 29 | Project participants have gotten parents of disadvantaged students to participate more in our school's activities. | —.47 |

*High scorers* are convinced that the project had little effect on nonparticipating teachers and administrators in their school, and that the effectiveness of the school in relating to disadvantaged children and their parents was not improved in any appreciable way.

*Low scorers* feel the project had a positive effect on the nonparticipating personnel of their school and on its practices relative to disadvantaged students.

*Cluster 6 (Value of the Project's Instruction)*:

| 38 | The discussion following formal presentation was valuable to me. | .74 |
| 36 | The lectures in the project were valuable to me. | .63 |
| 37 | The panel discussions in the project were valuable to me. | .62 |
| 53 | Consultants who worked with teachers individually or in small groups were helpful. | .37 |

*High scorers* found great value in the discussion, lectures, and panel discussions which were a part of the project, and in the consultants who worked individually or in small groups with teachers.

*Low scorers* were unenthusiastic about the instructional procedures mentioned above, and about the consultants.

*Cluster 7 (Change in Participants)*:

| 8 | I am more self-confident in the classroom (or office) as a result of this project. | .60 |
| 9 | I like disadvantaged students better as a result of this project. | .58 |

*Table 3 (cont.)*

ATTITUDE CLUSTERS RESULTING FROM FACTORING OF THE Q-SORT
AND QUESTIONNAIRE DATA

| *Item Number* | *Item Statement* | *Oblique Factor Coefficient* |
|---|---|---|
| 21 | My disadvantaged students like me better as a result of this project. | .58 |
| 12 | This project has led me to give disadvantaged students more individual attention. | .57 |
| 15 | I teach (or counsel, etc.) about the same way I did before the project started. | —.56 |
| 13 | My relations with the parents of my disadvantaged students are unchanged in spite of the project. | —.46 |
| 6 | This project increased my effectiveness with *all* students, not just the disadvantaged. | .46 |
| 4 | This project convinced me that disdvantaged students have more learning ability than I had given them credit for. | .46 |
| 14 | As a result of this project, I have become more of a leader in my school in improving the education of disadvantaged students. | .45 |
| 3 | I learned very little from the project about the effects of a deprived home environment on a student's school life. | —.42 |

*High scorers* firmly believe the project improved their self-confidence, their relations with disadvantaged children and parents, and their overall effectiveness in the schools.

*Low scorers* are not persuaded that they were helped much, personally, by the project.

*Cluster 8 (Value of Project's Media):*

| 41 | The replaying of activities through video or audio tapes was of value. | .74 |

39    The films, records, tapes, and similar materials were
      valuable to me.                                         .70

*High scorers* found the use of television, with replay, films, records, tapes, and so on to be very valuable.
*Low scorers* were indifferent or worse to the use of these media.

*Cluster 9 (Value of Project's Encounter Groups):*

43    The encounter group (sensitivity training, T-group,
      etc.) was helpful to me.                                .88

42    The role-playing we did in the project was of value.    .49

69    Those sessions when participants were absolutely frank,
      and even angry, were valuable.                          .29

*High scorers* found direct confrontation among participants, either through encounter groups or role-playing, or informally, to be very valuable, even though anger was provoked.
*Low scorers* were dubious about the value of forthright encounters among participants.

Before the relationship among the various clusters are considered, domain validity indices of the cluster scores, and the reliability coefficients of cluster scores on each set of defining items are shown. These indices are included to demonstrate the accuracy of the factor estimates shown in Table 3.

## RELATIONSHIPS AMONG DEFINED CLUSTERS

By item content alone, one would judge a project to have been successful (at least in the opinion of its participants) if low scores resulted on Clusters 1 (Change in Students), 2 (Evaluation of Project), and 5 (Change in Institution, i.e., School), and a high score on Cluster 7 (Change in Participants). It would be expected, therefore, that positive correlations would inhere among Dimensions 1 (Change in Students), 2 (Evaluation of Project), and 5 (Change in Institution, i.e., School), and that Dimension 7 (Change in Participants) would correlate negatively with each of the other three. Scores on Dimensions 4 (Value of the Project's Curriculum), 6 (Value of the Project's Instruction), 8 (Value of Project's Media), and 9 (Value of

*Table 4*

DOMAIN VALIDITY AND RELIABILITY COEFFICIENTS
FOR EACH CLUSTER

| Cluster | | Domain Validity | Relia-bility |
|---------|---|---|---|
| 1 | (Change in Students) | .94 | .89 |
| 2 | (Evaluation of Project) | .90 | .80 |
| 3 | (Relationship with Disadvantaged Students) | .85 | .72 |
| 4 | (Value of the Project's Curriculum) | .91 | .83 |
| 5 | (Change in Institution, i.e., School) | .91 | .83 |
| 6 | (Value of the Project's Instruction) | .84 | .70 |
| 7 | (Change in Participants) | .89 | .79 |
| 8 | (Value of Project's Media) | .83 | .69 |
| 9 | (Value of Project's Encounter Groups) | .78 | .61 |

Project's Encounter Groups) will probably correlate positively among themselves and with Dimension 7 (Change in Participants) and negatively with Dimensions 1 (Change in Students), 2 (Evaluation of Project), and 5 (Change in Institution, i.e., School).

The actual correlations that resulted among dimension scores are shown in Table 5.

Table 5 shows the predicted relations among clusters to have been borne out by the data. When a project is highly rated, it is judged to have changed the respondent himself, his students, *and* the school for the better, with the rating being most closely related to the participant's own self-evaluation. Similarly, if one set of means (for example, discussion, lectures, panels, and consultants) used to achieve the changes is approved, then the other means (curriculum, audiovisual materials, teaching methods, and encounter groups) are also approved. But, unfortunately, whether or not participants taught high percentages of disadvantaged and black students, and in ghettos, had almost

## Table 5
CORRELATIONS AMONG OBLIQUE ROTATED FACTORS

| | | | | | Clusters | | | | |
|---|---|---|---|---|---|---|---|---|---|
| | 1 (CS) | 2 (EP) | 3 (RD) | 4 (VC) | 5 (CI) | 6 (VI) | 7 (CP) | 8 (VM) | 9 (VE) |
| Cluster 1 | 1.00 | .26 | −.03 | −.37 | .60 | −.19 | −.67 | −.35 | −.08 |
| Cluster 2 | .26 | 1.00 | .07 | −.40 | .34 | −.59 | −.45 | −.24 | −.19 |
| Cluster 3 | −.03 | .07 | 1.00 | .08 | .01 | .00 | −.04 | .15 | .12 |
| Cluster 4 | −.37 | −.40 | .08 | 1.00 | −.35 | .30 | .24 | .31 | .06 |
| Cluster 5 | .60 | .34 | .01 | −.35 | 1.00 | −.24 | −.53 | −.30 | −.09 |
| Cluster 6 | −.19 | −.59 | .00 | .30 | −.24 | 1.00 | .28 | .50 | .41 |
| Cluster 7 | −.67 | −.45 | −.04 | .24 | −.53 | .28 | 1.00 | .21 | .22 |
| Cluster 8 | −.35 | −.24 | .15 | .31 | −.30 | .50 | .21 | 1.00 | .33 |
| Cluster 9 | −.08 | −.19 | .12 | .06 | −.09 | .41 | .22 | .33 | 1.00 |

no effect on opinions about the changes wrought by a given project or the means used to achieve these changes, if any.[5]

As for relationships between means and ends, estimated changes in *students* were correlated most highly (.37) with curricular materials and teaching methods relating to disadvantaged students and with audiovisual materials, including television (.35). Estimated changes in the *participants* were correlated only nominally, and almost equally (.21 to .28), with the four sets of means. Estimates of change in participants' *schools* showed a correlation of .35 with curriculum and teaching methods, .30 with audiovisual materials, and .24 with instructional procedures. Opinion about the value of direct confrontation among participants (which was highly positive) was virtually unrelated to estimates of change in students or schools, and showed only a .22 correlation with estimates of change in the participants themselves.

Evaluations of individual projects were most strongly related (.59) to ratings of the quality of instruction, and less closely to the quality of the curriculum (.40), media (.24), and encounter groups (.19). Project evaluations were more closely related to estimates of change in participants (.45) than to estimates of change in schools (.34) or students (.26).

RATINGS OF INDIVIDUAL PROJECTS

Cluster scores on each dimension were calculated for every respondent and scaled for a mean of 50 and a $\gamma$ of 10. A mean score for all participants in each project was then found for each dimension. Scale scores on Dimensions 1 (Change in Students), 2 (Evaluation of Project), and 5 (Change in Institution, i.e., School) were inverted (subtracted from 100) so that a high score on every scale would be "good."

Those mean scores are shown in Table 6, where individual

[5] With respect to the hypothesis that the most positive reactions to projects would come from young teachers in urban districts having high proportions of disadvantaged students, at least a part of that hypothesis is thus unsupported. Participants' position (teacher, counselor, administrator) and years of experience did not as variables appear in any of the clusters, but an examination of the intercorrelations among those two variables and those comprising Dimension 2 (Evaluation of the Project) shows those correlations to be close to zero. It can further be said, therefore, that the statistical results do not support the hypothesis in *any* part.

projects are identified only by a code number. Where more than one set of scores for a school district appear, it is an indication that the district had more than one project.

The highest scores on each dimension are those listed below:

*Cluster 1* (*Change in Students*): Redondo Beach (Remedial Reading for Educationally Deprived Children), Stockton (ITA Demonstration Teachers only), Kern County (Modern Approaches to Language in Teaching English to Disadvantaged Students).

*Cluster 2* (*Evaluation of Projects*): Monrovia (Reading Improvement), Redondo Beach (Remedial Reading for Educationally Deprived Children), University of Southern California (Teachers of Disadvantaged Youth and Social-Cultural Milieu), Paramount (In-Service Education for Teaching Staff of Educationally Disadvantaged Children).

*Cluster 3* (*Relationship with the Disadvantaged*): Willowbrook (In-Service Project), Compton (Summer Curriculum Revision through Industrial and Business Experience), Los Angeles (Reading-Centered Instruction only).

*Cluster 4* (*Value of the Curriculum*): Stockton (ITA Demonstration Teachers only), Monrovia (Reading Improvement), Norwalk-La Mirada (In-Service: Staff and Elementary Teachers).

*Cluster 5* (*Change in the Institution*): Redondo Beach (Remedial Reading for Educationally Deprived Children), Fresno (Reading Opportunity Teachers), Norwalk-La Mirada (In-Service: Staff and Elementary Teachers).

*Cluster 6* (*Value of the Instruction*): Colton (Improvement of Communication Skills), Stockton (ITA Demonstration Teachers), Monrovia (Reading Improvement), San Fernando Valley State College (Teachers of Disadvantaged American Indian Youth).

*Cluster 7* (*Change in Participants*): Los Angeles (Counseling and Teaching Educationally Disadvantaged Students only), Redondo Beach (Remedial Reading for Educationally Deprived Children), Chico State College (Teachers of Disadvantaged Youth from Migratory Farm-Labor and Rural Communities), Fresno (Reading Opportunity Teachers), Paramount (In-Service Education for Teaching Staff of Educationally Disadvantaged Students).

*Cluster 8* (*Value of Media*): Stockton (ITA Demonstration

## Table 6

### Mean Factor Scores of Participants for Each Project

| Code No. | Clusters | | | | | | | | |
|---|---|---|---|---|---|---|---|---|---|
| | 1 (CS) | 2 (EP) | 3 (RD) | 4 (VC) | 5 (CI) | 6 (VI) | 7 (CP) | 8 (VM) | 9 (VE) |
| ESEA *Title I*: | | | | | | | | | |
| 1 | 55.4 | 46.7 | 42.7 | 45.9 | 51.9 | 48.6 | 50.9 | 50.6 | 50.7 |
| 2 | 50.8 | 49.0 | 39.5 | 47.1 | 49.2 | 50.2 | 49.5 | 53.5 | 52.4 |
| 3 | 46.0 | 52.3 | 41.4 | 52.8 | 47.7 | 56.7 | 50.1 | 48.6 | 50.0 |
| 4 | 52.3 | 45.4 | 58.7 | 54.2 | 58.9 | 51.4 | 56.3 | 54.9 | 41.7 |
| 5 | 55.1 | 51.3 | 39.6 | 53.0 | 52.8 | 45.2 | 50.2 | 51.8 | 47.5 |
| 6 | 61.5 | 52.6 | 40.8 | 50.0 | 56.4 | 45.5 | 45.5 | 32.0 | 47.4 |
| | 54.7 | 48.5 | 44.2 | 50.4 | 55.2 | 47.4 | 53.2 | 46.4 | 50.3 |
| 7 | 57.6 | 50.0 | 59.8 | 54.3 | 53.0 | 48.8 | 52.0 | 53.4 | 46.0 |
| | 57.1 | 49.4 | 55.5 | 53.0 | 51.3 | 42.1 | 49.9 | 47.5 | 48.8 |
| | 47.9 | 50.5 | 60.8 | 52.8 | 47.0 | 53.0 | 49.1 | 51.9 | 50.1 |
| | 45.3 | 49.9 | 59.7 | 49.1 | 46.7 | 51.9 | 48.3 | 49.4 | 54.4 |

| Sample | | | | | | | | | | | | | | | | | |
|---|---|---|---|---|---|---|---|---|---|---|---|---|---|---|---|---|---|
| 8 | 55.5 | 50.2 | 48.0 | 48.9 | 48.9 | 49.2 | 49.1 | 50.1 | 49.2 | 49.2 | 46.2 | 48.3 | 49.7 | 46.0 | 50.5 | 50.1 | 47.8 |
| 9 | 46.7 | 59.4 | 47.4 | 48.5 | 51.0 | 56.0 | 45.9 | 42.3 | 57.4 | 52.2 | 42.8 | 52.4 | 46.3 | 58.8 | 54.8 | 50.5 | 49.3 |
| 10 | 63.2 | 48.5 | 48.9 | 54.2 | 48.6 | 53.7 | 48.7 | 46.0 | 48.7 | 54.6 | 50.6 | 44.0 | 43.8 | 48.4 | 56.0 | 57.1 | 47.2 |
| 11 | 53.2 | 51.0 | 49.9 | 51.1 | 44.1 | 54.2 | 50.2 | 41.5 | 50.4 | 44.4 | 42.7 | 52.7 | 50.4 | 48.3 | 48.7 | 49.0 | 53.0 |
| 12 | 47.4 | 54.3 | 49.6 | 48.9 | 51.3 | 55.0 | 57.3 | 46.7 | 58.0 | 58.3 | 58.6 | 39.8 | 40.0 | 50.0 | 57.7 | 61.4 | 48.9 |
| | 46.4 | 53.1 | 53.3 | 55.6 | 48.6 | 57.1 | 44.0 | 43.1 | 55.7 | 53.8 | 56.0 | 46.5 | 47.9 | 52.8 | 53.8 | 50.8 | 50.9 |
| 13 | 60.7 | 56.6 | 39.1 | 39.3 | 44.0 | 42.3 | 43.0 | 42.9 | 46.0 | 46.5 | 49.2 | 48.0 | 56.1 | 44.6 | 42.8 | 41.8 | 48.1 |
| 14 | 52.1 | 49.0 | 53.9 | 56.8 | 48.0 | 56.9 | 47.5 | 47.1 | 50.4 | 52.4 | 49.4 | 51.7 | 45.1 | 49.8 | 55.5 | 56.5 | 52.9 |
| 15 | 46.2 | 53.2 | 50.9 | 53.3 | 49.5 | 52.9 | 50.4 | 37.9 | 55.0 | 54.0 | 55.5 | 43.0 | 42.6 | 54.1 | 55.1 | 62.0 | 48.3 |

Table 6 (cont.)

MEAN FACTOR SCORES OF PARTCIPANTS FOR EACH PROJECT

| Code No. | 1 (CS) | 2 (EP) | 3 (RD) | 4 (VC) | 5 (CI) | 6 (VI) | 7 (CP) | 8 (VM) | 9 (VE) |
|---|---|---|---|---|---|---|---|---|---|
| | | | | | *Clusters* | | | | |
| ESEA Title I (cont.): | | | | | | | | | |
| 18 | 44.9 | 46.7 | 49.7 | 46.2 | 50.4 | 47.3 | 47.8 | 47.6 | 48.4 |
| 19 | 49.6 | 45.8 | 52.4 | 47.6 | 56.2 | 43.9 | 51.1 | 46.0 | 52.9 |
| 20 | 48.4 | 46.4 | 56.3 | 48.1 | 51.0 | 46.9 | 51.7 | 47.5 | 52.3 |
| | 45.9 | 47.2 | 54.7 | 51.8 | 50.1 | 48.0 | 48.8 | 48.9 | 49.0 |
| | 51.3 | 44.5 | 56.5 | 50.1 | 54.6 | 44.3 | 48.3 | 51.0 | 45.2 |
| | 40.9 | 48.0 | 52.3 | 46.6 | 49.9 | 42.8 | 45.7 | 47.8 | 42.6 |
| 21 | 55.4 | 44.8 | 41.0 | 49.5 | 55.0 | 52.4 | 50.9 | 51.5 | 52.5 |
| 22 | 43.4 | 50.9 | 41.0 | 37.5 | 50.4 | 47.0 | 51.7 | 40.6 | 55.0 |
| 23 | 54.0 | 55.1 | 37.2 | 55.2 | 53.1 | 52.5 | 53.6 | 55.4 | 51.2 |
| 24 | 47.9 | 45.4 | 45.0 | 55.1 | 46.8 | 47.0 | 42.6 | 47.8 | 50.0 |
| 25 | 54.3 | 37.2 | 68.7 | 48.9 | 50.2 | 48.7 | 46.2 | 48.4 | 48.4 |

160

**ESEA Title III:**

| | | | | | | | | | |
|---|---|---|---|---|---|---|---|---|---|
| 26 | 44.8 | 37.9 | 64.2 | 53.5 | 40.5 | 37.1 | 38.9 | 34.9 | 51.1 |
| 27 | 49.5 | 48.6 | 43.1 | 52.4 | 49.2 | 51.7 | 50.4 | 48.6 | 49.5 |
| 28 | 46.1 | 50.4 | 49.4 | 55.2 | 51.1 | 52.7 | 43.9 | 52.7 | 44.9 |
| | 52.2 | 47.0 | 46.2 | 57.1 | 48.4 | 49.8 | 50.3 | 57.4 | 48.3 |
| | 61.9 | 49.3 | 38.2 | 59.3 | 57.9 | 54.8 | 53.2 | 64.3 | 53.0 |

**NDEA Title XI:**

| | | | | | | | | | |
|---|---|---|---|---|---|---|---|---|---|
| 29 | 42.8 | 48.7 | 54.4 | 42.6 | 43.2 | 53.1 | 44.3 | 47.1 | 49.8 |
| 30 | 52.8 | 54.5 | 42.9 | 48.1 | 52.1 | 51.9 | 56.8 | 48.0 | 53.6 |
| 31 | 49.6 | 51.8 | 48.9 | 49.6 | 48.7 | 47.4 | 53.7 | 44.3 | 48.0 |
| 32 | 50.2 | 47.4 | 52.9 | 43.1 | 49.5 | 52.9 | 53.8 | 49.1 | 58.2 |
| 33 | 48.0 | 50.6 | 49.0 | 45.8 | 47.5 | 53.4 | 52.3 | 49.6 | 52.9 |
| 34 | 48.7 | 51.3 | 40.4 | 44.5 | 45.5 | 54.1 | 49.2 | 52.2 | 53.9 |
| 35 | 48.0 | 55.7 | 54.5 | 45.5 | 42.1 | 52.4 | 52.7 | 56.2 | 58.5 |
| 36 | 49.4 | 50.9 | 44.4 | 48.4 | 49.3 | 51.1 | 48.6 | 47.1 | 50.9 |
| 37 | 36.9 | 50.6 | 50.9 | 49.3 | 45.0 | 45.9 | 49.4 | 46.6 | 52.7 |

Teachers only), Orange (In-Service Education), Norwalk-La Mirada (In-Service: Staff and Elementary Teachers).

*Cluster 9 (Value of Encounters)*: University of Southern California (Teachers of Disadvantaged Youth and Social-Cultural Milieu), Pasadena College (Teachers of Disadvantaged Youth with Interracial Encounter Groups), Los Angeles (Counseling and Teaching Educationally Disadvantaged Students only), Santa Maria (In-Service: Sensitivity Training).

When all dimensions are taken into account, with special consideration for estimated changes in students, participants, and schools, the projects with the highest overall scale scores are Redondo Beach (Remedial Reading for Educationally Deprived Children), Stockton (ITA Demonstration Teachers only), Paramount (In-Service Education for Teaching Staff of Educationally Disadvantaged Children), and Monrovia (Reading Improvement). A number of factors might explain why these projects were evaluated highly: (1) the target population was small; (2) the projects themselves were small in terms of the number of participants; thus morale and *esprit de corps* were more readily achieved; and (3) the purposes were modest, direct, and specific; thus the highest rated projects tended to be the ones that apparently tried hardest to focus on a single objective and to achieve only this one goal.

Of nine projects that received particularly low ratings, five were in metropolitan areas in Southern California and four in the San Francisco Bay Area. Two of the nine were in a single big-city school district, one in a smaller nearby city, and one in an almost entirely white suburban district. Six of the nine were ESEA Title I projects, one a Title III, and two NDEA Title XI ventures, one in a university whose other Title XI project was well rated, the other in a state college. Analysis of responses on these low-rated projects shows that they had no specific characteristics in common.

## SUMMARY

Data were collected, by Q-sort and questionnaire, from 1,443 participants in twenty-five ESEA Title I, three Title III, and nine NDEA Title XI California projects for improving the teaching of disadvantaged students. In general, respondents were approving of the projects, believing that they had become less critical of disadvantaged students, understood their students' subcultures better, had become more knowledgeable about appropriate instructional materials and curricula, and were more effective with the general, not just the disadvantaged, learner.

Participants also believed, though not as firmly, that their disadvantaged students had benefited from the projects—being at least somewhat surer of themselves, less hostile toward teachers, less disinterested in school, less inefficient in their learning, and less productive of discipline problems. Respondents were dubious, however, about their disadvantaged students getting along better with teachers and classmates, having higher educational aspirations, participating more in school activities, improving their attendance records, or developing a better understanding of their own ethnic backgrounds.

As for changes in participants' schools brought about by the projects, it was thought that the attitudes of other teachers and administrators had been improved somewhat, that more appropriate instructional materials and curricula had been introduced, and that other in-service programs had benefited to some extent. Other changes suggested by items were not affirmed by the respondents.

The strongest approval by participants was that given to the instructional procedures and curricula of projects, which were supported more thoroughly than were the estimates of change in disadvantaged students, the participants themselves, or their schools. Chances to criticize different aspects of the projects were, on the average, declined, and a mean overall rating of 5.4 (on a 1 to 7 scale) was given for all projects.

On certain current education issues, participants took the position that the best thing schools could do for disadvantaged children would be to put them in smaller-sized classes; teachers-in-training can learn more in local schools than they can in colleges or universities; no expense should be spared to provide special help for disadvantaged students; and disadvantaged children should begin school at an earlier age than they do now, though the age at which students are legally permitted to leave school should not be lowered. Respondents also approved of the idea that unstructured interaction groups should become more a part of teacher education programs, even at the expense of some traditional topics, but did not agree that a disadvantaged student learns best from a person having a similar cultural background, or that children should be bused outside their own neighborhoods or that it is the most practical way to attain racial integration in a given school district.

When the responses were factor-analyzed, nine dimensions were identified, representing estimates of changes in students, participants, and their schools; the value of project curricula, instruction procedures, media, and confrontations (through organized encounter groups); the degree of job exposure to disadvantaged students; and evaluations of the individual projects. While consistent and predictable correlations among certain of the factors were found, it was not possible to establish particularly meaningful relationships between the instructional procedures and curricula of projects and their accomplishments—between means and ends—that had been hoped for. About all that can be said is that what were considered to be positive changes were brought about by a variety of approaches.

Factor scores for each respondent on each dimension were calculated, and mean scores found for the individual projects. Considering all dimensions, the projects having the best ratings were Redondo Beach, Stockton (ITA Demonstration Teachers only), Paramount, and Monrovia.

All things taken into account, the statistical results must be regarded as suggestive rather than as definitive. The confidence with which one accepts the "suggested" statistical results and the apparent ambiguities should be held in abeyance, pending the results of interviews with participants. These are presented in Chapter V.

# CHAPTER V

~~~~~~~~~~~~~~~~~~~~~~~~~~~~~~~~~~~~~~~~~~~~

# *Interviews with Participants*

~~~~~~~~~~~~~~~~~~~~~~~~~~~~~~~~~~~~~~~~~~~~

*It is the babes who want to climb the mountains, and the wise men who know the hills.*

Taylor Caldwell

*A* major effort of the California Component of the Four-State Project was the interviewing of a random sample of program participants. Four researchers, skilled in interview techniques and with a common interview guide, traveled throughout the state during the spring of 1968 to interview a few participants in each project studied to gain added insight on how teachers felt about the programs in which they had participated.

## MOST EFFECTIVE ACTIVITIES

### SMALL-GROUP INTERACTION

Many teachers stated that the most valuable aspect of the program they had attended was the interaction with fellow teacher-participants. A number actually resented such intrusions as speakers or films into the format of the program. These participants commonly recommended that future programs be designed to provide much more time for participants to interact regarding matters of mutual concern. This is not to say that these same participants did not find value in many of the informative aspects of the program, such as speakers, field trips, reading, and films, but they felt a great need to interact and sort out, via small-group work, the many facets involved in a true understanding of the plight of disadvantaged youth. Some of the most successful in-service programs involved live-in situations specifically designed to provide an encouraging atmosphere and time for participants to share and compare views. Teachers seemed to appreciate the fact that program directors were attempting to provide a rich environment by "parading by" a series of outstanding resources, but as one participant noted, "a rich environment, as a rich meal, demands time to digest."

Much of the small-group work provided within the projects was not a follow-up to speakers and other resource activities, but rather a conscious attempt to aid participants in gaining greater understanding about themselves and their views of others. This activity, commonly known as sensitivity training, was extensively used in many of the in-service programs studied. Generally, sensitivity training was well received by those teachers who participated in it. The common organ-

166

izational arrangement was either to bring in individual sensitivity group leaders (Title XI institutes generally) or to contract with a college or university to provide an expert, usually a clinical psychologist or psychiatrist, who would bring a staff of group leaders to the district to conduct the sessions (Title I projects generally). Meetings were sometimes spread out over weeks or even months, perhaps as an extension course, or in the case of the Title XI Summer Institutes, were run on a daily basis for a six- or seven-week period. One of the most successful encounter group activities was the effort of one college-based summer institute to provide sensitivity training for the participants in racially mixed groups (approximately 50 per cent black and 50 per cent white). Judging from the reactions of the interviewees, this proved to be highly successful. Participants cited the development of much greater tolerance and understanding regarding the views of others, particularly those with different skin color, as an outcome of the sensitivity training. They also noted that they became increasingly more perceptive about the feelings of others and also more perceptive about their own feelings and how these feelings affect their behavior within the classroom. Several of those interviewed in various projects that involved sensitivity training noted that for the first time in their lives, they were able to express their views to others concerning issues that had in the past remained mostly hidden below the surfaces of their personalities.

Although some concern was expressed about the use of sensitivity training for school staffs, it appears to be used more and more, and is certainly positively regarded by those who wish to change attitudes about the disadvantaged. Conservative factions of some communities and schools have at times been concerned about the possibly damaging effects of sensitivity training on staff relations, and as a consequence, in a number of in-service projects it was not always well publicized for this reason. Even in evaluation reports, apparently because of concern about adverse criticism, sensitivity training often was called a "human relations workshop." Nevertheless, sensitivity training was being used successfully and effectively in a majority of the projects visited.

Two other means being used, seemingly effectively, to sharpen teachers' perceptions of their classroom behavior were video taping and interaction analysis. Although both were viewed with positive feelings by the majority of participants who were exposed to them, they came nowhere near the high rating given to small-group discussions among participants and sensitivity group work. The success of both video taping and interaction analysis seemed to depend greatly on both the degree of expertise of the consultants and the organizational talents of the project director.

KNOWLEDGE OF DISADVANTAGED COMMUNITY

Next to getting to know oneself, including one's prejudices and behaviors, the participants saw a knowledge of the community from which their students came as being a most important factor in effectively working with disadvantaged youngsters. Several techniques, listed below, were viewed positively by the teachers interviewed.

Direct contact with members of the community immediately surrounding the school was viewed to be by far the most valuable means of developing an empathic understanding of disadvantaged youth. Participants found that going into the community in small groups with guides provided by the community itself was of inestimable value. Although there were difficulties in reaching the so-called hard-core members of ghetto communities, when the planning was carefully thought through and utilized those in the power structure of the community, effective interaction seemed to take place. For many teachers this was their first encounter with both a verbalized and actualized nonmiddle-class culture. This experience produced much trauma in a good proportion of those interviewed. Nevertheless, they viewed this encounter as essential in developing their effectiveness to work with their disadvantaged students.

RESOURCE PERSONNEL

Outstanding guest speakers provided from the community were viewed by many participants to be a valuable resource. Members of minority groups who came as consultants to the various programs were also viewed as making significant contributions. Generally speaking, guest lecturers who were willing to discuss the conflicts between staff and students from different cultural backgrounds were viewed as valuable. Speakers who were willing to interact with participants were generally rated high. Those who were able to work from a theoretical base, particularly in the areas of sociology and anthropology, and to apply these theories to the practical problems faced by teachers in their schools, also proved to be well accepted. Participants particularly enjoyed the opportunity to interact with consultants over an extended period of time, possibly two or three days. When resource people represented the community or a minority group and were actually members of the in-service program staff, that is, were involved in the program from beginning to end, a very high degree of value was perceived by a majority of those interviewed.

PUBLISHED MATERIALS

Readings, particularly those with a sociological or anthropological orientation and which dealt with the culture of poverty, were very well received by program participants. Many claimed that they had had their eyes opened for the first time to any theoretical base for dealing with the problems of the disadvantaged child. Bibliographies were often mentioned as being useful in helping teachers to learn more about the disadvantaged child and his total environment. Several of those interviewed mentioned their desire to develop a reading plan for themselves in order to continue to keep abreast of the latest information. It was mentioned on several occasions that it would be worth while for district consultants and principals continually to provide teachers with the latest written material on the disadvantaged child.

PUPIL SELF-IMAGE

Many of the interviewees noted that they began to realize that one of the most important things needed within the schools was to help the student develop a more effective self-image. Two means were perceived as highly effective in bringing about this insight: one was becoming more knowledgable about the principles of psychology, the second was the opportunity for teachers to work with disadvantaged children in less authoritarian settings. Camping, extended field trips, and in one case, working together as fellow participants, proved to have high catalytic value for changing the teachers' views of disadvantaged youth. Although many teachers who had been involved in the in-service activities studied by this project continued to see hope only in making students conform to middle-class values, the percentages of highly authoritarian teachers seem to be reduced when they are involved with young people in a nonacademic atmosphere. In general, little seems to have been done within the in-service programs studied to show teachers how to shift from authoritarian controls of the past to more modern means of involving students in the learning and decision-making processes.

Although participants viewed as valuable the new techniques and materials provided them as part of their in-service activity, they made almost no mention of using their increased knowledge of minority cultures to develop more relevant classroom activities. Students generally were not viewed as possessing the wide variety of expertise that they in fact do possess about the "real world," nor were they often seen as contributors to a classroom learning situation.

TEACHING STRATEGIES

Specific teaching techniques and new instructional materials that the interviewees were exposed to in their programs were viewed with less enthusiasm than the opportunities that enabled teachers to know themselves better, to know their pupils, and to understand their pupils' backgrounds. On the other hand, they found valuable the opportunities provided to view demonstrations and visit classrooms in which particularly effective teachers were using the latest in methods and materials. Released time from their own classroom duties as well as frequent opportunities to work with consultants were viewed as effective means of keeping the teacher abreast of new developments applicable to the classroom.

PARENT INVOLVEMENT

One interesting, though seldom used, activity provided in the programs studied was the concentrated effort to involve the parents in a direct and meaningful way in their children's education. Although certain problems of organization were encountered, particularly where parents were used in paraprofessional roles, a rather large percentage of participants interviewed found the opportunity to know and interact with parents about mutual concerns to be highly valuable. Despite the encouragement found in much of the literature on the disadvantaged, little seems to have been done to involve parents, particularly in decision making, in the in-service activities studied.

## LEAST EFFECTIVE ACTIVITIES

During the course of the interviews, participants were also asked to identify those things which they felt to be worst, or least effective, in the program they attended. Surprisingly, many were unable to identify anything fitting this category. There was also little repetition in the answers given. Three comments recurred several times in the course of the interviews. One was that the time was too tightly scheduled to provide for adequate interaction among the participants. A second point was that the approach to curriculum development was too theoretical and too much geared to the general school population and not enough to the educational needs of the disadvantaged. The third recurring comment was that there was poor organization of the field activities—that is, visits outside of the school proper to community agencies, other schools, and homes—and the lack of any direct relationship between what was seen and heard on these visits to what was being discussed by guest lecturers and staff.

## IN-SERVICE IMPLICATIONS

All participants interviewed were asked what they felt was working particularly well for them in their dealings with disadvantaged students. They were also asked if they could possibly identify how this effective activity or trait might be developed within the pre-service training activities that teachers receive. A wide variety of items was identified by those interviewed. Since the majority of these respondents were experienced, skillful teachers who had been the recipients of a rather intensive type of in-service activity to aid them in dealing with disadvantaged students, it seems appropriate to identify the techniques they emphasized.

Many participants noted success arising from the way they behaved with their pupils. Foremost among these was an increased awareness of the importance of the pupil's self-image. Many of these same teachers felt that in order to prepare teachers to recognize the importance of developing this in students, there should be ample opportunities in the pre-service training of teachers to study both individual pupils (by the case method technique, for example), and also to become aware of the sociological and psychological implications of a positive self-image. It seemed important to these interviewees that each teacher look for that which is good in a student and help the student identify these valuable traits.

Closely related to the above item was the often cited technique of treating students with respect. Several of the teachers who cited this technique as effective in working with their disadvantaged students also noted that it might be incorporated in the pre-service training of teachers by example—that is, college professors and master teachers might work with prospective teachers in a manner which connotes mutual respect. As an outgrowth of this point, several participants stated that an effective way to show students respect was to involve them in the decision-making aspects of both the school and the classroom. They suggested that an effective means of encouraging this in new teachers might be the involvement of college students in the decision-making processes of their institutions and their campus classroom, as well as extensive training for teachers-to-be in human relations and group dynamics.

Also mentioned as needed in the education of teachers is the successful efforts of teachers to let students know that they do care. Although it was difficult for them to suggest how they might train teachers to show this, some did mention that it is important for the teacher to show his lack of rigidity and authoritarianism by treating people as individuals and by not being preoccupied with consistency. Others noted that merely by learning to touch children, particularly members of minority groups, it is possible to convey to them that they are not feared, and that they are cared about.

Knowing the dialect or the language of the minority pupils with which these teachers deal was deemed important by many of them. Yet it was surprising to note that very few teachers of the Mexican-Americans had any knowledge of Spanish, and only about the same percentage had any but a passing knowledge of the Negro dialect. Those seeing the value of this knowledge felt that its incorporation into the pre-service training of teachers could be quite simple and direct.

As noted earlier, a knowledge and understanding of the disadvantaged was seen by teachers as extremely important in their effectiveness in working with their pupils. They felt that visiting the homes of their pupils and becoming familiar with and involved with the community in which they taught proved valuable in the class-room. These interviewees wanted pre-service programs to provide extensive opportunities for students to become involved early in their collegiate career with schools and the disadvantaged community and homes from which the pupils come.

Within the area of curriculum, several participants noted the success they were having using other than written materials. Although little seemed to have been done in the programs studied with nonverbal materials and activities, teachers felt that it was essential in the development of positive self-image to provide students with success experiences outside of the verbal realm. These teachers, particularly those in secondary schools, felt that their pre-service training had been exclusively devoted to the teaching of verbal activities.

Several of the interviewees noted the effectiveness of using materials that reflected the minority culture and gave status to the backgrounds of the young people in their class. They recommended that the pre-service training of teachers give guidance to the student teacher in locating and developing minority-culture-oriented materials for use with their classes. Others noted that those interested in teaching as a career should be given ample opportunity to become involved as true participants in the teaching-learning activities at the onset of this interest, whether in elementary school or in graduate school. Many interviewees felt that student teaching should provide ample opportunity for experimentation. It was felt that the rigidity with which many master teachers deal with their student teachers fails to provide the type of broadening initial experience necessary to start a teacher toward on-going professional growth.

Interviewees were also asked about the goals that they would set for the in-service programs designed for teachers of disadvantaged youth, and how they would go about reaching these goals. A wide variety of responses was elicited by this question. "Awareness" seemed to be the key word in most interviews while discussing this topic. Over and over again participants noted the importance of teachers being sensitive to the needs of young people, and stated that this awareness seems to be attainable in training programs that provide greater insight into the community and culture from which these young people come. These teachers were convinced that programs providing opportunities for interaction between parents and general membership of the community and the teaching staff of the school were absolutely essential. Many went on to recommend racially and economically mixed sensitivity training groups involving the professional staff of the school and community members. They also recommended using all possible types of activities to provide teachers and prospective teachers with knowledge about the culture of poverty. They judged particularly effective the use of minority-group members as lecturers and discussion leaders. Many stated that too many teachers were unwilling to become involved with the community surrounding their school. Many of these same participant-teachers were difficult to reach for interview because they had unlisted telephone numbers. This is particularly true in the urban areas. This may be symptomatic of a desire to divorce themselves from real involvement with the community.

Interviewees said that training programs should be designed to help teachers see what they are doing in the classroom and advocated the use of video tape and interaction analysis as a method of getting at this problem. They also suggested providing released time for teachers to visit one another and criticize each other's classroom activities.

A number of those interviewed pointed out the importance of providing time to work in small-group activities with fellow teachers, prospective teachers, teacher aides, and consultants to share problems and develop techniques and teaching materials relevant to the situation in a particular school. *On the whole, the teachers who were interviewed were convinced that training programs must be planned and conducted from and at the grass roots level rather than by and in the district office or on and at the college campus, removed as they usually were from the local school and neighborhood.*

## OBSERVATIONS

The participants who were interviewed, then, seemed to see as essential to the effective education of disadvantaged youth the development of training programs that will allow teachers to develop self-knowledge and greater sensitivity to their students and that are planned and conducted in the schools and neighborhoods "where the action is." As a group they seem highly dedicated, yet frustrated. They are generally concerned and creative, yet they seemed to lack the time and the resources to implement these talents. They apparently understood the value of openness and of expressing concern and care for the young people in their charge, yet they felt the restrictions of a rigid educational system and were discouraged by the defiance of militant students who rebel against an irrelevant curriculum. Most, however, have not lost hope. They seem willing to continue to try under the most adverse circumstances to provide young people with an "alive" educational program. Although the interviewers were disturbed by this sense of frustration that teachers face while working with young people alienated from the larger society, they were also encouraged by the teachers' willingness to apply new solutions to new problems.

# CHAPTER VI

~~~~~~~~~~~~~~~~~~~~~~~~~~~~~~~~~~

# *Conclusions,*
# *Recommendations,*
# *New Models*

~~~~~~~~~~~~~~~~~~~~~~~~~~~~~~~~~~

I *have seen the enemy, and*
*he is us.*

Pogo

$\mathbb{W}$hen the California Component of the Four-State Project was conceived, four hypotheses concerning the investigation were postulated. Let us examine each in the light of the findings reported in Chapters IV and V.

## HYPOTHESES

The first hypothesis states,

*Participants would express positive opinions about changes in themselves and estimate considerably less change in their students and the operation of their school.*

This hypothesis was based on the assumption that the projects we would be studying would regard special instructional programs as the instruments of change, dependent for their success upon the skilled efforts of dedicated teachers. That is, these projects would cast the classroom teacher in the role of change agent and regard him as the central figure in the process by which educational opportunities for disadvantaged youth would eventually be improved. This view of the teacher's role would be reflected in the rationale for the in-service teacher-training components of the projects under study. These programs would feature activities designed to stimulate and facilitate those changes in the attitudes, understandings, and behaviors of teachers thought necessary to ensure the changes in the self-images, attitudes, skills, and behaviors of their pupils that were the stated objectives of these projects' special instructional programs. We further assumed that the participants in the in-service programs we would study would identify themselves sympathetically with the role in which they had been cast. They would come to see themselves as change agents and to perceive changes in their pupils and in the operation of their schools as the beneficial result of changes in their teaching styles, procedures, and techniques. We hoped that they would relate these changes in themselves to specific features of the in-service program in which they had participated.

The findings reported in Chapter IV, which resulted from statistical analysis of data gathered by questionnaire and Q-sort, tend to support this hypothesis. Table 2, which reports mean responses on individual items of the Q-sort, shows items ranked by mean score within sections headed Estimate of Changes in Participants, Estimate of Changes in Disadvantaged Students, and Estimate of Changes in Participants' Schools. The average mean score in each of these sections is 3.82, 3.54, and 3.45, respectively. The differences among the three average mean scores and the difference between each of these and the sample mean of 3.5 on all items are not statistically significant, but the differences in absolute value are suggestive of those postulated by the first hypothesis.

The findings reported in Chapter V also support this hypothesis. As indicated there, participants interviewed reported considerable change in their attitudes toward problems of teaching disadvantaged pupils, in their understanding of their pupils' cultural and socioeconomic background, in their knowledge of special instructional programs, procedures, and materials for meeting the special educational needs and learning problems of their pupils, and in their teaching styles and general behavior in school. They also reported having observed gratifying indications of changes in their pupils. They mentioned particularly changes in their pupils' self-image and their attitude toward school and education. Some reported marked improvement in their pupils' learning skills and academic achievement. Participants were more cautious about estimating changes in their schools. When asked in the interviews to describe specific changes in the operation of their schools, participants would first attempt to characterize general improvements in the atmosphere and tone of human relations and then would tentatively cite one or two significant improvements in the organization, administration, or operation of their schools. Many, perhaps most, remained hopeful of further improvements, some of which they then proceeded to recommend in detail.

In sum, participants saw themselves in the role of change agents to just about the extent we had expected they would. They appeared to be generally optimistic that the process of change would continue—that they themselves would change further along lines and in directions on which they had reported a considerable beginning; that their pupils would, in time, show greater improvements, particularly in their learning skills and classroom performance; and that their schools would, with continued encouragement and support, eventually implement the improvements in organization, administration, operation, and especially facilities which they would recommend.

The second hypothesis states,

> *Participants would see themselves changing most in the acquisition of new knowledge about the disadvantaged and curricula to meet their special educational needs, less in their attitudes toward problems of teaching disadvantaged pupils, and still less in their teaching behavior.*

This hypothesis was based on the assumption that kinds and degrees of change in participants would be a function of two complex variables: the duration and intensity of their involvement with teacher-training activities in an in-service program, and the priorities and emphasis placed upon these outcomes by the stated objectives and instructional procedures of the program. The outcomes anticipated by this hypothesis reflect our expectation that most participants' involvement with teacher-training activities would be of relatively short duration and in relatively passive (not to say resistant) roles, and that both the stated objectives and instructional procedures of most in-service programs would emphasize these changes in participants in the order described by the hypothesis.

Findings resulting from statistical analysis of data gathered by questionnaire and Q-sort do not support this hypothesis; indeed, they tend to deny it. However, these findings, reported in Table 2, Mean Responses on Individual Items: Estimate of Changes in Participants, and Table 3, Attitude Dimensions Resulting from Factoring of the Q-Sort and Questionnaire Data: Dimension 7 (cluster name: Change in Participants), are ambiguous and inconclusive.

Findings resulting from content analysis of data gathered by interviews with participants and program directors, and reported in Chapter V, indicate that although there probably were differences of degree among the three kinds of change in participants, these differences were neither as great nor as significant as had been anticipated. In the more conducive setting of the interview situation, participants were able to be more informative about the changes they experienced. Many of them described openly and to some length the kinds and degrees of change in themselves which they regarded as important. They reported changes not only in their knowledge and understanding of their disadvantaged pupils and of ways and means for meeting their special educational needs, but also in their attitudes toward problems of teaching such pupils and in their actual teaching behavior in school and classroom.

Furthermore, the participants interviewed regarded the changes in themselves as outcomes of their participation in certain specific types of teacher-training activities. They associated these changes most particularly with their involvement in such activities as small-group discussion and interaction; visits to the homes and neighborhoods of their disadvantaged pupils; conferences with the parents of their disadvantaged pupils and with representatives of community social agencies also working with these children; lectures and panel discussions by authorities on the environmental conditioning of the disadvantaged who themselves came from minority-group backgrounds; visits, on released time, to observe instructional programs, methods, and materials in classrooms and schools other than their own; in-depth case studies of the learning problems of their disadvantaged pupils and efforts to prescribe remedial instruction to remove the disabilities and difficulties diagnosed; and in various types of clinical exercises—actual teachng performances and demonstrations—carried out with special classes of disadvantaged pupils under supervised laboratory conditions and often involving the use of video taping and interaction analysis or some other form of self-appraisal. A number of participants commented that they probably would have changed even more if they had had more extensive and more intensive opportunities of this sort. Several remarked that they might have changed sooner if they had had opportunities to undergo such training during the period of their pre-service teacher education.

In sum, participants saw themselves as having changed both more fundamentally and more fully than we had expected they would.

The third hypothesis states,

> *Projects which participants report as having caused the most change would be those in which there was a maximum amount of interaction between and among participants and in which there was maximum and deliberate exposure to the culture of the disadvantaged.*

This hypothesis was based on the assumption that, although the in-service programs we would be studying would feature a variety of curricula and instructional procedures, participants would experience their most dramatic and engaging encounters with problems of teaching disadvantaged students in the confrontations and interactions between and among themselves and in the activities (practicums, observations, consultations, and visitations) that brought them in direct contact with the culture of the disadvantaged. We assumed that the greaer the number of such confrontations, interactions, and exposures, the greater the amount of human interest and concern they would generate in the participants, thereby providing the strongest motivating force for change in the participants themselves and, through them, in their disadvantaged students and their schools.

The findings based on statistical analysis of questionnaire and Q-sort data and reported in Chapter IV support this hypothesis to some extent. Examination of participants' opinions of curricula and instructional procedures used in in-service programs, which are reported in Table 2, Mean Responses on Individual Items, indicates that the mean scores on interaction items, Items 41 through 48, range from 4.1 to 5.5 and average 4.8 on a scale from 1 to 7. Likewise, the mean scores on exposure items, Items 50 through 55, range from 5.4 to 5.8 and average 5.6 on the same scale. Opinion about the value of direct confrontation and interaction among participants is reflected in Cluster 9, Value of Projects' Encounter Groups. Examination of Table 5, Correlations among Oblique Rotated Factors, indicates, however, that Cluster 9 correlates only .22 with Cluster 7, Changes in Participants, and is virtually unrelated to Cluster 1, Changes in Participants' Disadvantaged Students, and Cluster 5, Changes in Participants' Schools. Opinion about the value of direct exposure to the culture of the disadvantaged is not reflected in any of the nine clusters described in Table 3, Attitude Clusters Resulting from Factoring of the Q-Sort and Questionnaire Data.

Content analysis of data gathered by interviews with participants and program directors yielded results that also support this hypothesis. As reported in Chapter V, participants felt that time provided for interaction among themselves was extremely valuable; in fact, most felt that more time should have been allowed for this type of activity. They generally noted that, although the learning environment provided by the program proved to be catalytic, more time was needed to digest the new information and ideas they had gained. Participants who were involved in programs that provided opportunities for confrontation as well as interaction valued such opportunities very highly. They were especially enthusiastic in their praise for opportunities for direct confrontation and frank interaction between teachers of the black and white races. White teachers, in particular, tended to rate these activities highly.

Interviews with participants revealed one reason why their opinions regarding the value of direct contact with the culture of the disadvantaged, though strongly favorable, were not reflected in an attitude cluster. Many reported that, although their involvement with minority-group members, through activities conducted in their communities, proved to be extremely valuable, opportunities for such involvement were seldom as extensive or intensive as would have been desirable. These participants were somewhat disappointed that their programs were usually unable to provide opportunities for direct contact with the most alienated members of minority groups and their communities.

In sum, participants valued interaction among themselves and exposure to the culture of the disadvantaged as highly as we expected they would. They did not, however, relate these activities to changes in themselves, their students, and their schools to quite the extent we had anticipated, primarily because most did not feel that their programs had provided them sufficient opportunities for such activities.

The fourth hypothesis states,

> Persons who would express the most positive reaction to the project in which they participated would be younger teachers from urban districts who taught classes with a high proportion of disadvantaged students in them, who themselves came from lower social-class backgrounds, and who were strongly desirous of changing the present school structure.

This hypothesis was postulated on the assumption that such participants would be most enthusiastically in favor of the changes specified in their project's stated objectives and most appreciative of in-service programs designed to help them achieve such objectives. We assumed that these persons would be most ready to assume the role of change agent and most eager to praise efforts encouraging and supporting them in that role.

As indicated in Chapter IV, findings resulting from statistical analysis of questionnaire and Q-sort data do not support this hypothesis. None of the variables named in the hypothesis (number of years of teaching experience, school setting, proportion of disadvantaged students taught, social-class background, or attitudes toward certain educational issues expressed in Items 83 through 90) is significantly correlated with items offering participants an opportunity to evaluate or criticize the project in which they were involved. Furthermore, none of these variables is included in any of the clusters described in Table 3, Attitude Clusters Resulting from Factoring of the Q-Sort and Questionnaire Data. It would appear, therefore, that none of these variables is significantly related to the attitudes reflected in these clusters.

Content analysis of data obtained by interviews with practicipants and program directors and reported in Chapter V indicates that younger teachers are, generally speaking, more inclined to express liberal views and to demand more radical changes in the teaching of disadvantaged students and, indeed, in the organization, administration, and operation of the schools. There is no indication, however, that young teachers in urban schools with a high proportion of disadvantaged students in their classes were significantly different in this regard from young teachers in other types of school settings with fewer disadvantaged students in their classes. Nor is there any evidence that younger teachers are more inclined than their more experienced colleagues either to praise or to blame the aims and efforts of the projects with which they were involved. Since younger teachers working with disadvantaged students in particularly problematic school districts are neither unusually demanding nor especially critical of their projects, it would appear that their desire for change and their dissatisfaction with halfway measures is nicely balanced by a willingness to support projects that are well intended even though they are only mildly effective. Or, to put it another way, while younger teachers in problem schools welcome almost any and all efforts whatever to improve the teaching of disadvantaged students, they are just as cognizant as their more experienced colleagues that all too many of these efforts fail to achieve substantial results.

In sum, viewed either way, younger teachers' reactions to the projects and in-service programs in which they participated are very similar to those of their more experienced and presumably more conservative colleagues, who apparently expect less and are therefore more easily satisfied with what they see being done to improve educational opportunities for disadvantaged youth.

## ADDITIONAL FINDINGS

While clearly not a part of the hypotheses, some additional but nonetheless important findings of the investigation may be summarized as follows:

Opinions held by respondents on some educational issues, apart from the projects, are: that no expense should be spared to provide special help in the schools for disadvantaged children; the best thing which could be done for those children would be to put them in smaller-sized classes; disadvantaged children should begin school at an earlier age and the legal age for leaving school maintained; unstructured interaction groups should be used more; and teachers-in-training can learn more in local schools than they can in the colleges and universities. If these opinions were taken at face value the implications would, of course, be considerable.

More in-service training is being done at the elementary than at the secondary level, and far more in reading and language development than in any other subject areas. While this emphasis on younger children is generally supported, a number of project directors are of the opinion that much greater effort ought to be directed to even earlier years of childhood, and they urge the expansion of preschool programs. At the same time, the tensions in the target elementary schools appear to be of a substantially lesser degree than in the corresponding secondary schools, and projects at the higher level are easily justified. No one wants to diminish any programs at any level; what is deplored is the lack of resources to do a thorough job all along the line. A good deal of frustration is generated by the knowledge of what could be accomplished with more funds.

Research and evaluation on the effectiveness of individual in-service projects is very sketchy, but what exists is overwhelmingly approving. Rigorous evaluation designs should be required of all future programs.

In the nearly all-white districts of, especially, southern California, the boards of education are dubious of federal aid if not outright hostile. On the other hand, they are unable to bring themselves to turn it down. Despite the lack of board support in such districts, the directors of Title I and other projects relating to the disadvantaged segment of the school community still seem able to operate effective programs that eventually exert some positive influence on the boards and communities as well as on teachers and students. The project directors were impressive both in their conception of the problems and their ability to organize and administer programs to begin to solve those problems. Teachers too often are unaware of the comprehensive efforts that the directors have in mind, but are nevertheless supportive.

Teachers and administrators are now aware that a much larger part of the problem of educating disadvantaged children must be dealt with in the home than was earlier realized. Despite this awareness, and the contacts with parents arranged through many of the projects, teachers are still limited in their time, ability and, sometimes, willingness to continue and expand those contacts. The use of community workers, often themselves from a disadvantaged background and relatively untrained, appears to be increasing.

Teacher aides are welcomed, though there seem to be at least three problems to be overcome: (1) teachers are sometimes reported to use aides for more lower-level, clerical tasks than is intended by project directors instead of utilizing them to work directly with children; (2) aides who are also parents of children in that school occasionally give teachers some concern about their own authority; (3) teachers are sometimes defensive about aides from a disadvantaged community who have a greater rapport with, or speak the native language of, the children.

To change attitudes about the disadvantaged and about closely related racial issues, sensitivity training is coming more and more to be utilized and positively regarded. Though some concern exists about its criticism by conservative factions of the community and the schools, and about its possibly damaging effects on staff relations, the overwhelming opinion was that sensitivity training was an unusually potent procedure for improving attitudes, and with that, behavior. This element of in-service projects is not always well publicized, even in evaluation reports, apparently because of concern about adverse criticism; but sensitivity training is nevertheless being used or planned in a majority of the districts visited. The usual procedure is to contract with a state college, university, or private organization to provide an expert, usually a clinical psychologist or perhaps even a psychiatrist, who brings a staff to the district or other place of meeting to conduct the sessions. Meetings are sometimes spread out over weeks or even months, perhaps as an extension course, or more often take place in one- to five-hour periods on several different days or during intensive one- to three-day periods. It should also be noted that some sensitivity training among students is occurring, usually as "group counseling."

While districts commonly seek out institutions of higher learning for assistance with their compensatory programs, the cooperation between public schools and the higher institutions is not what it should be and proceeds too often in only the one direction. Colleges and universities offer expertise, but the schools are the laboratories where that expertise is properly developed and applied—and the schools have developed considerable understanding of their own about the problems of teaching disadvantaged children. When asked for suggestions of how teacher education could better prepare teachers for target schools, the response is almost invariable that teachers-in-training should have more and earlier experience with the whole disadvantaged milieu—students, schools, homes, and communities. In this connection several proposals were examined for a combined district college plan to bring college juniors and seniors into target schools as paid teaching assistants, passing them into internships in the fifth year, with classes being taught at a school site and largely by school personnel, and culminating with full-time teaching appointments in the schools where the candidates were trained.

The need for more minority-group teachers is everywhere conceded, though the claim is made that they are extremely hard to find in any number, especially Mexican-Americans. (American Indian teachers are, by all accounts, not available at all.)

Teachers and administrators generalize the differences between Negro and Mexican-American students in target schools as being, with obvious exceptions, that Negro children are more aggressive and more volatile, principally because of community unrest over current racial strife, while Mexican-American children are more passive and less inclined toward the whole school establishment, largely because of their cultural background. Though generally agreeing with their white counterparts on these differences, the minority-group teachers and administrators place the blame both for the aggression and the passivity on those unknowing, uncaring, or outright bigoted persons in authority who fail to provide the kind of education that minority-group children need.

A perplexing paradox exists in that while the trend of the times is toward greater freedom for students and more involvement in decision-making, teachers over and over again voiced their conviction of the need to maintain control over students lest the present fragile system of discipline disintegrate. An important function training programs could perform would be to show teachers how to shift from the authoritarian controls of the past to more modern modes of involving students in the learning process and in making decisions about what that process should be. Demonstrations of flexible scheduling, discovery and inquiry methods of learning, teacher-student "contracts," "simulations," tutorial plans, group counseling and the like would be in order.

A number of unusual projects, all of them promising, were observed, involving self-evaluation by video tape preceded by training in the setting of behavioral objectives and in interaction analysis, new approaches to continuation training, the rewriting of academic subject matter to incorporate material essential to modern vocational training, the development of highly sophisticated diagnostic and prescriptive techniques in reading, and preschool education beginning even in infancy—all requiring appreciable pre-service and in-service training.

Districts having high proportions of minority-group students have such pronounced and overwhelming problems that unusual and creative solutions are absolutely necessary. Bold and unusual in-service and pre-service training programs should be encouraged through clearly supportive state and federal guidelines, along with the immediate and massive intrusion of saturating funds.

## IMPLICATIONS

At first blush, the results of this investigation are disappointing. They certainly are not very dramatic, and they appear to be inconclusive, but suggestive. In fact, our findings are somewhat inconsistent among themselves, and even contrary to several of our hypotheses. For the most part, they are too ambiguous to be susceptible of easy interpretation or broad generalization. Certainly no one program, single technique, specific set of purposes, or principles of operation emerge as an ideal model. No magical, far-reaching, or dramatic changes emerge in the behavior of teachers, their pupils, or their schools; no one set of features distinctly characterizes the most effective and the least effective projects. Our findings seem to indicate that, like the profession and institutions that sponsor it, the process of teacher education is an essentially conservative one, relying for its best effects on time-tested and proven methods and materials used in combination with some few experimental and innovative ones.

The effective in-service training programs that are suggested by these findings cannot be characterized as dramatic new possibilities for marked improvement over actual ones presently in operation—no panaceas, no miracles, no brave new world! The curricula suggested can most properly be regarded as somewhat new and different ways in which traditional, conventional, experimental, and innovative methods and materials of teacher education can be combined and coordinated in order to provide coherent, continuous, and comprehensive programs for the pre-service and in-service training of teachers of the disadvantaged.

Yet the projects we investigated all were successful in that participants judged them to "go well." The participants thought that they themselves changed to some extent, their pupils did too, and their schools also—all for the better and in descending order. The various means used to achieve project objectives met with participants' approval, one technique being rated positively about as high as another. Thus the approval of a project's purposes, its means, and its results tended to be "across the board." Changes identified were unrelated to the extent or kind of pupil or school disadvantageousness. The teachers tended to see change happening all around them. They were receptive and they were enthusiastic.

For weeks the project staff pondered the results. We talked again with project directors, participants, and State Department of Education personnel who were closely identified with the programs.

We came to this conclusion: *the teachers of the disadvantaged who responded to our inquiry are desperate.* They are so desperate they welcome *any* in-service training activity that seems likely to help them even a little bit in their struggle to cope with the problems of teaching disadvantaged students. In these circumstances, they do not seem to have very strong preferences for one type of activity over another; they like them all for their purposes, if they are conducted well enough to serve their purposes at all. Since most of the activities we studied *were,* for the most part, conducted well enough to serve the participants' purposes, most of them can be recommended as effective means for achieving one or more objectives of a training program for teachers of the disadvantaged. So our first discussion of implications will be concerned with curricula—how particular means can be combined in a comprehensive program designed to achieve specific objectives.

The findings of the study indicate that in-service programs designed to train teachers of the disadvantaged are organized and operated to achieve four primary objectives by means of a few principal components, or activities, as follows:

*Primary Objective 1:* To change teachers' attitudes toward the problems encountered in teaching disadvantaged pupils. More specifically, to heighten teachers' sensitivity to their own needs, desires, feelings, ideas, and values, and to their present attitudes toward themselves, their profession, their colleagues, their pupils, and their schools; and also to increase teachers' awareness of the constructive and destructive effects of their present attitudes on their teaching and its expected outcomes. Ultimately, to bring about a fundamental restructuring of the teachers' perceptions, preferences, prejudices, predispositions, and purposes regarding themselves, their teaching, and its outcomes.

*Principal Activities for Achieving Objective 1:* Small-group discussion and interaction focused on the participants themselves and on the objectives and activities of the special instructional program for disadvantaged pupils with which they are involved. This procedure is carried out in a variety of formats, including seminars and workshops explicitly oriented toward accomplishment of specific teaching objectives; sensitivity training sessions (T-groups), which may be explicitly task-oriented but implicitly oriented toward the exploration of human relationships among the participants and the discovery of dynamic principles of group processes; the basic encounter session ("pure" T-group), which is explicitly oriented solely and entirely toward the individual participants' experience of and responses to the encountering process—the process by which they encounter each other and cope with the mutual impacts resulting therefrom. In each of these formats, the discussion and interaction procedure may be supplemented by the use of video tape-recorded materials and interaction analysis techniques to expose and explicate group processes and to evaluate their appropriateness and effectiveness for certain instructional purposes.

*Primary Objective 2:* To increase teachers' personal knowledge, understanding, and appreciation of their disadvantaged pupils. More specifically, to inform teachers about the personal characteristics, cultural and historical background, socioeconomic circumstances, and environmental conditions of their disadvantaged pupils; and also to enhance their understanding of the special educational needs and learning problems of disadvantaged pupils resulting from their environmental conditioning and economic and educational deprivation. Ultimately, to broaden the perspective within which teachers regard their disadvantaged pupils, particularly in relation to their own personality, character, background, training, and experience; and also to extend and expand teachers' capacity for recognizing, accepting, and valuing the implications of cultural and social differences as these are exemplified by the problems that confront them in their efforts to be helpful to pupils who have been deprived of many of the cultural, social, economic, and educational benefits they themselves have enjoyed.

*Principal Activities for Achieving Objective 2:* Authoritative and scholarly presentations of information about the environmental conditioning of disadvantaged pupils and its effects on their motives, interests, abilities, and achievements in the learning of school subjects. This procedure is carried out in a variety of formats, including lectures, panel discussions, symposiums (involving disadvantaged pupils, their parents, and other members of their community), films and guided tours or field trips to observe disadvantaged neighborhoods. Usually this procedure is augmented by some form of discussion following the presentation—often an exchange of questions and answers between speakers and members of the audience, sometimes informal exchange of ideas and opinions among members of the audience subdivided into small groups. An additional procedure, employed in NDEA Title XI institutes and only rarely in ESEA Title I in-service programs, is the home visit and interview with individual disadvantaged pupils or their parents, or both. More than one home visit and interview may be made part of a case study of the individual pupil's needs and problems. Another procedure, employed by NDEA Title XI institutes, is the live-in experience, an arrangement whereby participants reside with disadvantaged families whose children are among the pupils in their classes. The authorities and scholars who present information and opinion, guide field trips, arrange home visits and interviews, and direct case studies are often, themselves, members of racial or ethnic minority groups that have been disadvantaged. Their relationship to the total program varies from single-occasion guest speaker to consultant and to full- or part-time staff member.

*Primary Objective 3:* To improve teachers' professional knowledge and skills and increase their effectiveness in providing instruction that meets the special needs of disadvantaged pupils. More specifically, to extend teachers' familiarity with curricula, instructional programs, and units developed especially for teaching the disadvantaged; also to enlarge teachers' repertory of instructional procedures and techniques and their store of instructional media, materials, and equipment that have proved especially effective in such teaching. Ultimately, to extend the range of effective alternatives within which teachers can choose roles, styles, facilities, materials, and techniques likely to prove helpful for individualizing the instruction they offer their disadvantaged pupils.

*Principal Activities for Achieving Objective 3:* Workshops on the curricula, methods, and materials for teaching specific school subjects. The workshop procedure is carried out in a variety of formats, combining such approaches and activities as lectures, demonstrations, films, video tapes, kinescopes, slides, and other presentations; field trips to visit other classrooms, schools, and districts to observe demonstrations of instructional programs, procedures, techniques, media, materials, and equipment; grade-level and department meetings for group discussion and exchange of information, opinion, and suggestions; individual consultations and small-group conferences with specialists in curriculum and instruction; individual and group attendance at local, county, regional, state, and national curriculum conferences and meetings of professional organizations; and small-group projects for designing, developing, testing, evaluating, and revising instructional units, methods, media, and materials. Workshops are conducted in a variety of settings, including school libraries and instructional materials centers, special instructional and supplementary services centers, curriculum planning and development centers, demonstration-laboratory schools, and college and university institutes.

*Primary Objective 4:* To modify teachers' personal and professional behaviors in the classroom and school, especially in their work with disadvantaged students. More specifically, to provide teachers with opportunities to improvise, innovate, experiment with and evaluate new modes and styles of behavior toward their pupils and their colleagues; also to permit them to practice, under sympathetic observation, guidance, and supervision, behaviors that are more appropriately expressive of the new insights, knowledge, understandings, and appreciation gained from other training activities. Ultimately, to encourage teachers and support them while they try out new and hopefully better ways of working with their disadvantaged pupils and of cooperating and collaborating with their colleagues.

*Principal Activities for Achieving Objective 4:* The clinical experience, or practicum, in teaching and counseling with disadvantaged pupils. This procedure is carried out in a variety of settings and arrangements, including case work with individual disadvantaged students (diagnosing pupils' educational needs and learning problems and prescribing and conducting individualized remedial or developmental instruction to meet them), practice teaching in special instructional programs or classes in a regular school, practice teaching under close supervision in a demonstration-laboratory school, counseling with and guiding the studies of selected individuals or small groups of students in a special instructional program or school activity, and field work with community social agencies under the supervision of regular staff members. The clinical experience or practicum in teaching and counseling is sometimes facilitated by the use of video tape recording and playback of practice teaching performances (often on the microteaching model), audio tape recording and replay of counseling interviews, interaction schedules and rating forms for structuring observations of classroom and playground activities, and various other instruments and techniques for analyzing interactions between teachers and pupils or among pupils. The practicum usually includes some provision for individual and small-group conferences wherein the practicing teacher can gain from open and frank discussion the benefit of his supervisor's observations, criticisms, and suggestions.

This list of what was intended and what was tried can doubtless be extended somewhat. Nevertheless, it is sufficiently detailed to serve as a basis for suggesting means that should have been tried to achieve the four primary objectives of the in-service programs investigated. Furthermore, the list suggests the problems in assigning priorities to both means and ends because of limitations on money, time, talent, interest, commitment, and other resources necessary for the operation of an effective in-service program.

Assuming, as we do, that our respondents gave care and thought in answering our questions and had sufficient intelligence and tact to evaluate their experience, we can interpret our findings to mean that the participants believe that all four primary objectives are equally worth while—not to say necessary—and that all of the means for achieving them were about equally appropriate and effective. From this, we conclude that they are telling us that training programs for teachers of the disadvantaged should be *comprehensive:* that is, they should be planned and conducted to pursue all four primary objectives *simultaneously,* by including at least one activity designed to achieve each one. If this is what our findings indicate, our model curricula should be the means whereby various training activities, each designed to achieve one or more of the four primary objectives, can be combined with one another in a comprehensive program. The resulting programs should stand a better than even-money chance of successfully achieving all four primary objectives simultaneously and, thus, of instigating those further and ultimate changes, in students and schools, for which changes in teachers are a necessary, though hardly sufficient, condition.

In proposing model curricula, and in formulating recommendations for implementing them in model training programs, we have been obliged to consider both the *desirability* and the *feasibility* of certain procedures and expected outcomes. The question of feasibility necessarily entails questions of priorities, whether these priorities are only differences of emphasis, or whether they are tangible differences in the amounts of money, time, talent, and energy allocated for each of the training activities to be included in the total program. We have, for this reason, dropped the idea that we should prescribe different model curricula for different settings—types of communities, minority-group populations, concentrations of disadvantaged students, and the like. Instead, what we are suggesting is different curriculum models for different purposes, just as long as the overall program objectives are sufficiently comprehensive, regardless of the community settings in which the training programs are to be conducted and the specific objectives of the projects of which they are to be components.

At this point, it seems appropriate to assert that local school districts, in cooperation, and even collaboration, with colleges and universities, are the agencies most likely to be able to provide the experiences, activities, and facilities necessary (or at least desirable) for the comprehensive training programs we are proposing for teaching of the disadvantaged. At issue is the matter of how these two agencies—local school districts and colleges—can effectively combine their resources with those of the communities in which the disadvantaged live and have their being.

In offering suggestions for model curricula and programs for training the teachers of disadvantaged pupils, we have emphasized our view, supported by our findings, that, if they are to be fully effective in achieving desirable outcomes, they must be comprehensive. That is, we have said that they should combine training activities designed to achieve four primary objectives: simultaneous changes in teachers' attitudes, knowledge and understanding, skills, and behavior. In making recommendations for implementing these models, we have emphasized our view that such activities must be carefully planned and coordinated, and that they must be conducted in strongly supportive institutional settings that provide adequate resources, facilities, and equipment; readily accessible opportunities for field trials and rigorous evaluation of procedures; and, above all, sympathetic, knowledgeable, and deftly expert supervision. It is our considered judgment, therefore, that the curriculum models we have proposed, whether designed to provide *in-service* or *pre-service* training for *teachers of the disadvan-*

*taged* or for *all teachers,* can be most efficiently and effectively mounted by an institution that is (1) situated more advantageously in relation to the resources, opportunities, and problems of local communities and school districts than colleges and universities usually are, and (2) operated more independently from social, economic, and political pressures for particular uses of resources and opportunities and for specific solutions to those problems than local school districts usually are. The institution we regard as most appropriate for the professional education and training of teachers—not only teachers of the disadvantaged but all teachers—would have the following features: It would (1) provide training centered in the ghetto, the *barrio,* the reservation, and similar neighborhoods; (2) emphasize participation, encountering, confrontation of all persons involved as the basis for the teachers' (or prospective teachers') learning about theories, concepts, principles; (3) be governed by representatives of *all* of the groups providing the necessary resources—the local community, the local school district, the college or university, the trainees themselves, and the profession; and (4) draw its staff from *all* agencies providing the resources, thus employing as teachers of teachers the students, parents, community agency workers, and civic leaders of the local community, as well as the public school teachers and supervisors in the local school district, the faculty and graduate students of colleges and universities, and other professional specialists.

## A NEW MODEL

Assuming that there is merit in the suggestions we have offered, the question remains: How and where can the model curricula and programs best be mounted, and under what administrative arrangement is there the best chance of immediate and effective implementation? The clue to a new model institution has appeared again and again in this report; the clearest description of its most characteristic feature is contained in a statement made in Chapter V, from the summary of our interview findings: "These teachers were convinced that training activities must be planned and conducted *from* and *at* the grass roots level, rather than *by* or *at* the district office or the college, removed as they are from the local school and neighborhood."

Several projects in our investigation operated an institution that had this characteristic feature, at least to some degree. The institution was a multipurpose center, either a special learning center that offered remedial, developmental, and supplementary instruction for disadvantaged pupils, such as the Yuba County Reading-Learning Center operated by the Marysville ESEA Title I project; a curriculum and instructional materials center that developed, field tested, and evaluated innovative instructional units for disadvantaged pupils, such as Initial Teaching Alphabet Program operated by the Stockton ESEA Title III project; or a demonstration-laboratory center that was either a comprehensive school program or a program of special classes for disadvantaged pupils (and their parents), such as the Laurel Elementary Demonstration School operated by the Santa Cruz ESEA Title I project, or the Special Evening Demonstration Classes conducted by the Healdsburg ESEA Title I project.

The organization and operation of the multipurpose center was a cooperative and collaborative arrangement between a college or university and a local school district or school. The instructional and administrative staff of the center was drawn from both agencies. The principal activities of the center were conducted in a public school or in a facility immediately adjacent to one, and not regularly and exclusively on a college campus. The program of the center included, in addition to other activities, an offering of workshops, seminars, extension courses, and similar training activities for the teachers of disadvantaged pupils. In sum, the multipurpose centers operated by several projects we studied conducted comprehensive, coherently articulated, coordinated, cooperative, and collaborative programs for the immediate and direct benefit of disadvantaged pupils, their parents, and their teachers.

The institutional model embodied by the multipurpose centers we studied seems to us to be, in almost every respect but one, worthy of being exported as is. *The one respect in which this model can, and, in our view, should be improved is in its control and governance.* The governing authority of the centers investigated was either a local school district, a consortium involving a district and a nearby college or university, or a trusteeship including representation from these agencies and local community agencies. We believe the joint-power authority formed to govern the model institution we have in mind can and should provide for more equitable delegation of responsibility and distribution of decision-making functions.

From what we know of the paradigm of change,[1] of the bureaucracy of the establishment, and the cement of tradition in which most schools and colleges are mired, it is difficult to see how the center can be the long-term answer for the radical reforms and dramatic changes needed in order to successfully recruit, train, and retrain teachers of the disadvantaged.

In several previous publications we have pointed out the failure of traditional teacher education,[2] a failure that is particularly alarming with respect to our total lack of accomplishment in recruiting, training, and retraining ghetto teachers. This failure may be summarized as that of the colleges, the schools, the state, and the profession.

*The Colleges:* Most colleges—as institutions—have *not* taken seriously their responsibility to educate teachers. As institutions their efforts have been largely incidental—tangential to other (and more important) missions like preparing liberal arts graduates, or, at the professional level, doctors and lawyers. Certainly, in the present most crucial need of teacher training—preparing teachers of the disadvantaged—most colleges and universities are far removed from the problem. Since institutions of higher education have not taken seriously this social obligation of teacher training, since they cannot be forced into active social responsibility, and since the most significant aspect of this training should occur in the ghetto and in classrooms of disadvantaged children, why not move this unwanted stepchild from the colleges?

*The Schools:* For years schools merely accepted teachers trained

---

[1] As applied to school curriculum projects, see Mario D. Fantini and Gerald Weinstein, *The Disadvantaged: Challenge to Education,* New York: Harper and Row, 1968, pp. 298–300. As applied to innovations in collegiate programs, see James C. Stone, *Breakthrough in Teacher Education,* San Francisco: Jossey-Bass, 1968, pp. 178–180.

[2] James C. Stone, *ibid.,* Chap. 12, *passim,* and James C. Stone, "Reform or Rebirth?" *NEA Journal,* Vol. 57, No. 5 (May, 1968), p. 23. Also James C. Stone, "Whither Reform in Teacher Education?" *Educational Leadership,* Vol. 25, No. 2 (November, 1967), p. 127; reprinted in *The Education Digest,* Vol. XXXII, No. 5 (January, 1968), pp. 40–42.

by the colleges, however adequate or inadequate, and sent them back
to college for refresher courses and advanced degrees. Similarly the
public schools have merely accepted student teachers and intern teachers and passively provided them with whatever laboratory experiences
the college or university requested. In more recent times, aided and
abetted by federal grants, school systems have developed their own
in-service education programs that teachers have flocked to and generally applauded.

Building on this know-how, it would be logical for the schools
also to become the pre-service educators of teachers, replacing the
institutions of higher education. For the increasing numbers of public
schools involved in internship programs, this would be a logical and
simple step. Assistant superintendents in charge of staff development
are being found with greater frequency in the schools; such persons
are the individuals obviously qualified to direct and organize pre-
service teacher education as they now successfully organize and direct
in-service training. An obvious benefit would be to close the gap that
has so long existed between pre-service and in-service education and
which internship programs were expected to achieve but few have.

In publicly supported education this shift of responsibility
would involve a simple transfer of funds from higher to public education. Such a shift would create in every school system a division of
teacher education—in-service and pre-service—that is closer to the
operational level and not so removed as present education departments
and schools are now, bound up as they are in the bureaucracies, politics, and distractions in higher education. The teacher-education center previously described would be an example of this administrative
model. Yet to expect public education—which has failed in the ghetto,
bound up as it is by the inertia, irresponsive bureaucracy, middle-class
traditions, overlegislation, underfinancing, and other distractions of
public education—to mount and sustain such centers on a wide-scale
basis and at high levels is to expect what is not and what is not likely
to be.

*The State:* The education of teachers has long been recognized as a state responsibility. Originally states took this obligation
seriously and provided special institutions—the normal school, the
teachers college—as their prime vehicle for pre-service and in-service
education. The last decade has seen the demise of these institutions.

Most have evolved into state colleges interested in the education of all occupational groups, including teachers. Gradually teacher training has lost its importance in these institutions, their subsequent conversion to state universities has continued and hastened the decline of interest in teacher education on the collegiate level.

Meanwhile, state departments of education have been content with confining their teacher-education obligations to the certification of teachers and the accreditation of colleges and universities for teacher education. In most states the accreditation function amounts to an approval system based primarily on whether the institutions offer the specific courses prescribed by the certification office and, as a recent Teacher Education and Professional Standards (TEPS) publication points out, has failed to provide leadership.

> Thus a no-man's land is created for the college . . . school function (of teacher training) which is typically characterized by dual administration, improper financing, and conflicting supervision.[3]

*The Profession:* World War II created a critical shortage of teachers and was followed by an unprecedented increase in the birth rate, which worsened the teacher shortage. Out of this crisis came the "professional standards movement" in which the NEA took the leadership through the formation of its Commission on Teacher Education and Professional Standards in 1946. While all of us connected with this movement over the past twenty-five years—at local, state, and national levels—can enthusiastically testify about its many accomplishments, the simple fact is that, despite these efforts, the average teacher still is disinterested in and uninformed about teacher education and the professional processes such as certification, accreditation, in-service training, personnel standards, and the like which undergird and support it. If you doubt this statement, look around at the next school conference you attend. Check how few general sessions are given over to the topic of teacher training. Visit the section meetings on Training, Certification, Accreditation, or Ethics and note the paucity of teachers at these section meetings in contrast to the standing-room-only signs on doors marked Salary, Negotiating Councils, Col-

---

[3] "A New Order in Student Teaching," National Commission on Teacher Education and Professional Standards, NEA, Washington, D.C., 1967, p. 21.

lective Bargaining, and the like. Check on who goes to conferences on teacher education—a few public school master teachers and personnel directors, yes, but mostly college or university professors of education. We can't blame the teachers—we've never really opened the doors of teacher education to them. When it comes to pre-service training, we college people have given a few supervising teachers a look inside, but we've not dared to let them get further than *recommending* the grade the student or intern teacher should receive. (We, the college supervisors, who only visit the student teacher about two or three times a semester are empowered with the final judgment!) When it comes to in-service training, teachers are merely the recipients of our ideas, seldom involved in the planning for what is *needed* and desirable for them!

We could open the door wider—make supervising teachers faculty members, give them pre-service teaching responsibilities for the whole professional sequence instead of the student teaching problems seminars we typically toss to a few of them. We could set up procedures whereby teachers actually plan, organize, and conduct their own in-service training. Any such moves would be in the right direction, but there is scant hope that from these forms of tokenism, the profession will be moved to a concern for teacher education.

*Social Institutions:* All attempts to reform teacher training[4] have failed to recognize that the social institutions in which teacher education is embedded—the schools, the colleges, state departments of education—were created by society *not* for the purpose of bringing about change and innovation, but rather that of preserving the status quo. As guardians of the establishment, the schools, institutions of higher education, and state regulatory agencies were specifically created to see that change does not take place. The primary function of these educational agencies, in common with education since the days of primitive man, is to pass on the cultural heritage to the upcoming generation. Designed to preserve "what is," they have been staffed largely by those who are wholly committed to this end. Few teach-

[4] There have been many reform efforts. Among the major attempts have been the Commission on Teacher Education of the American Council on Education (1938–1946); the NEA TEPS Commission (1946 to date); the Fund for the Advancement of Education (1950–59); the Ford Foundation's "Breakthrough Programs" (1960–66); NDEA, ESEA, and other Federal Grants (1964 to date).

ers, for example, see their role as agents of change. The result is that reform efforts have done little to break the patterns of traditional teacher education.

As long as education and its handmaiden, teacher education, remain fixed in the concrete of college, public school, and state department traditions, both likely will remain substantially as they are now, and reform efforts will continue to come and go without making an appreciable impact on either higher education or public education, or on state departments of public instruction where teacher education has its roots.

If ever we hope to break what George Counts, writing some twenty-five years ago, called "the lock-step in teacher training," we must create new organizational structures; we must be willing to go one step further than modifying the present establishment. We need to cut the ties, plough over the old college-school ruts in which teacher training is quagmired, and begin fresh.

Our summation of the failures of teacher education and its traditional role in society brings to mind the statement by Felix Robb, the long-time former president of George Peabody College for Teachers, one of the two remaining teachers colleges still in existence in the United States: "If the successors to teachers colleges become mediocre and abandon their concern for teachers, another generation will have to start teachers colleges all over again."[5]

While not wishing simply to go back as Robb suggests, we do propose a new model that takes something from the past—the idea of a separate social institution for teacher training—while adding several new dimensions crucial for the education of teachers of the disadvantaged: training that is "planned and conducted from and at the grass roots level" and intimately involving the local school and neighborhood—an agency controlled by the client-groups that comprise the local community.

We have called this new social institution an *EPI—Education Professions Institute*. We offer it as our major recommendation for training teachers of the disadvantaged, if not for all teachers. For those of us who have been in teacher education most of our professional lives, proposing an alternative and competing agency to the

[5] Henry C. Hill, "Wanted: Professional Teachers," *The Atlantic Magazine* (May, 1960), p. 39.

one that has nurtured us these many years is a difficult task. As Minnis has said: "No one likes to point out that the king is naked. If you are the tailor, it is especially difficult."[6]

## EDUCATION PROFESSIONS INSTITUTE (EPI)

The EPI would be a separate agency of higher education with a distinct, unique, and differentiated function.[7] The unique purpose would be to provide professional training for teachers-to-be, teacher aides, associate teachers, intern teachers, regular teachers, master teachers, and teachers of teachers through the bachelor's and master's degrees. It would recruit adults of all ages from the ghetto community in which it was located as well as from the ranks of high school graduates, the junior colleges, four-year colleges, and universities. Those teachers and prospective teachers who had not themselves grown up

[6] Douglas Minnis, "Rebellion in Teacher Education: Requiem for a Fossil in White Tie and Tails," CASCD Conference Address (Nov. 21, 1968), p. 2 (mimeographed).

[7] Hobert Burns, a member of the Task Force of the NDEA National Institute for Advanced Study of the Disadvantaged and a key member of the California Advisory Committee for this Four-State Project, has arrived at a somewhat comparable idea to that of an EPI. Coincidentally, he hit upon his proposal, not from the results of this study, but through his concern for the problem of the disadvantaged, his impatience with present modes of teacher education, and his training as a philosopher. In an address to the California Council on the Education of Teachers, he stated: "It is no longer possible for colleges and universities, through the instrumentation of schools or department of education, adequately to prepare teachers within the relative isolation of the campus—even when that preparation involves, as it usually does, some cooperative efforts between the colleges and the public schools. The coalition between colleges and schools should be expanded to include representatives from student and community groups and, since neither the college nor the public school is able by itself to provide for that kind of extension of the teacher education coalition, the creation of new institutions responsible for the training of educational personnel. Put simply, the creation of quasi-governmental or multi-institutional consortia or corporations for the preparation of educational personnel. While such an institution must and would include schools and colleges it would also include other groups now excluded; and the full meaning of that, of course, is to suggest that the present school-college coalition surrender some of its present sovereignty over teacher education to a new quasi-governmental institution. . . ." [Hobert Burns, "The Public Schools as Trainers of Teachers: A (Modest) Proposal," California Council on the Education of Teachers, Yosemite, California, Oct. 31, 1968 (mimeographed).]

in a ghetto would be expected to both live in and work in the local community for a significant part of their training period.

Fiscal support for the institute might come from a variety of sources. Some might be funded entirely by the state or the federal government, others might be supported in whole or in part by private foundations, industrial groups, or professional associations. *Initially, they would offer an alternative to present agencies of teacher training, thus providing healthy competition to existing college and university and school district operations. In time, the EPI might completely replace colleges and schools as the trainers of teachers.*

Regardless of source or sources of financial support, the EPI should be viewed as a natural extension of the state's responsibility for teacher education; better stated, it would be a case of the state's returning to itself the responsibility it has always had but has failed to exercise since the end of the teachers colleges. The institute would be accredited by the state for developmental and experimental purposes. Special and unique licensing provisions might be needed in some states for those completing EPI training. This is not to suggest a lowering of standards, but rather different standards for a different group to accomplish a purpose not now adequately served by any existing social agency.

The EPI would draw its faculty from the communities in which it was located, the local schools, adjacent colleges and universities, and other social, governmental and industrial agencies. While strictly a professional institution, the EPI might admit prospective teachers and paraprofessionals at any point in their college career when they were deemed ready to embark on a semester of professional education. During any semester of enrollment, the trainees would be paid by the state or the local school, or both, for rendering teaching or community services of various kinds. This "paid to learn" feature is especially significant in terms of recruiting from the ghetto community itself. In-service teachers would enroll in the institute for afternoon or evening workshops and seminars or summer colloquiums, conferences, institutes, sabbaticals, and the like, using scholarships provided by local, state, and federal governments, foundations, the business community, professional associations, and school district sabbatical leaves.

The single most distinguishing feature of the EPI would be

that it is a *teaching* institution. Its educational style would be to "learn to teach by teaching" so all trainees would be involved in some form of teaching as the central focus of their learning activities.

The EPI is envisioned as a prestige agency, paying better salaries, for example, to its faculty than do traditional colleges, universities, or school systems. This would be a truly professional school analogous to the medical school, the law school, the divinity school. Its program for the education of teachers of teachers would encompass research focused on professional problems in the teaching-learning process.

There would be equality of status and prestige for those faculty having differentiated responsibilities for the so-called theoretical and practical aspects of teacher training since any one individual would be expected to be equally involved in both. The heart of the EPI would be an exemplary school or school system that it would adopt or organize. The institute and the school would be housed together. Professional education would grow out of the instructional problems of children. Laboratory experiences in classrooms and neighborhoods of the disadvantaged would be the central focus of the in-service and pre-service teacher-training program. The professional curriculum would be tailored to each individual and would be so organized that every trainee, during his stay at the institute, would be simultaneously involved in a stream of classroom or community experiences and a concurrent stream of theoretical seminars, both taught and supervised by a team of instructors working with a particular group of trainees. The EPI would have the advantage of being close to the schools, yet removed one step from the politics of local school systems. Though ultimately responsible to the state, it would be characterized by "home rule" from the local community and the trainees themselves. However funded, it would be administered by and for the local community and trainee clientele. The state department of education, the local school district, and adjacent institutions of higher education would have a cooperative and consultative relationship with the institute.

The EPI would be chartered by the state under a joint powers agreement (see Figure 1). This is a legal entity provided for in most states, but until now seldom used in education circles except in connection with the federally sponsored Research and Development Laboratories. The powers brought together to organize the EPI and to

*Figure 1*

STATE ORGANIZATION OF EDUCATION PROFESSIONS INSTITUTE (EPI)

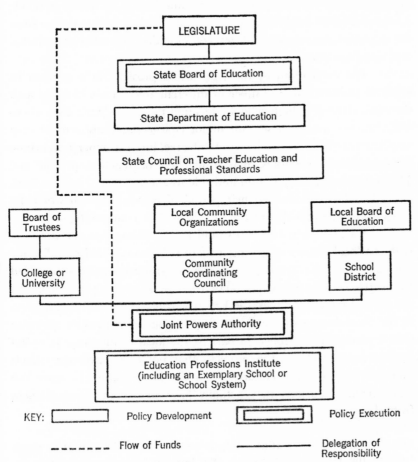

formulate policy for it (within broad state guidelines) would be (1) a local community, (2) the trainees, (3) a college or university, (4) a school system, and (5) the organized profession. These powers would establish an independent local board of control that would have fiscal and administrative authority to operate the EPI. The five powers initially comprising the governing board might appoint additional representatives, including the public-at-large.

Within state departments of public instruction, there would be a specific unit of higher education with responsibility to provide lead-

ership for the EPI and coordinate their efforts. The permanent staff
would be a small cadre of higher education and disadvantaged teaching specialists. This nucleus would be augmented by yearly appointments of a much larger number of consultants and faculty drawn from
the institutes, the schools, colleges, communities, and other educational
and social agencies.

The curriculum of the EPI would provide for a number of
levels of training for a number of different roles. Thus mothers with
the equivalent of a high school education might enter the EPI to become teacher aides; those with junior college preparation to become
associate teachers; those with an AB degree, intern teachers; and those
with teaching credentials, master teachers or teachers of teachers.
Movement from one program and role to another would be provided.
All would be paid during their period of training, for all would be
serving in some capacity in the local school or community.

A school in the ghetto would be the "home" of the institute,
with the local district supplying a room for seminars and an office for
the staff. Academic preparation needed by trainees would be provided
by nearby colleges on a contractual or cooperative arrangement. In
the vernacular of the times, the EPI would be "where the action is"—
in the disadvantaged community. And it would stay there in the sense
that it would be controlled in part by the local community. It would
address itself solely to the problem that not only have our schools
failed to help enough children from the lower classes to enter the
mainstream of society, they actually have prevented many of them
from doing so.

> We are now educating students whose lives will be lived as much
> in the next century as this one, but our schools and colleges are
> . . . still based on structures, functions, and curricula more apropos
> of the last century than the next. . . . For many . . . the judg-
> ment has been made that the urban schools are failures because the
> present ends of the schools are not aceeptable as the proper ends
> by . . . students and parents from impoverished or minority groups.[8]

And if our schools have failed, teacher training likewise has
failed. Both are part and parcel of the present establishment. We
teacher educators thus are admitted failures, but we can also be part

[8] Burns, pp. 11, 12.

of the solution through the EPI. We can draw a lesson from a parallel problem that has long been prevalent in rural America. Like the present ghetto, rural teachers have been and are in short supply. An attempt to solve the rural problem was made by recruiting from the country young women to be trained at colleges located in the towns and cities. Upon qualifying for teaching certificates, however, very few returned to the country to teach. The EPI would draw from its area many of those who were local residents but it would train them on the spot, with a greater likelihood of their remaining in the area after training to serve in the local schools.

Since the EPI is *the model* that emerges from our findings, we feel obliged to underscore and reiterate the fact that in an EPI the ghetto community and its trainees would be active participants in determining their own and their children's education. They clearly would have a stake in it—a piece, perhaps *the* piece, of the action. The growing belief by ghetto communities that schools and teacher-education institutions no longer are serving ends they believe in is the cause of the increasing demands and increasingly intense confrontations by black power, Mexican-American, Puerto Rican, and American Indian groups. In an EPI, the ghetto community and the trainees would have not only a *voice* but also a *vehicle* for remaking their own education and the education of their children.

No one doubts the difficulty of establishing such a new social institution, especially not those of us who have been "the tailors" (Minnis' term) for so many years of conventional training in traditional colleges and universities. Yet surely the times demand action, new approaches, radical departures, brave new worlds. Henry David Thoreau once wrote:

> Why should we be in such desperate haste to succeed, and in such desperate enterprises? If a man does not keep pace with his companions, perhaps it is because he hears a different drummer. Let him step to the music which he hears, however measured or far away.

Let those of us who are committed to training teachers for ghetto communities and retraining present staffs who teach the disadvantaged be given the opportunity to march to a different drummer whom now we hear in ever increasing crescendo.

# PART THREE

---

*Appendices*

---

# APPENDIX A

---

# *The Questionnaire*

---

TO:   Participants in In-service Projects under ESEA Titles I and
      III, and NDEA Title XI

FROM: James C. Stone, Director
      California Project
      National NDEA Institute for Advanced Study in Teaching
      Disadvantaged Youth

I am writing to ask if you would help in a project to improve the education of teachers of disadvantaged students. With the special needs
of educationally deprived children becoming increasingly understood,
the need for teachers who can work effectively with these children is
critical.

The NDEA Institute which I represent is sponsoring studies in four
states—one of them California—to evaluate the teacher-education
components (only) of projects funded under ESEA Titles I and III,
and NDEA Title XI. Better projects should result from this evaluation.
The first step in this undertaking must be to consult with participants,
like you, who have taken part in projects related to the teaching of the
disadvantaged. Having participated in such a project, you are in a
position to offer good advice for future efforts. I am hoping, therefore,
that you will be willing to answer the questionnaire and complete the
card sort which are enclosed. Following your return of the materials,
our staff will wish to talk personally with some of the participants in
order to develop the lines of thought initiated by the questionnaire and
card sort. Approval to circulate these materials has been given us by
appropriate persons associated with the project.

GENERAL INSTRUCTIONS

I realize that the term *disadvantaged* is difficult to define precisely.
You will have your own definition of it, based upon your experience
with disadvantaged students and your participation in a project designed to help you in your work. The term *disadvantaged student* is
defined by Title I of the ESEA as a student who comes to school from
a family whose income is below $3,000 per year. It is used first of all,
therefore, to designate socioeconomic status and refers to the condition
of being economically impoverished. Inevitably, however, it will also

**212**

designate some members of racial or ethnic minority groups who comprise the largest proportion of persons in this socioeconomic category and will refer, in such cases, to the condition of being culturally different. In any case, as used in these materials, the term *disadvantaged student* ultimately designates the consequence of both socioeconomic deprivation and cultural discrimination and refers primarily to the condition of being *educationally disadvantaged*. I hope you will be guided by this sense of the term as you respond to the enclosed questionnaire and card sort.

As I have mentioned earlier, our study seeks to evaluate *only the inservice teacher-training component* of what may have been a much more comprehensive program overall. It may be difficult for you to isolate your participation in that component from your participation in the total program and to evaluate the former experience independently, but I ask you to try.

Our study has no interest in identifying individuals. Therefore, your name does not appear anywhere in these materials. A number appears on the questionnaire, but it will be used only for the purpose of classifying responses according to project. Your anonymity will be strictly maintained. Do not, therefore, identify yourself by name on any of the enclosed materials.

INSTRUCTIONS FOR ANSWERING THE QUESTIONNAIRE

Please turn now to the attached sheet headed QUESTIONNAIRE. At the top of it you will find a brief description of the particular project which we are asking you to evaluate.

Each question is followed by a choice of responses ranged in order along a line. Please indicate the response which best answers the question for you by making a check mark at the appropriate point on the line. For example, if you have taught school for eight years, you would indicate your answer to question 2 thus:

<pre>
     0       5      10     15     20+
     |       |     ∨|      |      |
     |_____|_____|_____|_____|
</pre>

*Please answer the questionnaire now and, when you have finished, return to this page for instructions about the card sort.*

INSTRUCTIONS FOR COMPLETING THE CARD SORT

Enclosed is a packet of 70 cards, each containing a statement with which you may or may not agree as a result of your participation in the in-service training project identified at the top of the questionnaire. Also enclosed are seven envelopes, labeled as follows:

> 7—I *strongly agree* with these statements.
> 6—I *agree* with these statements.
> 5—I *barely agree* with these statements.
> 4—I *feel neutral* about these statements.
> 3—I *barely disagree* with these statements.
> 2—I *disagree* with these statements.
> 1—I *strongly disagree* with these statements.

You are asked to select the *ten cards for each envelope* which best fit the label on it. If the teacher-training component of the project did not include some feature which you are asked to evaluate, place that card in Envelope X, labeled "I am unable to respond to these statements because of the nature of the project." If you put any cards in Envelope X, you obviously will be unable to place ten cards in each envelope, but you are still asked to keep the number of cards in each envelope as nearly equal as possible. For example, if you put four cards in Envelope X, then four envelopes will have only nine cards, the other three having ten.

To accomplish the final result of your sorting, proceed as follows:

1. Go through all of the cards, arranging them first in *three* piles: one for statements with which you agree, another for those about which you feel neutral, and a third for those with which you disagree. (If you cannot respond to a statement place that card in Envelope X.) You may put any number of cards in each of the three piles in this first sorting, but you will find that subsequent sorting goes more efficiently if you put roughly the same number in each.

2. From the first pile, select the ten cards with which you *strongly agree* and place them on top of Envelope 7. Do not put them inside the envelope yet, because you may wish to shift some later.

3. Next, select the ten cards with which you *agree* and place them on Envelope 6.

4. Now it is best to start at the other end. From the third of

the original three piles, select the ten cards with which you *strongly disagree* and place them on Envelope 1.

5. Next, select the ten cards with which you *disagree* and place them on Envelope 2.

6. You will now have thirty or fewer cards left, depending on how many you put into Envelope X. Sort these remaining cards into three piles, depending on whether you *barely agree, feel neutral,* or *barely disagree,* and put each pile on its corresponding envelope.

7. Go through each pile a final time, changing cards from pile to pile if you like, but making sure that, when you have finished, each pile has the same number of cards in it (or within one of the same number, if it is impossible to equalize them exactly). Then put each pile of cards into its corresponding envelope.

*IMPORTANT:* You may find it difficult to force the same number of cards into each pile and have the feeling, when you are finished, that some of the cards are mismatched with the labels on the envelopes into which you have put them. Nevertheless, it is essential to our treatment of the data that *you follow these instructions exactly,* despite the reluctance you may feel.

Happy sorting! When you have completed the card sort, please return to this sheet for final instructions for returning these materials.

INSTRUCTIONS FOR RETURNING THE MATERIALS

When you have answered the questionnaire and completed the card sort, check through one final time to be sure you have all of the completed materials (one filled-out questionnaire and eight envelopes containing cards) and place them all in the enclosed stamped, self-addressed envelope and mail them.

Thank you for your time and very great help!

## QUESTIONNAIRE

Institution:
Project:
Period of project:
Project no.:

1. What is your present position?

2. For how many years have you taught or otherwise worked in schools?

3. At what grade level(s) are the students with whom you are presently working?

4. In what setting is your school located?

5. What per cent of your students do you estimate to be disadvantaged?

   What per cent of your students come from each of the following groups?

   6. White

   7. Oriental

   8. American Indian

   9. Mexican, or other Spanish-speaking

   10. Negro

11. What overall rating would you give the in-service project named at the top of this page?

12. In how many other projects related to disadvantaged youth have you participated?

13. What do you consider the socioeconomic status of your own family to have been during your childhood?

14. What is your own ethnic background? (If you prefer not to answer, leave the response line unchecked.)

    How do you feel about the following statements?

    15. No expense should be spared to provide special help for disadvantaged students in the schools.

    16. The best thing schools could do for disadvantaged children would be to put them in smaller-sized classes.

    17. Children should be bused outside their own neighborhoods if that is the most practical way to attain racial integration in a given school district.

    18. Disadvantaged children should begin school at an earlier age than they now do.

    19. The age at which students are legally permitted to leave school should be lowered.

    20. A disadvantaged student learns best from a person who has a similar cultural background.

21. Unstructured interaction groups should become more a part of teacher education programs, even at the expense of some traditional topics.

22. Teachers-in-training can learn more in local schools than they can in colleges or universities.

Please turn back to page 2 of the original instruction sheets for the card-sort directions.

# Appendix B

# Q-Sort Items

1. This project increased my knowledge of the subcultures of disadvantaged groups.
2. I learned very little from the project about instructional materials and curricula for disadvantaged students.
3. I learned very little from the project about the effects that a deprived home environment has on a student's school life.
4. This project convinced me that disadvantaged students have more learning ability than I had given them credit for.
5. This project showed me that disadvantaged students are actually *superior* to other students in certain ways.
6. This project increased my effectiveness with *all* students, not just the disadvantaged.
7. I have had little success in using what I learned in the project to influence the attitudes of my colleagues regarding disadvantaged children.
8. I am no more self-confident in the classroom (or office) than I was when the project started.
9. I like disadvantaged students no better than I did when the project began.
10. I am more supportive of disadvantaged students as a result of this project.
11. This project led me to collect more information about the backgrounds of my own disadvantaged students.
12. This project has led me to give disadvantaged students more individual attention.
13. I have no better relations with the parents of my disadvantaged students than I had before the project started.
14. As a result of this project, I am more of a leader in my school in improving the education of disadvantaged students.
15. I teach (or counsel, and so on) about the same way I did before the project started.
16. My disadvantaged students have greater knowledge of their own ethnic backgrounds as a result of this project.
17. My disadvantaged students have higher educational aspirations as a result of this project.
18. My disadvantaged students are as disinterested in school as they were when the project started.

19. My disadvantaged students are as hostile toward teachers as they were when the project started.
20. My disadvantaged students are as unsure of themselves as they were when the project began.
21. My disadvantaged students like me better as a result of this project.
22. My disadvantaged students get along better with their classmates because of the project.
23. My disadvantaged students read better because of this project.
24. My disadvantaged students are absent from school as often as they were before the project began.
25. My disadvantaged students cause as many discipline problems as they did before the project started.
26. My disadvantaged students participate more in school activities as a result of this project.
27. Overall, my disadvantaged students are learning no more than they would have if this project had not existed.
28. This project has led my school to collect more comprehensive data on our disadvantaged students.
29. Project participants have gotten parents of disadvantaged students to participate more in our school's activities.
30. Project participants have had little effect on the attitudes of other teachers and administrators concerning disadvantaged youth.
31. This project has had little effect on the (other) in-service programs at my school.
32. Project participants have been influential in getting special instructional materials for disadvantaged students introduced in my school.
33. Project participants have had little success in my school in achieving a curriculum which would be more appropriate for disadvantaged students.
34. Project participants induced my school to establish, or enlarge, a cultural enrichment program for disadvantaged students.
35. This project has raised the morale of our whole school staff.
36. The lectures in the project were valuable to me.
37. The panel discussions in the project were of little value to me.

38. The discussion following formal presentations was valuable to me.
39. The films, records, tapes, and similar materials were valuable to me.
40. The reading that I did as part of the project was of little value to me.
41. The replaying of activities through video or audio tapes was of little value to me.
42. The role-playing we did in the project was valuable to me.
43. The encounter group (sensitivity training, T-group, and so on) was valuable to me.
44. Doing the assigned written work was of little value to me.
45. The actual teaching or tutoring that I did as part of the project was valuable to me.
46. Observing the teaching of disadvantaged students was of little value to me.
47. Those activities in which all the participants were together in one large group were of little value to me.
48. Working together in small groups was valuable to me.
49. Meeting agency workers, community leaders, or other non-school personnel who work with the disadvantaged was valuable.
50. Visiting the homes, neighborhoods, or communities of disadvantaged students was valuable to me.
51. Working by myself was of little value to me.
52. Visiting other projects similar to ours was of little value to me.
53. Consultants who worked with teachers individually or in small groups were of little help.
54. The material on the history and characteristics of minority-group peoples was valuable.
55. The material on the learning problems of disadvantaged children was of little value.
56. The material on teaching English as a second language was valuable.
57. The material on reading improvement was of little value.
58. Being introduced to special instructional materials for disadvantaged children was valuable.

59. The material on curricula appropriate for disadvantaged children was of little value.
60. The material on teaching methods appropriate for disadvantaged children was valuable.
61. The material on how to teach specific subjects to disadvantaged students was of little value.
62. The participants were involved in the planning of this project.
63. Participants made few of the decisions about the day-to-day operations of the project.
64. Too often in the project, I was just listening or watching, rather than actively *doing* something.
65. Persons who were members of minority groups themselves offered valuable advice on teaching disadvantaged children.
66. I got valuable advice from the leaders and others who spoke to the project group.
67. I got valuable advice from my fellow participants in the project.
68. Activities that hadn't been planned ahead of time turned out to be of little value.
69. Those sessions when participants were absolutely frank, and even angry, were valuable.
70. The project was too middle-class in its philosophy and operation.

# APPENDIX C

---

# *Summaries of ESEA Title I Programs*

---

# ALAMEDA CITY UNIFIED SCHOOL DISTRICT
## (Alameda County)

Average per pupil expenditure in fiscal year 1966: $563.83
Number of schools: 16 (K–12)
Total enrollment in fall 1966: 12,254
Number of pupils from low-income families: 1,610 (12%)

ESEA TITLE I PROJECT, 1966–67

Title: Program to Meet the Special Needs of Educationally Deprived Children from Low-Income Families
Amount of federal funds: $373,484
Number of target schools: 8
  6 Elementary
  1 Junior High
  1 Senior High
Number of target pupils: 1,610
   90 Prekindergarten
 870 Elementary
 300 Junior High
 350 Senior High
Percentage of minority-group pupils:
  6.5% Mexican-American
  4.4% Negro
  3.1% Oriental
  1.0% Others
Special instructional activities:
  Reading and Language Arts
  Preschool
  Kindergarten
  Physical Education
Special supplementary services:
  Reading laboratory and clinical services
  Library facilities and services
  Counseling and guidance
  Nursing and health care
  Work experience

Teacher aides
In-service training

IN-SERVICE PROGRAM

Amount of federal funds: $9,000
Number of participants: 25
Objectives:

To orient staff members of target schools to the objectives and activities of the ESEA Title I project.

To help school personnel gain increased understanding of the characteristics, cultural background, educational needs, and special learning problems of disadvantaged children.

To assist teachers in improving their knowledge of instructional programs, procedures, techniques, media, and materials that are especially effective in meeting the educational needs of disadvantaged children.

To improve the ability of teachers and other school personnel to develop personal relationships characterized by humane understanding of children from different cultural and racial backgrounds.

Activities:

A two-and-one-half-day orientation session to acquaint school personnel from target schools with the organization and operation of the ESEA Title I project.

A series of training meetings held in the individual target schools, at which school personnel viewed video tape-recorded discussions presented by resource persons.

Informal individual and small-group consultations conducted by specialists in curriculum, instruction, and pupil personnel services for teachers and parents.

Released-time attendance of teachers at counseling sessions conducted by consultant psychologists and psychiatrists.

Periodic case conferences, in which guidance counselors discussed the problems of individual children with their teachers for training purposes.

Parent-teacher conferences and teacher attendance at parent-group meetings, in which teachers were assisted by guidance counselors for training purposes.

IN-SERVICE TRAINING ACTIVITY

The in-service teacher training component of Alameda City Unified School District's ESEA Title I project was carried out in close conjunction with the Improvement of Instruction phase of the project. The California Project asked the thirty-four teachers, teachers aides, and other school personnel who participated in the in-service program to evaluate the several activities which comprised it.

The in-service teacher training program began in the fall of 1966 with a two-and-one-half-day orientation meeting for all staff of the ESEA Title I project's target schools. This meeting was held to acquaint the staff with the philosophy, objectives, organization, programs, and procedures of the project. Project staff and guest speakers from Bay Area teacher-education institutions presented lectures and conducted discussions of a wide variety of background matters, including social and economic environments from which disadvantaged children come to school; techniques and proven ways of providing effective preschool classes and activity; audiovisual and other approaches to special communication problems of disadvantaged children; techniques of classwork and individual instruction planning to permit accommodation of children with specific learning difficulties within normal school operations; and development of personal relationships and human understanding with children from cultural and racial backgrounds different from those of staff members.

Following the orientation meeting, an extensive program of in-service training sessions was conducted for classroom teachers and other school personnel in all target schools, using short discussions by resources persons presented on video tapes. The staff of each target school was furnished with a catalogue of available video tape-recorded materials created by Academic Resources of Berkeley especially for the ESEA Title I project. Staff members then selected from the catalogue those materials which they thought would serve their purposes and ordered them through the project office or the school principal. The video tape-recorded materials were accompanied by all the television equipment necessary for presenting them and a technician to operate this equipment, and also by a trained discussion leader who, using the discussion guide especially prepared for each program, kept the ensuing discussion focused on ways to apply the resource information directly to classroom situations. The format for each of these training sessions, conducted in the target schools, was a short television presentation to a small group of the school's staff of a talk or demonstration by the resource person, followed by a group discussion of his subject led by the trained discussion leader (or, in some cases, by one of the teachers in the group using the discussion guide). A total of sixty-two such in-service training sessions were held in the target schools during the year, covering the full range of topics related to teaching disadvantaged children and youth.

In addition to the in-service training sessions, the project provided specialists in curriculum, instruction, and pupil personnel services who conducted informal individual and small-group consultations and conferences with teachers in the target schools and with parents of disadvantaged pupils. These consultations and conferences were concerned with such matters as remedial reading, speech correction, vocational education, physical education, teaching English to non-English speaking pupils, identification of specific learning difficulties, library operations and the use of library facilities and services in the classroom instructional program, and parent orientation to school activities.

At the conclusion of the fall orientation meeting, the participants were asked to indicate their reactions and evaluations by responding to a questionnaire. At each in-service training session, the discussion leader maintained a tally of comments and discussion in the following categories:

| | |
|---|---|
| Learned something new | Seemed to gain motivation |
| Felt information was valuable | Wanted further programs |
| Suggested classroom uses | Suggested needed topics |
| Expressed confusion | Expressed unsatisfactory atti- |
| Disagreed with resource per- | tude or motivation |
| son | |

(The last is a general category for those opposing federal funds, lacking interest in teaching, critical of attempts to help disadvantaged students, and similar "undesirable factors.") No attempt was made at a formal evaluation of the informal consultations and conferences conducted by specialists with teachers and parents.

The distinguishing feature of the district's in-service program was the use of video tape-recorded presentations by resource persons. These presentations, conducted in the format of guided small-group discussion meetings, were an economical and efficient means of providing a wide range of useful information and expert opinion for a large number of teachers and other school personnel in order to increase their knowledge of the personal characteristics, cultural and social background, educational needs, and special learning problems of disadvantaged students and to guide their efforts to apply that knowledge in their efforts to find solutions to the problems they encountered in teaching these students. Judging from the carefully detailed evaluations of these meetings, they also proved an effective means for achieving at least two of the in-service program's primary objectives.

## ANAHEIM UNION HIGH SCHOOL DISTRICT
### (Orange County)

Average per pupil expenditure in fiscal year 1966: $576.69
Number of schools: 20 (7–12)
Total enrollment in fall 1966: 29,656
Number of pupils from low-income families: 2,837 (9.1%)

ESEA TITLE I PROJECT, 1966–67

Title: A Project to Enhance the Achievement, Abilities and Attitudes of Disadvantaged Youth
Amount of federal funds: $114,750
Number of target schools: 9
   6 Junior High
   3 Senior High
Number of target pupils: 13,148
   8,045 Junior High
   5,103 Senior High
Percentage of minority-group pupils:
   6%    Mexican-American
   .01% Negro
   .9%   Oriental
   .38% Others

Special instructional activities:
Reading and Language Arts
Communicative Skills
Family Life and Sex Education
Science
Special supplementary services:
In-service teacher training (Family Life and Sex Education)
Curriculum and materials development (Science)

IN-SERVICE PROGRAM

Amount of federal funds: $10,400
Number of participants: 62
Objectives:
To help teachers achieve increased awareness and understanding of their own and others' interaction in a group.

To help them achieve increased awareness of the possible resolutions for problems presented in the Family Life and Sex Education classes.

To assist them in learning the functions of various resources and the procedures and methods of effective referral.

To help them gain increased understanding of the methods that will encourage parents to participate in the education of their children in the area of family life and sex education.

To help teachers gain increased knowledge of recent developments and research in the field of family life and sex education.
Activities:
An orientation, planning, and organization meeting of two days for director and new teachers of Family Life and Sex Education classes.

An intensive four-day summer workshop on Family Life and Sex Education for all teachers, conducted in a conference facility arranged with live-in facilities away from the district.

IN-SERVICE TRAINING ACTIVITY

The in-service training component of Anaheim Union High School District's ESEA Title I project was carried out in conjunction with the Family Life and Sex Education program of that project. The

California Project asked the sixty-two participants in this in-service activity to evaluate their experience.

The goal of the Family Life and Sex Education Program was to educate disadvantaged students to become effective members in the family in which they are now living and to establish competent and effective families of their own in the future. The in-service training for teachers of the Family Life and Sex Education classes began with a two-day meeting, on August 24 and 25, 1967, between the workshop director and nine new teachers in the program. At this meeting, the curriculum guide and other materials distributed the previous June were reviewed and discussed, as were the philosophy of the program and the procedures and techniques by which it was to be conducted.

Following the two-day meeting for new teachers, a four-day intensive workshop was conducted for all teachers of Family Life and Sex Education classes on August 28 through 31, 1967. It was felt that the objectives of this workshop would be met more efficiently and effectively by conducting the workshop in a conference facility that provides for living-in arrangements. Accordingly, the workshop was held at a motel some distance from the local area. The workshop director, assisted by trained leaders of small-group discussions, met with the participants in small groups of approximately ten persons each. The discussions were conducted in just the way the workshop staff hoped the teachers themselves would conduct their classes; that is, the experts unobtrusively facilitated relaxed, open, and frank discussion of all matters relating to family life and sex education, and to the means by which that subject might best be presented in a school classroom setting as a learning experience for disadvantaged students.

Participants in the workshop were paid a uniform salary of $50 each for the four days, approximately ten hours of discussion per day. In addition, their travel and subsistence expenses were paid from funds allocated for the Family Life and Sex Education Program of the project.

The workshop director conducted a subjective evaluation at the conclusion of the workshop, inviting participants to comment upon their experience and to make recommendations for further training sessions. During the 1967–68 school year, he conducted a follow-up evaluation of the workshop by visiting each of the target schools and observing the teachers conducting their Family Life and Sex Education Classes. The results of these evaluative efforts seem to indicate that the task-oriented approach to sensitivity training through small-group discussion and interaction was an appropriate and effective means for increasing the participants' awareness and understanding of their own and each other's attitudes and interactions, and also of the possible resources and solutions they might use to solve the problems they confronted in teaching Family Life and Sex Education classes for disadvantaged youth.

## MODESTO CITY SCHOOL DISTRICTS (Stanislaus County)

Average per pupil expenditure in fiscal year 1966: $439.81 (K–8), $688.25 (9–12)
Number of schools: 27 (K–12)
Total enrollment in fall 1966: 19,378
Number of pupils from low-income families: 3,635 (37%)

ESEA TITLE I PROJECT, 1966–67

Title: A Comprehensive Program of Compensatory Education
Amount of federal funds: $584,379
Number of target schools: 9
  7 Elementary
  1 Intermediate
  1 Senior High
Number of target pupils: 6,753
  495 Kindergarten
  2,989 Elementary
  1,692 Junior High
  1,577 Senior High
Percentage of minority-group pupils:
  18.0% Mexican-American
  5.0% Negro
  0.5% Oriental
  0.3% American Indian
Special instructional activities:
  Remedial Reading
  Physical Education
  Cultural Enrichment (study trips)

Outdoor Education
Instrumental Music
Kindergarten
Saturday Recreation and Crafts
Summer School
Special supplementary services:
Counseling and guidance
Psychometric testing
School nursing care
Home visitations
Parent meetings
Financial assistance to needy pupils
Curriculum and materials development
Teacher aides
In-service teacher training

IN-SERVICE PROGRAM

Amount of federal funds: $3,067
Number of participants: 155
Objectives:
To encourage professional staff improvement in working with disadvantaged students.

To assist teachers in understanding educational hardships and learning problems of disadvantaged students.

To assist teachers in making the best use of teacher aides, audiovisual equipment, and instructional materials in the classroom.
Activities:
Summer school course on the disadvantaged student at Stanislaus State College.

One-day, district-wide conference on the disadvantaged student in Pleasanton.

Workshops on the use of audiovisual equipment.

District-wide grade-level meetings.

Attendance at regional and state conferences.

Visits, on released time, to observe demonstrations of instructional programs, units, procedures, techniques, media, materials, and equipment in other schools and school districts.

Consultations with curriculum specialists and social workers from outside the district.

Ten-week evening course, three-day orientation conference, and six workshops with master teachers, conducted by the district in cooperation with Modesto Junior College, for teacher aides.

IN-SERVICE TRAINING ACTIVITY

The stated intent of the Modesto City Schools and High School District was to assist the teachers in its target schools in gaining a better understanding of the educational hardships and learning problems of disadvantaged children and a better appreciation of the best methods of providing realistic learning situations for them. The in-service teacher training component of its ESEA Title I project therefore attempted to be as comprehensive as the project itself: it included a wide variety of activities in which all or some of the approximately 170 classroom teachers, eighty-six teacher aides, and other personnel in its target schools were expected to participate. The California Project asked all of the classroom teachers and other school personnel who participated in any of these activities to evaluate their experience.

The training activities which comprised the in-service program included:

A summer session course on Education of the Disadvantaged at Stanislaus State College, from July 19–28, 1966, attended by twenty-six teachers.

A one-day conference on the disadvantaged sponsored by the district and held in August in Pleasanton, attended by 110 elementary grade teachers.

A series of workshops on the use of audiovisual equipment—three on television and three on the overhead projector—conducted by a representative of the Stanislaus County Schools Office.

A series of district-wide meetings of teachers working at the various grade levels in the target elementary schools.

A lecture on the needs of the disadvantaged child by a professor from the School of Criminology, University of California at Berkeley, attended by the faculty of Modesto High School.

A series of regional and state conferences, including the California Reading Association State Conference in Fresno, attended by fifteen teachers; the International Reading Conference in San

Francisco, attended by four teachers; the Mathematics Curriculum Conference at the University of California at Davis; the University of the Pacific Music Conference at Stockton; the Conference of the California Association of Psychologists and Psychometrists at San Francisco; and the Early Childhood Education Conference in Berkeley.

Visits to observe demonstrations in the city schools of Berkeley, Stockton, and Tulare; to observe facilities and equipment at Granada School in Corte Madera, William Wilson School in Santa Clara, the School for Cerebral Palsied Children in San Francisco, the Livermore Schools Library in Livermore, the San Jose Schools Library in San Jose, the Random House Display at Keyes, the Yuba County Reading-Learning Center in Olivehurst, and the Stanford Planning Laboratory at Palo Alto; and to observe activities at Project Discovery in Daly City and the Outdoor Education Workshop in Columbia.

Consultations in the target schools with curriculum specialists from nearby colleges, universities, and social agencies, particularly regarding instructional programs, procedures, media, and materials in reading, science, and art.

Each participant in any of these in-service training activities was asked to prepare a résumé of his experience and submit it to the project director and also to report briefly on his experience to the faculty of his school.

Future plans for the development of the in-service component of the District's ESEA Title I project include a two-day sensitivity training session at Asilomar in August, arranged for the district by SRA to provide an all-expenses-paid opportunity for about sixty persons to participate in T-group activities with ten to twelve persons in each group. If this experiment with sensitivity training is successful, the district plans to offer further opportunities for such training in the future to teachers in its target schools. From these plans it would appear that the district intends to expand an already complex and comprehensive in-service program to include sensitivity training, in order to achieve a further objective which it regards essential to the attainment of all the others; that is, to bring about fundamental changes in teachers' attitudes toward problems of teaching disadvantaged youth.

## MT. DIABLO UNIFIED SCHOOL DISTRICT
(Contra Costa County)

Average per pupil expenditure in fiscal year 1966: $514.06
Number of schools: 54 (K–12)
Total enrollment in fall 1966: 46,000
Number of pupils from low-income families: 1,642 (3.3%)

ESEA TITLE I PROJECT, 1966–67

Title: Program for Compensatory Education
Amount of federal funds: $326,230
Number of target schools: 6
  4 Elementary
  1 Intermediate
  1 Senior High
Number of target pupils: 6,528
  279 Kindergarten
  883 Elementary
  219 Junior High
  147 Senior High
Percentage of minority-group pupils:
  16.0% Mexican-American
  13.0% Negro
   0.3% Oriental
   0.5% American Indian
Special instructional activities:
  Remedial Reading
  Kindergarten
  Expanded Music Program
  Extended Day Study and Recreation
  Cultural Enrichment (study trips)
  Outdoor Education
Special supplementary services:
  Counseling and guidance
  Instructional materials centers
  In-service teaching training

Amount of federal funds: $5,000.00

Number of participants: 108

Objectives:

To provide teachers and administrators in the target area with a better understanding of the community served by the schools.

To bring together members of the community and the schools in a workshop setting in order to establish the basis for community involvement in the total compensatory education program.

To provide teachers and administrators with a broad view of compensatory education, its purposes and methods.

To develop attitudes that will ensure success for the compensatory education program.

Activity:

Summer Workshop in Compensatory Education.

IN-SERVICE TRAINING ACTIVITY

The in-service teacher training component of the Mt. Diablo Unified School District's ESEA Title I project consisted of a summer workshop in compensatory education, in 1966. The California Project asked the 108 participants in the workshop to evaluate their experience.

The summer workshop was held in the project's target high school, Pacifica High School in Pittsburg, for a total of fourteen days beginning on Monday, June 20, and ending on Friday, July 8, 1966. The workshop staff, which was under the direction of the project coordinator, included guest lecturers and panelists, specialists, and consultants from colleges, universities, and other educational and social institutions outside the district, as well as curriculum coordinators, pupil personnel specialists, and demonstration teachers employed by the district. The 108 participants in the workshop included teachers, administrators, counselors, media specialists, and other school personnel. The daily schedule of activities began at 8:30 A.M. and ended at 3:00 P.M. Participants were paid at the rate of $5.50 per hour.

The summer workshop's instructional program emphasized three areas of study: (1) the local community: socioeconomic levels, educational and cultural backgrounds, attitudes toward school and education, social and civic agencies, churches, industries, and other institutions; (2) human relationships: sensitivities, processes, group relations, and intercultural relationships; (3) instructional planning: working as a team, working with auxiliary services, using additional resources (librarians, aides), using new instructional materials, planning for specific procedures and techniques of instruction, diagnosing needs and individualizing instruction. Within these three areas, the program focused on such matters as the nature of the disadvantaged child, his family and his home, his experiences, his needs, and the services available to him; parent-teacher and home-school relationships and the problems of communication arising within these relationships, the value of cooperation and collaboration within these relationships for working out solutions to the school and learning problems of disadvantaged pupils; contemporary teaching and learning theories related to the disadvantaged student; existing and new instructional programs, procedures, techniques, media, and materials appropriate for the teaching of disadvantaged students; and effective cooperative arrangements between schools and community agencies also concerned about the education of disadvantaged youth.

The summer workshop's program was carried out by means of a variety of activities, including lectures and panel discussions presented by guest speakers, teachers, parents, and students; demonstrations of lesson units and instructional methods, equipment, and materials; audiovisual materials production sessions; films, filmstrips, video tapes, and slides; home visitations and parent conferences; field trips and tours. The effectiveness of these various activities as means of achieving the summer workshop's objectives was evaluated by asking the participants to complete a questionnaire and by observing the long-range outcomes—changes in teachers' and pupils' attitudes and behavior and developments in the instructional programs and procedures of the target schools.

Plans for a teachers institute in August, 1967, whose program was to have been similar to though not as extensive as that of the summer workshop in 1966, were not carried through because of the decrease in the district's entitlement to funds in the 1966–67 school year.

The Mt. Diablo Unified School District's ESEA Title I project concentrated its efforts upon a relatively small target area—a small number of target schools (only six of the district's fifty-six) and a small group of disadvantaged pupils (only about 1,300 of the district's 46,000). The in-service teacher-training component of this project was also a concentrated effort—an intensive and extensive program comprising a wide variety of activities all carried out in the fourteen daily sessions of a summer workshop. Because the district's project was not fully approved and funded until mid-March, 1966, most of its proposed activities were not operational in the 1965–66 school year. Because the district's entitlement funds were cut back for the 1966–67 school year, the in-service teacher-training component of the project was not carried out as planned. The district's problem, therefore, has been to plan, organize, conduct, and evaluate its compensatory education project and the in-service component thereof as a coherent and continuously sustained effort to enhance the educational opportunities of disadvantaged youth living in its target area.

## OAKLAND UNIFIED SCHOOL DISTRICT
### (Alameda County)

Average per pupil expenditure in fiscal year 1966: $587.53
Number of schools: 88 (K–12)
Total enrollment in fall 1966: 63,191
Number of pupils from low-income families: 13,686 (19.6%)

ESEA TITLE I PROJECT, 1966–67

Title: ESEA Program of Compensatory Education
Amount of federal funds: $2,384,685
Number of target schools: 15
   11 Elementary
   3 Junior High
   1 Senior High
Number of target pupils: 12,198
   1,211 Kindergarten
   7,233 Elementary
   2,840 Junior High
   914 Senior High

Percentage of minority-group pupils:
  6.30% Mexican-American
  88.90% Negro
  0.54% Oriental
  0.47% American Indian
Special instructional activities :
  Cultural Enrichment
  English Language Arts
  Reading, Remedial Reading and Language Instruction
  Kindergarten
  Teacher Aides
Special supplementary services:
  Integration component
  Health services
  Psychological services
  Guidance and attendance
  Guidance and counseling
  Library services
  Curriculum materials center
  In-service teacher training

IN-SERVICE PROGRAM

Amount of federal funds: $25,562
Number of participants: 1,045
Objectives:
  To develop new aspects in curriculum that give promise of helping disadvantaged children improve their academic attainment.

  To develop curriculum and instructional materials that assist disadvantaged children to improve their attitudes toward school.

  To develop techniques that will foster the team approach toward meeting the special educational needs of disadvantaged children.

  To assist teachers to improve their expertise in small-group instruction.

  To assist professional and nonprofessional personnel and community residents to develop improved intergroup relationships.

  To institute human relations programs that will develop the appreciations and understandings essential to relating significantly with disadvantaged children.

Activities:

A district-wide meeting to orient the professional staffs of target schools to the goals of the project, followed by on-site meetings conducted by target school principals to prepare them for project activities in their schools.

A Summer Workshop on Teaching Disadvantaged Children.

A Summer Workshop on Human Relations, sponsored by the College of the Holy Names, in connection with the district's summer workshop.

Numerous district-wide and target school-sponsored workshops, institutes, and training meetings for the development of human relations, intercultural and intergroup relations, and curriculum materials.

Visits, on released time, to observe instructional programs, procedures, techniques, media, materials, and equipment in use in other classrooms, schools, community agencies, and school districts.

Consultations with curriculum specialists and media specialists.

District-wide grade-level and department meetings of teachers and administrators.

Teachers on special assignment to coordinate in-service training activities, and teaching assistants in reading and language development.

IN-SERVICE TRAINING ACTIVITY

Prominent among the many teacher-training activities which comprised the in-service component of Oakland Unified School District's ESEA Title I project was the Oakland Teachers' Summer Workshop on teaching disadvantaged children. The California Project asked ninety-six persons who participated in this workshop to evaluate their experience.

The Oakland Teachers' Summer Workshop was held at Hamilton Junior High School during the four weeks from June 26 through July 21, 1967. The workshop was directed by the ESEA Title I project coordinator and was planned and staffed, for the most part, by district personnel from the Divisions of Urban Educational Services, Elementary Education, Secondary Education, and Administrative and Special Services. The staff included seven curriculum specialists and consultants from nearby state colleges and universities, nine instructional specialists in reading, creative writing, mathematics and other subjects chosen from the district's teaching staff, a consultant in intergroup relations, a specialist in instructional media, two audiovisual specialists, a librarian, and a representative from the Neighborhood Youth Corps. It also included a large number of guest speakers from all over the state and nation, and also several from local racial and ethnic minority-group communities. Approximately 200 teachers, teacher aides, administrators, and other school personnel participated in the various phases of the workshop. Facilities available to workshop participants included an audiovisual laboratory, a materials duplication and reproduction laboratory, the school library, and a curriculum and materials center. The total budget for the workshop was approximately $63,100.

The principal concern of the workshop's program was the development of curricula and of instructional units, procedures, techniques, media, and materials especially appropriate for teaching disadvantaged students. The underlying theme of the workshop was the necessity for effective human relations to the solution of problems involved in the teaching of disadvantaged children. Most of the activities of the workshop were organized by grade level—elementary and secondary. Courses for elementary teachers placed particular emphasis on the relation of instructional units to the nature and needs of disadvantaged pupils and on human relations involved in the teaching of disadvantaged children. Among these courses were: remedial reading techniques; working with children unable to read the textbook; oral language development and techniques; motivation for creative writing; using newer media of instruction; developing lessons with the tape recorder; individualized reading; and mathematics. Some of these courses ran for one week, some, for two. Courses of study for secondary teachers were usually organized around individual curriculum projects: secondary reading; human relations; guidance and counseling; English as a second language; mathematics and computers; foreign language instruction; family life education; and audiovisual work. Participants met in small classes to pursue these courses of study for two periods a day, five mornings per week, from 8:30 A.M. to 10:00 A.M. and from 11:00 A.M. to 12:30 P.M. The period from 10:00 to 11:00 A.M. was used for a coffee break and the Special Events Session.

Both elementary and secondary curriculum development teams pursued the following objectives: to provide for a variety of student activities stressing oral and written language and relating school experiences to life and to the world of work; to locate and develop instructional materials on ethnic minorities suitable for teaching children of various ages and ability levels; to further incorporate into the conventional school curriculum instructional units on the contributions of ethnic minorities; and to relate the goals of compensatory education to the comprehensive educational plans of the district. The elementary curriculum development teams worked at developing courses of study for fourth and fifth grade social sciences. The fourth grade course was entitled "California-Japan-Nigeria: A Comparative Study"; the fifth grade course, "Our Country and Its Expanding Frontiers." The secondary curriculum development teams prepared curriculum materials for junior and senior high school grade levels, emphasizing the contributions of ethnic minorities, particularly Negroes, to the history and culture of the United States. Also, a vocational guidance team was formed to provide a three-year program to help junior high school students develop positive attitudes toward work and society and to explore vocational interests and aptitudes.

Included within the framework of the workshop was a graduate seminar and television lecture course on Education and Human Relations. This course, a special two-unit class offered through the College of the Holy Names, was open to all summer school and Summer Workshop personnel in the district. The plans for this course were developed by the district's human relations staff in cooperation with consultants and specialists. The basis for the course was an Educational Television In-Service Course created by the Massachusetts Department of Education in collaboration with the Lincoln Filene Center for Citizenship and Public Affairs at Tufts University. The course was designed to help each participant define human and intergroup relations; develop more factual knowledge and understanding of the various ethnic groups existing in American society; and help participants translate what they have learned into more positive attitudes, techniques, and methods to use in their work with disadvantaged students. In addition to the films and small-group discussion sessions in each of the twenty two-hour sessions, the forty participants in this course heard guest speakers express various viewpoints on issues raised in discussion.

The Special Events Sessions of the workshop was a program that presented individual speakers, panel discussions, and demonstration teams emphasizing human relations and language learning in the education of disadvantaged children and youth. This program also provided opportunities for workshop participants to visit and observe sessions of the Roosevelt Junior High School Demonsration Program, which emphasized English as a second language, and the Durant Elementary School Internship Program's In-Service Institute, in which teaching interns with a primary interest in teaching in disadvantaged schools were being trained. Additionally, several participants attended a NASA Aerospace workshop at the Chabot Science Center.

Also included in the workshop program was a special six-day session for teacher aides. Twenty-one aides, each of whom had served at project target schools during the preceding regular school year, participated in this session; eighteen of them took leave from current summer school teacher aide positions to attend the workshop. In addition to attending the Special Events Sessions with other teacher participants, the teacher aides held separate discussion meetings of their own to consider such matters as the characteristics of good aides, role playing, oral reports, and to practice with materials duplicating equipment.

The Oakland Teachers' Summer Workshop was open to all teachers—to those from the more advantaged schools and from other nearby districts as well as those from ESEA Title I project target schools—in accordance with the rationale that solution to the problems of teaching disadvantaged children are vital to the future of education in all public schools. Invitations announcing the summer workshop were sent to all elementary and secondary teachers in the district. These teachers were given the opportunity to indicate the instructional areas of the workshop's program in which they would like to participate. Course and class assignments were then made on the basis of these indications of preference. Teachers and other school personnel who enrolled in the summer workshop received four units of credit on the district's salary schedule for four weeks of successful participation in workshop activities. Upon completion of the workshop, all participants were asked to complete a questionnaire designed to help them evaluate their experience and make recommendations for future in-service training activities to be offered by the project.

The Oakland Teachers' Summer Workshop on Teaching Disadvantaged Children, with its component Seminar on Education and Human Relations, provided a fully comprehensive—intensive as well as extensive—program of training activities to achieve the objectives of the project's in-service component. It proved to be a highly effective way to introduce target school teachers, administrators, counselors, and other school personnel to the problems of teaching the disadvantaged and to some of the means for solving those problems. But a four-week summer workshop, however comprehensive, nevertheless cannot provide all the assistance and support that teachers need and expect in order to meet the challenges of their work with disadvantaged pupils. An extensive program is necessary to follow up and continue the training begun in the workshop. Oakland's project provided such a program through the carefully planned and coordinated efforts of the Teacher on Special Assignment, whose responsibility it was to direct all in-service training activities for the project; the Teaching Assistants in Reading, who coordinated in-service and curriculum development activities in each of the target elementary schools; and the Teaching Assistants in Language Development, who coordinated these activities in each of the target secondary schools. Each target school sponsored its own program of in-service training activities for members of its staff, in addition to the program of district-wide activities sponsored by the project. These target school-sponsored activities—grade-level and department meetings, workshops, institutes, consultations, and conferences—were planned and conducted in more immediate response to the needs and demands of teachers than the district-wide activities could possibly be. For this reason, there was considerable variety and differences of emphasis among the in-service programs sponsored by target schools. In the main, however, these programs focused on topics treated in the summer workshop, particularly upon the development of human relations—intercultural and intergroup relations—and the development of curricula and instructional materials. They deliberately sought to provide a coordinated, coherent, and consistent continuation of the exploration of these topics begun in the summer workshop.

## SACRAMENTO CITY UNIFIED SCHOOL DISTRICT
(Sacramento County)

Average per pupil expenditure in fiscal year 1966: $520.93
Number of schools: 73 (K–12)
Total enrollment in fall 1966: 52,000
Number of pupils from low-income families: 10,746 (18.32%)

ESEA TITLE I PROJECT, 1966–67

Title: Project Aspiration: Raising Educational Attainments
Amount of federal funds: $931,000
Number of target schools: 18
   14 Elementary
    2 Junior High
    2 Senior High
Number of target pupils: 4,800
    432 Kindergarten
  2,582 Elementary
    618 Junior High
  1,168 Senior High
Percentage of minority-group pupils:
   10% Mexican-American
   13% Negro
    8% Oriental
Special instructional activities:
  Reading, Remedial Reading and Language Development
  English Language Arts
  English as a Second Language
  Kindergarten-Primary Grades Summer Session
  Cultural Enrichment (study trips)
  Reduction of Class Size
Special supplementary services:
  Counseling and guidance
  Health services
  Psychological and psychometric
  Food service (free breakfasts and lunches)

Bus transportation
Community school centers
Curriculum materials development centers
Teacher aides (orientation and training)
In-service teacher training

IN-SERVICE PROGRAM

Amount of federal funds: $72,600
Number of participants: 147
Objectives:

To assist school personnel better to understand disadvantaged pupils and their families.

To change positively teachers' insight, sensitivity, and skill in working with disadvantaged pupils.

To train teachers in the use of newly developed curricula, materials, audiovisual aids, and instructional techniques for working with disadvantaged pupils.

To survey all possible resources for materials, media, techniques, and equipment appropriate for effective teaching of disadvantaged pupils and to demonstrate their uses to classroom teachers and administrators.

To provide specialized training for teachers that will enable them to emphasize improvement of reading and communication skills.

To raise the general level of teacher competence in all target schools in the compensatory education program.

To assist in the development and evaluation of curricula and instructional materials used by teachers of the disadvantaged.

Activities:

Summer Teacher Workshop on Compensatory Education.

Summer In-Service Training Institute on Compensatory Education.

Demonstration teachers, serving classroom teachers in target schools throughout the school year.

In-service training meetings for all classifications of school personnel working with disadvantaged pupils in target schools.

IN-SERVICE TRAINING ACTIVITY

The principal in-service training component of Sacramento City Unified School District's ESEA Title I project has been the Summer Teacher Workshop on Compensatory Education, 1966, and the Summer In-Service Institute on Compensatory Education, 1967. The California Project asked the 147 participants in the latter institute to evaluate their experience. (The organization and operation, as well as the instructional program and procedures, of the two summer in-service training activities were very similar, so only the latter was studied in detail.)

The Summer Teacher Workshop on Compensatory Education, 1966, was conducted for teachers, counselors, department chairmen, and administrators working with compensatory education pupils in public and nonpublic schools. Its objective was "to provide these personnel with a unique opportunity to analyze the problems of the disadvantaged child, to suggest practical ways of dealing with these problems, and to develop and share techniques and materials useful in teaching disadvantaged children."

The Summer Teacher Workshop was conducted for a period of five weeks, holding daily sessions three and one-half hours long from July 5 through August 5, 1966. These sessions were held at the Luther Burbank Senior High School, a new, modern facility located conveniently near to freeway travel and having a sizable automobile parking capacity. A director and six staff members, assisted by seventeen consultants and forty-eight demonstration teachers, conducted training activities for 144 participants. Each participant received $250 for the five-week period and four units of salary credit on the salary schedule. Each daily session was composed of three parts: (1) the development of concepts relative to the problems of disadvantaged youth was provided through the use of outstanding resource persons, primarily from outside the district, as lecturers and discussion leaders; (2) demonstration lessons were provided to present practical teaching techniques which would be helpful in working with these children; and (3) a materials development laboratory was established where special supplies and resources were provided in order to give teacher participants an opportunity to create and prepare instructional materials for use in their classrooms the following fall semester.

The In-Service Training Institute on Compensatory Education, Summer 1967, was in most respects similar to the Summer Teacher Workshop of 1966. Its objectives were to help school personnel "to identify pupils' ability levels, to understand disadvantaged pupils' environmental handicaps, and to develop instructional techniques and materials which will be of practical use in the classroom."

The In-Service Training Institute was also conducted at the Luther Burbank High School, holding daily sessions during the five weeks from June 26 through July 28, 1967. The director and staff, assisted by sixteen consultants and twenty demonstration teachers, carried out the program for 147 participants. The participants, who were teachers, counselors, and administrators working in compensatory education target or receiving schools and others who had expressed interest in working at such schools, again received $250 and four salary credit units for their participation. The program concentrated on the basic areas of attitudes and instructional techniques designed to upgrade the performance of socially deprived pupils. Qualified consultants worked daily with teachers and administrators to develop an awareness of the most advanced techniques for working with disadvantaged pupils. Members of the Sacramento City Unified School District staff demonstrated techniques and presented practical methods by which classroom teachers can be more effective in helping these pupils. A major feature of the institute was the daily period devoted to the development and production of instructional materials (charts, tapes, transparencies) by participants for use in their classrooms during the coming school year.

In designing the in-service teacher-training components of its ESEA Title I compensatory education projects, the Sacramento City Unified School District's Staff Training Services Department has focused its principal effort on providing an articulated, coordinated, and integrated program for its summer workshop (institute) on compensatory education. It has sought to provide continuity for its principal effort through its use of demonstration teachers, who demonstrate instructional techniques and materials for classroom teachers throughout the school year and also help in the planning and conduct of the summer workshop. It has supplemented its principal effort with a series of one-day in-service training sessions held throughout the school year for all classifications of school personnel who work with culturally deprived and educationally disadvantaged pupils. One prominent and noteworthy feature of the district's in-service teacher-training program, then, is the high degree of efficiency and economy of effort achieved by the overall coordination of training activities. This overall coordination is made possible by the fact that all of the district's in-service teacher-training activities, including those that are components of its compensatory education program, are under the direction of its Staff Training Services Department. In this particular institutional setting, a high degree of centralization and specialization of in-service teacher-training responsibilities results in a high degree of efficiency and economy of effort to enhance the professional growth of teachers who work with the district's disadvantaged pupils.

## SAN BERNARDINO CITY UNIFIED SCHOOL DISTRICT
### (San Bernardino County)

Average per pupil expenditure in fiscal year 1966: $540.61
Number of schools: 56 (K–12)
Total enrollment in fall 1966: 37,721
Number of pupils from low-income families: 9,755 (21%)

ESEA TITLE I PROJECT, 1966–67

Title: A Comprehensive Compensatory Education Program
Amount of federal funds: $1,137,985
Number of target schools: 13
  9 Elementary
  3 Junior High
  1 Senior High
Number of target pupils: 4,953
    30 Prekindergarten
  583 Kindergarten
2,963 Elementary
1,277 Junior High
  100 Senior High
Percentage of minority-group pupils:
  19% Mexican-American
  14% Negro

Special instructional activities:
  Cultural Enrichment
  English Language Arts
  English as a Second Language
  Reading
  Mathematics
  Music
  Physical Education/Recreation
  Prekindergarten
  General Elementary
  Summer School
  Teacher Aides and Other Subprofessional Help
  Administration and Evaluation
Special supplementary services:
  Food services (lunch)
  Clothing services
  Health services
  School social work services
  Guidance and counseling
  Tutoring and after-school study
  Transportation service
  Services and instructions for parents
  In-service training of teachers, teacher aides and administrators

IN-SERVICE PROGRAM

Amount of federal funds: $51,256
Number of participants: 214
Objectives:
  To sensitize professional and nonprofessional school personnel to the special needs and problems of pupils and parents from families with low-income status and increase their awareness and acceptance of cultural differences that exist in the society.
  To provide the opportunity and leadership for school personnel to plan improved ways of working with disadvantaged pupils and their parents.
Activities:
  A seminar on The Disadvantaged Pupil, consisting of a regularly

scheduled series of lectures, films, panel discussions, large- and small-group discussions, for new teachers in target area schools.

A seminar on the teaching of reading and English language arts for experienced teachers in target schools.

A seminar dealing with improved ways of working with small groups of students and parents for adjustment teachers (school social workers) working with community agencies to alleviate the children's problems.

An orientation, pre-service, and in-service training program for teacher aides.

IN-SERVICE TRAINING ACTIVITY

The in-service teacher-training component of San Bernardino City Unified School District's ESEA Title I project has featured a seminar on The Disadvantaged Pupil, consisting of a regularly scheduled series of lectures, panel discussions, film presentations, community tours, home visits, demonstrations, and large- and small-group discussion meetings. In 1965–66, the emphasis was on the first broad objective enumerated above—increasing teachers' sensitivity to and awareness of the personality, cultural background, environmental conditioning, educational needs, and special learning problems of disadvantaged pupils; in 1966–67, the emphasis shifted to the second objective—helping teachers work out solutions to the special learning problems of disadvantaged pupils, especially those related to their self-image and their reading and language skills. The California Project asked 271 of the teachers who took part in either seminar to evaluate their experience.

In 1965–66, the in-service seminar on The Disadvantaged Pupil met weekly for ten three-hour after-school and evening sessions between February 14 and May 23, 1966. A total of eighty-three elementary and 191 secondary teachers attended one or more meetings of the seminar; fifty-eight elementary and 136 secondary teachers participated in substantially all of the in-service training sessions. The program of the seminar included eight lectures by guest speakers and consultants followed by large- and small-group discussions on the following topics: The Culutre of Poverty; The Dynamics of Prejudice; Aspects of Mexican-American Culture; The Negro-American Child:

His Background and School Problems; Thirty Characteristics of the Disadvantaged Validated by Research; Health Needs of the Disadvantaged Child; Working with the Parents of the Disadvantaged Child; and The Use of Community Resources. It also included a showing of the film "Children Without" and a panel discussion of "The Schools" presented by a group of local school youth. Reading lists of books and articles and mimeographed excerpts and pamphlets were distributed to all participants to guide their reading and discussion of the various topics related to teaching the disadvantaged.

All teachers were paid a nominal sum ($2.75 per meeting) for their participation in the seminar. At the end of the seminar, they were asked to evaluate their experience by responding to a questionnaire that included items about the effectiveness of the various topics and media, about the influence and outcomes of their participation, and about their suggestions concerning topics, media, structure, and procedures for future sessions of the seminar. The principals of target schools were also asked to evaluate the effectiveness of the in-service seminar and report changes and other outcomes resulting from the participation therein of teachers in their schools.

As a result of evaluations and suggestions offered by participants and principals, the district shifted the emphasis of the seminar on The Disadvantaged Pupil. In the fall of 1966, it continued the seminar with its format and program virtually unchanged for one semester for the benefit of new teachers on the staffs of target schools and teachers in schools not involved directly with the ESEA Title I project but soon to become receiving schools under the district's open enrollment plan. The program of this seminar included nine lectures by guest speakers and consultants, followed by large- and small-group discussions, on these topics: The Culture of Poverty; The Nature of Prejudice; The Mexican-American in Southern California Today; The Negro in Our Society; Desegregation and Integration; Growing Up as a Member of a Minority Group; Parent Involvement in School Activities; Sources of Help in the Community; and The Health Needs of Disadvantaged Children. It also included a tour of the communities in which San Bernardino's racial and ethnic minority-group citizens live and a panel discussion of "Classroom Procedures." Again, bibliographies and other mimeographed materials were distributed to the participants.

For those teachers who had already been involved in the ESEA Title I project for one year and who had participated in sessions of the seminar held the previous spring, the district offered additional in-service training sessions conducted in a somewhat different format. These sessions focused more specifically on the learning problems of the disadvantaged pupil resulting from either his self-image or his reading and language disabilities and on practical classroom solutions for these specific problems. This seminar met thirteen times in two-hour sessions held in the late afternoon or evening approximately every two weeks from October 3, 1966 through June 15, 1967. At some of these sessions the participants met in one large group to hear a speaker or a panel discussion, but then they broke up into smaller discussion groups, organized by grade level or department, to consider specific problems and solutions. Then they took their ideas from the small-group discussions back to their schools for trial, practice, and closer scrutiny by analysis and evaluation. At the in-service meetings held in individual target schools, teachers with particularly good understanding of specific learning problems and ideas for their solution demonstrated these ideas for their fellow participants.

Of the 157 public school teachers and administrators who participated in the in-service training activities of the 1966–67 program, 128 completed substantially the entire series. Some of the participants, approximately 60 per cent, elected to be paid the district rate of $2.75 per meeting for attendance at in-service training sessions; the rest elected to receive credit on the district's salary schedule in lieu of payment. Those participants who played a more active role in the program of the seminar, by giving demonstrations, making home visits, and the like, were paid at the rate of $6.36 per hour.

At the conclusion of the seminar in June, the participants and target school principals were again asked to evaluate the effectiveness of the program and make suggestions for its further development.

In the subsequent development of the project's in-service program, the format of the seminar on The Disadvantaged Pupil has been retained for the purpose of providing a comprehensive general introduction to this subject for teachers who are new to the district or to the staffs of its target schools. This format has been modified considerably, however, to provide continuity and reinforcement in the training of experienced teachers who have already had the benefit of this general introduction. Particularly noteworthy among these modifications are the provisions for small-group discussion and interaction following lectures, films, panels, or other presentations; for follow-up meetings, organized by grade level or department, in each of the target schools; for demonstrations of lessons, materials, and equipment at these follow-up meetings by teachers with strong interests in and good understanding of specific problems considered in the seminar; and for experimentation and innovation, field trial and evaluation, of instructional procedures, techniques, media, and materials demonstrated by these teachers or developed in these meetings. As the result of these modifications, experienced teachers have become increasingly more actively and productively involved in a coordinated effort to improve the teaching of disadvantaged pupils through effective in-service training activities. And, of course, the project's district-wide in-service program in particular, and its special instructional programs in general, have benefitted greatly from such intensification of target school in-service activities.

## SAN DIEGO UNIFIED SCHOOL DISTRICT
### (San Diego County)

Average per pupil expenditure in fiscal year 1966: $535.82
Number of schools: 147 (K–12)
Total enrollment in fall 1966: 121,705
Number of pupils from low-income families: 11,364 (8.11%)

ESEA TITLE I PROJECT, 1966–67

Title: Equal Educational Opportunity Program
Amount of federal funds: $2,211,481
Number of target schools: 36
   25 Elementary
    5 Junior High
    6 Senior High (1 Continuation High)
Number of target pupils: 10,751
   200 Ungraded
   816 Kindergarten
 4,932 Elementary

2,852 Junior High
1,951 Senior High
Percentage of minority-group pupils:
  20.68% Mexican-American
  42.69% Negro
   3.95% Oriental
   .09% American Indian
Special instructional activities:
  English Language Arts
  English as a Second Language
  Reading
  General Elementary and Secondary
  Special Education for Handicapped
  Reduction of Class Size/Additional Staff
  Teacher Aides and Other Subprofessionals
  Cultural Enrichment (General)
  Kindergarten
  Speech Therapy
  Work-Study (Career)
  Prekindergarten
Special supplementary services:
  Curriculum materials
  Transportation services
  In-service training
  Library services
  Health services (nurse)
  Psychological services
  Guidance
  Food services

IN-SERVICE PROGRAM

Amount of federal funds: $23,831
Number of participants: 162
Objectives:
  To strengthen teachers' understanding and deepen their respect for the culturally and educationally disadvantaged child.
  To develop specific instructional programs, procedures, tech-

niques, and materials for use in classroom teaching of the disadvantaged.

To provide orientation and training for teachers new to the district.

To provide experienced teachers with opportunities to further their understandings and skills in teaching disadvantaged pupils so that they can actively participate in and give continuity to school in-service activities.

Activities:

District-sponsored college and university extension courses, seminars, and workshops.

District-sponsored workshops and conferences.

Local school-sponsored lectures, panel discussions, group discussions, seminars, workshops, and in-service meetings.

District-wide orientation and planning meetings for new teachers in project target schools.

Distribution of program development materials, including curriculum guides, instructional innovations, and curriculum plans.

Attendance at local, regional, state, and national conferences and meetings of professional organizations.

Consultations with curriculum specialists and pupil personnel specialists.

Orientation and training activities for teacher assistants, teacher aides, and kindergarten helpers.

## IN-SERVICE TRAINING ACTIVITY

San Diego Unified School District's ESEA Title I project included a comprehensive and extensive in-service program, the principal activities of which are enumerated above. The California Project asked a sample of 200 teachers who participated in one or more of these activities to evaluate their experience. The sample of participants was drawn by the ESEA Title I project director and includes both elementary and secondary teachers and both experienced and inexperienced teachers of the disadvantaged in the project's target schools.

In cooperation with colleges, universities, and other organizations and institutions, the district conducted courses, seminars, and workshops that provided staff members in the target area with opportunities for professional growth necessary for successful work in a compensatory education program. Courses included such subjects as The History of the Negro in America, The Negro's Contributions to American Culture, The Mexican-American in Transition, The Role and Contributions of the Mexican-American to American Culture. Also included were a Seminar on the Attitudes and Values of the Culturally Deprived, a Workshop in Meeting the Needs of Deprived Youth, a Workshop in Human Relations Techniques and Communication Skills in Dealing with Disadvantaged Youth, as well as a number of workshops dealing with specific subject areas, such as English as a second language, reading, and mathematics. These courses, seminars, and workshops usually ran for one semester (some for two), and met weekly or biweekly for two to three hours each session. The number of participants in each varied considerably with the nature of the subject and the interests of the teachers, but the heaviest enrollments were in the lecture-and-discussion courses dealing with the historical and cultural background of disadvantaged pupils.

Consultants were brought to the district to lecture and to conduct workshops on such topics as Counseling and Guidance for Disadvantaged Youth, Team Teaching and Staff Utilization, and Spanish for Teachers of Minority Groups. District personnel conversant with the purposes and programs of compensatory education spoke to groups of teachers about the district's ESEA Title I project and its various on-going activities.

The in-service program also included local district-wide orientation and planning meetings. New teachers on the staffs of project target schools were asked to report early before the opening of school in fall 1966 in order to attend a three-day orientation meeting designed to help them develop an understanding of the pupils, the school, and the community in which they were to work; to make them aware of methods and techniques that have been found most successful in teaching disadvantaged pupils; and to help them appreciate the potential of the pupils and the nature of the problems they face in achieving their potential. Experienced teachers participated in a curriculum and materials development workshop in the summer of 1966, to draw together, for the benefit of teachers and administrators working with culturally deprived pupils, the instructional programs, procedures, techniques, and materials that have proved most effective. Curriculum guides were written, published, and disseminated to the staffs of project target schools and throughout the district. Guides were prepared on such topics as remedial, corrective, and developmental instruction in reading, the language arts, mathematics, science, social studies, and music; team teaching and staff utilization; small-group instruction; use of the library as a resource center; English as a second language; counseling the disadvantaged; and training in various occupational skills.

District school personnel, particularly those serving on the staffs of project target schools, attended a large number of professional conferences sponsored by regional, state, and national organizations and held both in and outside the local district. These teachers, counselors, and administrators took part in virtually every professional meeting held within reasonable distance that was of particular interest to education involved in compensatory education programs.

District schools, particularly project target schools, sponsored in-service meetings for their own staffs. Lectures, demonstrations, films, panel discussions, group discussions, and workshops were conducted on topics covering the full range of matters related to the teaching of disadvantaged children and youth. At some of these meetings, experienced teachers, counselors, and administrators who had participated in district-wide in-service training activities passed along to their school colleagues the information and understandings they had gained from such participation.

School personnel who took part in the project's in-service training activities were rewarded for their participation in a variety of ways, depending on the nature and duration of the activity and the participant's position on the district's salary schedule. Some meetings were held after school, in the late afternoon or evening, some on Saturdays or during summer and other vacation periods. Other meetings were held on released time or on minimum days. The time of meeting was, of course, a consideration in setting the amount of remuneration or credit participants received. Participants in extension courses, seminars, and workshops offered under the auspices of colleges and universities also received either academic or salary credit for successful completion of these courses.

The project's in-service program was evaluated by two questionnaires, one for participants and one for school principals. Both groups were asked to judge the effectiveness of the program, to assess the outcomes of its various activities, and to make suggestions for future in-service training activities. Complete inventories of both distrct-sponsored and school-sponsored in-service activities were maintained, showing the number of meetings of each activity and the number of participants in each. Questionnaire responses and comments of participants and principals were tabulated, analyzed, and interpreted to provide bases for modifying and developing future activities in the program.

Two features of the San Diego project's in-service program appear to be particularly noteworthy: its extensive use of resources provided by nearby colleges and universities—extension courses, guest lecturers and panels, and consultants—as the expertise necessary for planning and conducting its district-wide in-service training activities; and its widespread reliance on school personnel who had participated in these district-wide activities for coordinators, instructors, guest speakers, and demonstration teachers in target school-sponsored in-service activities. By these arrangements the project has been able to get maximum benefit from its investment in expertise and, at the same time, it has been developing personnel and procedures to extend its in-service program and expand the range of its activities into an increasingly more comprehensive and better coordinated institution for the continuing education and training of teachers of the disadvantaged.

## SONORA UNION HIGH SCHOOL DISTRICT
### (Tuolumne County)

Average per pupil expenditure in fiscal year 1966: $481.24
Number of schools: 13 (K–12)
Total enrollment in fall 1966: 3,426
Number of pupils from low-income families: 302 (10.4%)

ESEA TITLE I PROJECT, 1966–67

Title: Language Arts Development and Remediation
Amount of federal funds: $43,400
Number of target schools: 13
   11 Elementary and Intermediate
   2 Junior and Senior High

Number of target pupils: 206
  12 Kindergarten
  112 Elementary
  41 Junior High
  41 Senior High
Percentage of minority-group pupils:
  3.00% Mexican-American
  .30% Negro
  .23% Oriental
  1.70% American Indian
Special instructional activities:
  English Language Arts
  Reading, Remedial Reading and Language Development
    (Summer Session)
    (Work-Study Continuation)
    (Handicapped and Retarded)
Special supplementary services:
  In-service teacher training

IN-SERVICE PROGRAM

Amount of federal funds: $2,500
Number of participants: 73
Objectives:
  To train teachers in the testing and diagnosis of reading and language disabilities.

  To help teachers develop special instructional skills for teaching reading and English language arts.

  To train teachers in the use of special instructional materials and equipment for teaching remedial classes in reading and language arts.

  To guide teachers in the development of English language arts curricula for all children in all cooperating school districts.
Activities:
  One-week intensive training course for summer school teachers prior to the beginning of the summer session, sponsored by Stanislaus State College.

Weekly (four) training meetings (Friday afternoon) throughout the summer session, under the auspices of Stanislaus State College.

County-wide in-service meetings throughout the regular school year.

School-sponsored in-service meetings conducted by the reading specialist.

Consultations and conferences, individual and small-group, with the project reading specialist and other curriculum specialists.

Summer, 1967: One-week intensive training in the teaching of reading as it relates to secondary instruction for teachers in both of the county high schools. The course, conducted by three highly skilled specialists from the college level, offered two units of credit from Stanislaus State College.

### IN-SERVICE TRAINING ACTIVITY

Sonora Union High School District has participated in the Tuolumne County School Cooperative ESEA Title I project, and its in-service teacher-training program has been carried out in conjunction with the total in-service component of that project. One of the principal activities of that project has been a summer school program of remedial and corrective instruction in reading and the language arts for disadvantaged students who have been identified as having serious reading disabilities and learning problems. The in-service training component of the project has therefore emphasized the preparation of teachers to offer such instruction. The California Project asked the twenty teachers who participated in the 1966 Summer Workshop in Reading and the Language Arts and the twenty-three teachers who participated in the 1967 Summer Workshop in Secondary Education: Reading and Language Arts to evaluate their experience.

The in-service teacher-training program for teachers on the staff of the project's summer school was developed by the project director and the reading specialist in collaboration with Stanislaus State College. The program began with a one-week intensive training session conducted during the week just prior to the opening of the summer school. During this session, daily meetings were held to discuss such matters as the objectives to be achieved by the program of remedial and corrective instruction in reading and language arts; the nature

and causes of specific reading difficulties; the uses of testing and diagnostic techniques to identify specific reading disabilities; the general
principles of developing instructional programs, procedures, techniques,
and materials for remedying and correcting reading difficulties; and
means of enriching the environment and experience of culturally disadvantaged children to provide them with a better background for
understanding basic concepts and the vocabulary necessary to the development of reading and language skills. These meetings consisted of
lectures, demonstrations, and group discussions conducted by the workshop staff and by guest speakers and consultants to the project.

Throughout the four weeks of the summer session, the staff
held Friday afternoon training meetings to consider specific instructional procedures, techniques, and materials and to share experiences,
exchange ideas, and evaluate the specific reading disabilities of individual pupils. Participants in these weekly meetings were divided into
two discussion groups, one for elementary and one for secondary teachers. Discussion in these groups emphasized understanding of the special
reading and learning problems of disadvantaged children and the especially appropriate means for meeting their educational needs. Workshop activities carried out in these meetings included demonstrations
of the uses of specific tests of reading and language skills and of specific
instructional materials and equipment for presenting them, as well as
selecting the teaching materials for use during the coming week from
among those available in the library-instruction center.

Teachers who participated in the summer school session and
its in-service training program received three quarter units of credit
from Stanislaus State College for taking part in training sessions, teaching under supervision, and preparing and submitting an intensive case
study of some aspect of the instructional program. Those who completed a report of an individual action or research project received an
additional two quarter units. All participants received a salary of $5.50
per hour for their work in the training and teaching programs.

During the regular school year following their participation
in the project's summer school session and in-service program, these
teachers continued their training by attending several county-wide
meetings conducted more or less regularly once a month in their individual target schools, and by consulting and conferring with the proj-

ect's reading specialist on the occasions of his visits to their respective schools. The county-wide in-service workshops were concerned with such practical aspects of reading and language arts instruction as demonstrations of the Frostig Program of Visual Perception by the project's reading specialist and demonstrations of instructional materials and equipment for teaching reading by representatives of manufacturers and commercial suppliers. The target school in-service meetings, which were held in the late afternoon after school hours or on minimum days, were usually devoted to discussions of the results of group testing and the analysis of individual cases of specific reading disabilities, though they also included some discussions of more general matters such as the use of tests and diagnostic techniques, grouping of pupils and other instructional procedures, the use of various instructional materials and equipment. Individual and small-group consultations with the project's reading specialist, which usually took place during preparation periods or after school, were concerned with problems of diagnosing and remedying the specific reading disabilities of individual pupils.

At the end of the year, the coordinator of the program sent a questionnaire to a random sample of twenty-eight teachers who had participated in the project's in-service training activities, asking them to evaluate the benefits they had received from their participation and to make recommendations for further planning and development of the program.

The in-service program from which the teachers of Sonora Union High School District receive assistance and support in their work with disadvantaged students is noteworthy for three features: its limited objectives and specific focus on training teachers of reading and language arts, its status as a component in the Tuolumne County Schools Cooperative ESEA Title I project, and its close and collaborative relationship to the teacher-education programs of Stanislaus State College. These arrangements enable teachers in a small rural one-school district to benefit from an in-service program whose training activities are more expertly planned and conducted and more efficiently coordinated than any the district could provide for them within the limits imposed by its very small entitlement to ESEA Title I funds.

## VALLEJO CITY UNIFIED SCHOOL DISTRICT
### (Solano County)

Average per pupil expenditure in fiscal year 1966: $538.89
Number of schools: 24 (K–12)
Total enrollment in fall 1966: 16,510
Number of pupils from low-income families: 1,769 (8.6%)

ESEA TITLE I PROJECT, 1966–67

Title: The Vallejo Compensatory Education Plan for Eliminating
Dropouts by Helping Children Attain Their Potential
Amount of federal funds: $381,411
Number of target schools: 12
9 Elementary
2 Junior High
1 Senior High
Number of target pupils: 4,317
608 Kindergarten
3,209 Elementary
250 Junior High
250 Senior High
Percentage of minority-group pupils:
2.5% Mexican-American
18.9% Negro
.5% Oriental
1.9% Other
Special instructional activities:
Reading, Remedial and Developmental
English Language Arts
Social Studies
Mathematics
Science
Cultural Enrichment (study trips)
Summer School
Reduction of Class Size
Special supplementary services:
Counseling and guidance
Psychometric testing and speech therapy

School nursing services
Food service (free lunch)
School-community relations work
Teacher aides
In-service teacher training

IN-SERVICE PROGRAM

Amount of federal funds: $8,000
Number of participants: 220
Objectives:
To assist teachers better to understand the special needs of educationally disadvantaged children.

To present information and demonstrations on many varied innovative materials, techniques, and teaching aids.

To increase awareness of teachers and parents of the importance of nutrition and health in relation to children's educational progress.

To constantly seek methods to improve children's skills in the areas of communication and reading.

To sharpen sensitivity to the importance of pupils' needs to perceive themselves as persons who can succeed because they have experienced success.

To continually strive to understand the humanistic concept of education so that we value each child because he is a human being.
Activities:
Curriculum Materials Production Workshops sponsored by the district.

Extension courses in Curriculum Development sponsored by Sonoma State College.

Film series on the socioeconomic and educational problems and needs of disadvantaged children.

District-wide in-service grade-level and department meetings of target school personnel.

Attendance at local, regional, and state professional conferences.

Consultations with curriculum specialists and demonstration teachers.

In the in-service component of its ESEA Title I project for 1966–67, the Vallejo Unified School District emphasized training in curriculum and materials development. The California Project asked forty-two teachers who had participated in such training to evaluate their experience.

During the summer of 1966, the district sponsored three Materials Production Projects that lasted for nine days, from August 22 to 31, and met for five or six hours each day. Each project was conducted by a curriculum specialist on the faculty of Sonoma State College who was engaged as a consultant by the district. Each project involved twelve to sixteen teachers in workshop discussions of instructional programs, procedures, materials, and media that are especially appropriate for teaching disadvantaged (and, consequently, low-achieving) students. Each project set up a program of instruction in its particular subject field that would meet the needs of such students, reviewed the instructional materials and media available for teaching these programs, and began developing a syllabus for a course of study that would coordinate these programs, materials, and media. The three Materials Production Projects worked on the development of curricula and materials to meet the particular educational needs of disadvantaged, low-achieving students in (1) seventh and eighth grade social studies, (2) eleventh and twelfth grade social studies, (3) and tenth, eleventh, and twelfth grade English language arts.

At the conclusion of the Materials Production Projects, the sixteen teachers who participated in the one concerned with developing curricula and materials for seventh and eighth grade social studies requested the district to sponsor an in-service activity that would enable them to continue their work during the following year. As a result, the district arranged for these teachers to be enrolled in an extension course, a Curriculum Development Workshop, offered by Sonoma State College and conducted by the same curriculum specialist-consultant who had conducted the Materials Production Project. This extension course was set up as a forty-five hour (three unit) session to meet for three hours one night each week throughout the first semester of the college academic year. The participants met with their instructor in a district school classroom and continued their work on a course in social studies for the seventh and eighth grades in Title I project target schools. At the end of the first semester, the participants in this Curriculum Development Workshop again requested that this activity be continued, and again the district made the necessary arrangements for the extension course to continue on the same terms throughout the second semester. At the end of that time, the participants in the workshop were ready to write an initial draft of the course they had been developing, so the district employed them during the summer of 1967 to make a first draft of a course in social studies for disadvantaged, low-achieving students in the seventh and eighth grades of the two target junior high schools in the ESEA Title I project.

At the end of the Materials Production Project, the twelve teachers who had been working on curricula and materials for eleventh and twelfth grade social studies also requested that the district sponsor the continuation of their efforts in an in-service activity. The district set up a Curriculum Development Workshop for them, too, arranged as a forty-five hour (three unit) extension course offered through Sonoma State College and conducted by the curriculum specialist-consultant who had previously conducted the Materials Production Project. Shortly after the end of the first semester this instructor became ill, however, and was forced to discontinue the workshop. The chairman of the Social Studies Department of the target senior high school was released for one period each week through the second semester to coordinate the program and supervise the use of instructional materials that had been developed up to the point at which this phase of the project ceased to operate.

As a result of the recommendations of the teachers who had participated in the English Materials Production Project, the district engaged a curriculum specialist on the faculty of the School of Education, University of California at Berkeley, to consult with target school teachers on matters related to the teaching of reading and the language arts to disadvantaged students in secondary schools. These teachers also requested that an extension course in Linguistics be set up and offered by Sonoma State College, and plans for such a course were begun.

The teachers who participated in the Materials Production Projects during the summer of 1966 received a salary at an hourly rate based on their position on the salary schedule and also three units of credit toward an increment on that schedule. Those who continued

268 Teachers for the Disadvantaged

their training in curriculum and materials development for disadvantaged students by enrolling in the extension courses offered by Sonoma State College received three units of professional credit toward advanced degrees for each semester's work and also three units of credit per semester toward an increment on the salary schedule.

Upon completion of the Materials Production Projects and the Curriculum Development Workshops, participants were asked to prepare brief résumés of their experience, including recommendations for continuing these types of in-service activities and for establishing new ones in the future. The district has been guided by these evaluations and recommendations in its planning for further in-service training of teachers in the ESEA Title I project target schools. In the district's planning proposal for 1967–68, the project director wrote, "Our feeling is that too many teachers are not fully aware of the problems of the deprived child, and we will attempt to change this lack of awareness and, at the same time, change the attitudes of many of the teachers. The in-service program [for 1967–68] will be made up mostly of sensitivity training. . . ."

# Index